Attachment and Interaction

The International Library of Group Analysis

Edited by Malcolm Pines, Institute of Group Analysis, London

The aim of this series is to represent innovative work in group psychotherapy, particularly but not exclusively group analysis. Group analysis, taught and practised widely in Europe, has developed from the work of S.H. Foulkes.

Other titles in the series

Active Analytic Group Therapy for Adolescents

John Evans
International Library of Group Analysis 6
ISBN 1 85302 617 4 hardback
ISBN 1 85302 616 6 paperback

Circular Reflections

Selected Papers on Group Analysis and Psychoanalysis

Malcolm Pines
International Library of Group Analysis 1
ISBN 1 85302 492 9 paperback
ISBN 1 85302 493 7 hardback

Self Experiences in Group

Intersubjective and Self Psychological Pathways to Human Understanding

Edited by Irene Harwood and Malcolm Pines
International Library of Group Analysis 4
ISBN 1 85302 596 8 hardback
ISBN 1 85302 597 6 paperback

Taking the Group Seriously?

Towards a Post-Foulkesian Group Analytic

Farhad Dalal
ISBN 1 85302 642 5 paperback

INTERNATIONAL LIBRARY OF GROUP ANALYSIS 3

Attachment and Interaction

Mario Marrone

with a contribution by Nicola Diamond

Foreword by Malcolm Pines

Jessica Kingsley Publishers
London and Philadelphia

First published in the United Kingdom in 1998 by
Jessica Kingsley Publishers Ltd
116 Pentonville Road
London N1 9JB, England
and
1900 Frost Road, Suite 101
Bristol, PA 19007, U S A

Copyright © 1998 Mario Marrone
Foreword Copyright © 1998 Malcolm Pines

Library of Congress Cataloging in Publication Data
A CIP catalogue record for this book is available from the Library of Congress

British Library Cataloguing in Publication Data
A CIP catalogue record for this book is available from the British Library

ISBN 1 85302 587 9 hb
ISBN 1 85302 586 0 pb

Printed and Bound in Great Britain by
Athenaeum Press, Gateshead, Tyne and Wear

Contents

To my children, Valerie, Daniel and Melissa

Acknowledgements

The skeleton of this book is formed of what I learned through regular and personal contact with John Bowlby over a period of ten years. Bowlby's wife, Ursula, and his son, Richard, have encouraged me to write this book; they provided important information and helped to make corrections to an early draft.

Nicola Diamond has been my closest interlocutor throughout the process of writing the book. The clarity and rigour of her thinking has been an essential aid, and I have made references to her comments throughout. However, her thought is independent of mine and I have used her remarks in the context of my own ideas. We have written Chapter 9 jointly and she has also written the final chapter.

The publication of this book also owes a great deal to Malcolm Pines – who has seen this project as worthwhile – and to my current analyst, Eric Rayner, who has played a very enabling role in my recent life.

It is a pleasure to acknowledge my debt to Tirril Harris for her careful and able scrutiny of the whole manuscript. Lisa Crandell, Earl Hopper, Ruth Robinson, Howard Steele and Estella Welldon have not only advised me in relation to particular sections of the book, but have also helped me to acquire greater insight into the significance of the overall message I am trying to convey. However, they should not be held responsible for what I say in this book, since I have used their critical remarks at my own discretion. Colin Murray Parkes has read the references I have made to his work and confirmed that they are accurate.

My father, Roberto Marrone, and a large group of friends and colleagues have encouraged me to bring this project to a satisfactory conclusion. Finally, I would like to express my gratitude to four senior psychoanalysts: Arthur Couch, Pearl King, Martin Miller and Clifford Yorke, who have given me generous support and understanding at crucial stages of my career.

Mario Marrone

Foreword

Attachment and Interaction is notable; attachment theory fully outlined is extended by taking into account such areas as self psychology (Kohut *et al.*), theory of mind (Fonagy, Steele *et al.*) and other research into early infant–caregiver experiences. In his exposition of Bowlby's theories Mario Marrone also gives us vivid glimpses of John Bowlby as his supervisor which contributes to the book's personal flavour. Marrone is a psychoanalyst and a group analyst, trained in the Independent Group of British psychoanalysts and Foulksian group analysts, and relates his personal and professional experiences to this context. A further dimension is given by his knowledge of Latin American psychoanalysis, and group analysis which is too little known in the Anglophone world. His collaborator, Nicola Diamond, educated in sociology, analytic psychotherapy and continental philosophy, through her knowledge of French psychoanalysis and sociology also introduces us to theoretical issues that do not receive sufficient attention in our literature: the underlying philosophical assumptions of classical psychoanalysis, how that theory 'has to jump over the irreconcilable gap' between separate minds, a gap that does not appear when the intersubjective approach is adopted. I appreciate her clear exposition of some aspects of Lacanian theory and of the philosophical basis of intersubjectivity.

In this book, psychoanalysis and Foulkes' group analysis meet and do not have to occupy separate irreconcilable domains. A shift away from drive theory in psychoanalysis to object relations theory and to self psychology has led to rich harvests in our knowledge of the intercommunicational matrix, that intertwined double helix of self and other, of togetherness and separateness that is intrinsic to the human life cycle. We explore this matrix through the different vectors of psychoanalysis and group analysis. A mirroring, resonant, echoing group analytic circle amplifies our exposure to and appreciation of the power of empathy as a way to discover and to uncover otherness; self in the other, other in the self. In our work as individual and group analysts and therapists we engage in the dialectical process of finding and creating meaning.

Another volume in this series, *Self Experiences in Group: Intersubjective and Self Psychological Pathways to Human Understanding* (Harwood and Pines 1998), explores similar issues from a standpoint of Kohut's self psychology which arose in the North American context. By reading these two volumes, one which reflects the British context and the other the North American, the reader will undoubtedly deepen his/her understanding of developmental and clinical issues, and will find new perspectives for work in both group and individual contexts.

Malcolm Pines
The Group-Analytic Practice

How to Read this Book

I believe that the reader will make better sense of this book if seeing it in relation to multiple layers of political contexts. Some of these contexts have an international dimension; others are to be located in Britain, where Bowlby spent most of his life and where I, personally, have been working as a clinician for many years.

Bowlby's ideas and findings are obvious for many. However, the fact that he became a pariah of psychoanalysis (to the point that his work is rarely given a substantial place – if any – in psychoanalytic and psychotherapy training programmes) seems to be partly related to political exclusion. His message was, however, heard by academic psychologists and empirical researchers, most of them based in the United States of America.

Since then, attachment theory has become predominantly the province of the academic world. Late in his life, Bowlby still hoped that one day there would be cross-fertilization between empirical research and clinical psychoanalysis. However, this association may not easily come about. Empirical researchers and psychoanalysts have different styles of acquiring respectability, validating data and withdrawing or publishing information. These differences have made dialogue somewhat difficult.

Attachment researchers have created a body of knowledge which may prove to be essential in mental health promotion. The idea that better parenting may result in more extensive good mental health in a given society is now scientifically substantiated. But parenting does not take place in a vacuum. There cannot be good enough parenting without social support. Where inequality, violence and/or parent-unfriendly employment policies prevail, the parental function is bound to be grossly impaired.

The field of attachment studies (and its roots in psychoanalysis) overlaps with general psychiatry. The latter is also riddled with political problems. The practice of general psychiatry is heavily influenced by two major factors: (1) the biological trend in psychiatric thinking; and (2) administrative policies that put constraints on hospital services. In biological psychiatry, the patient's emotional and subjective experiences of past and present interpersonal events seem only to be important in that they help to make a diagnosis. Continuity of sensitive care by key members of the staff, and detailed exploration of the patients' inner experiences, seem to be secondary to social containment and psycho-pharmacology (which is, of course, encouraged by the powerful interests of the pharmaceutical industry).

As Thomas, Romme and Hamellijnck (1996) point out, psychiatry cannot be separated from politics. A careful analysis of the relationship between psychiatry and socio-cultural context makes it difficult to support the view that we should keep political and psychiatric discourse apart.

What role can attachment theory play in these multiple contexts? The answer is: a great deal. Attachment theory holds the principle that psychological and psychosomatic well-being are contingent upon the stability and strength of a supportive network, where genuine concern for the other is paramount. If this is the case, then attachment theory can inform politics in a fruitful way (Roberts and Kraemer 1996).

As Peter Marris (1996) puts it, our society needs strategies of reciprocal collaboration which depend on trust, and trust implies a shared morality. He says:

> if one cannot deal with economic or even political relationships confidently in moral terms, the trust that would make these relationships more manageable and less destructive is hard to conceive, and harder to promote. The risk is that this yearning for a moral community capable of governing our collaboration will lead, out of frustration and suspicion, to an even more destructive exclusiveness and intolerance. (p.171)

The kind of morality that we need to promote should be grounded on the basic discoveries of attachment studies: optimal functioning of individuals and societies is contingent upon the hard-won development of the capacities for sensitive responsiveness, reflective thinking, reciprocal support, deep-seated trust and stability in relationships.

I believe that attachment studies may contribute to avert iatrogenia in psychoanalytic therapy (where, through faulty technique, the treatment becomes counter-productive). To me, this is a matter of utmost importance. However, this exploration should not be interpreted as an attack on clinical psychoanalysis. There are many good practitioners, and psychoanalysis is, and will continue to be, the treatment of choice for many human problems.

Finally, although the contribution of attachment theory to psychoanalytic thinking is emphasized – and perhaps overstated – I do not imply that attachment theory emerged in isolation. By and large, it is based on, and compatible with, the work of many other psychoanalysts: it has crystallized as part of a long tradition of independent psychoanalytic thinking. Such links are explored in Chapter 8, as well as in subsequent chapters on transference and technique.

In principle, this book is addressed to psychoanalytic therapists. Nonetheless, it may also be useful for other mental health workers and professionals concerned with parents' guidance and mental health promotion. Although the book is fairly comprehensive in certain respects, it cannot be all-encompassing. I have omitted many interesting issues and debates to avoid making the text interminable or perhaps diffused.

Loan Receipt
Liverpool John Moores University
Library Services

Borrower Name: Krzyzowska,Agnieszka

Borrower ID: **********5110

Attachment and interaction /
31111008459347
Due Date: 27/09/2013 23:59

Total Items: 1
16/07/2013 13:47

Please keep your receipt in case of
dispute.

PART 1

Background

An outline of attachment theory
and its historical, methodological
and theoretical features

CHAPTER 1

John Bowlby

Introductory remarks

Perhaps the best way of introducing attachment theory is to talk first about John Bowlby, its creator. In doing this, I shall mix some biographical details with some personal impressions and give an outline of the way his ideas developed. I hope to be able to maintain a certain coherence in spite of some 'free associations' which, in this context, may be inevitable. However, the main theme of this book relates to the study of: (1) the evolution of John Bowlby's ideas; and (2) his legacy: how attachment theory has developed up to the present day and its clinical applications.

I do not expect this synthesis to be impeccable and comprehensive, because we are dealing here with a paradigm which is developing quickly, with all sorts of implications and ramifications. There is thus no way of encompassing all the available information. I shall be satisfied if I succeed in producing a coherent reference framework from which the reader can develop his/her own inquiries.

I had regular contact with John Bowlby during a period of ten years (from 1980 until shortly before his death in 1990). Initially we met regularly at the Tavistock Clinic in London, often once a week, to discuss clinical cases and psychoanalytic theory. In later years I often visited him at his home. Also, as I shall explain later, we met in seminars held at the Institute of Group Analysis. I remember him with the greatest affection. I can still hear him, when I knocked on the door of his room on the fourth floor of the Tavistock Clinic and he said in his strong low-pitched voice: 'Come in, Mario!'.

He was a tall, well-built man, not very expressive. Yet he had a natural and amicable freshness. He dressed neatly but informally. During the time of our relationship, he often wore cotton checked shirts and a light-coloured sports jacket.

Bowlby was not prone to intrusive questioning or to unnecessary self-disclosure. He never commented on my personal issues unless I offered them for discussion. Similarly, he was reserved about his personal life, including his family. His wife, Ursula Bowlby, says that this style of self-restraint was part of his character.

Bowlby's early years

Bowlby was born in London on 26 February 1907. His father, Major-General Sir Anthony Bowlby, son of a journalist, was a successful surgeon. His mother, May Mostyn, was the daughter of a clergyman who lived in a Huntingdonshire village. John was one of six children in the family.

His parents' attitude was rather aloof, with little capacity to express affection and show playful enjoyment of life. John made valiant efforts as a boy to lighten the sombre, bad-tempered atmosphere at home. Ursula Bowlby says that this side of his family never left him completely. However, there were long family holidays in Scotland, when the family atmosphere improved. Probably, John also found secondary attachment figures in Minnie, his first, much-loved nurse maid and, subsequently, in Nanna Friend, an intelligent disciplinarian.

Colin Murray Parkes (1995) says:

> it is hard to explain why [Bowlby] showed so few of the cognitive and other impairments which he attributed to such deprivation, for John Bowlby stands as one of the most brilliant and intrepid thinkers of his time and those who knew him well found loyalty and warmth behind his reserved behaviour. Perhaps the question that we need to ask is how the many influences on his life converged to influence the formation of his truly exceptional character. (p.247–248)

In 1914, when John was seven years old, the war came. He and his elder brother were sent to boarding school. John deplored the emotional atmosphere in that school. Yet his intellectual development was not impaired and he did well with his studies.

His father worked as Surgeon-General in France for most of the war. When the war came to an end, John went as a naval cadet to Dartmouth. However, he did not find the navy satisfying and decided to move on. In 1925, he went to university in Cambridge, where he stayed until 1928. There he read Natural Sciences and Psychology. He then became interested in what we would now call 'developmental psychology'.

Subsequently, John spent a year in a progressive school for maladjusted children, which was run like a home. There he learned that behavioural disturbances in children seemed to be related to family dysfunction. John began to think that real-life experiences in childhood had an effect, often a pathogenic effect, on personality development. This idea is in fact the hallmark of attachment theory.

Perhaps we are now ready to jump to a formulation of the central point of attachment theory. The individual lives from the moment he is born until the moment he dies in an interpersonal or intersubjective context. In this context he becomes attached to his parents or parental substitutes and a few other people with whom he develops a close relationship. In the course of the experiences he has with these people (or in relation to them, both in their presence and in their absence), he develops mental representations of the quality of these attachment relationships. These mental representations act as organizing factors in the individual's intrapsychic world and influence personality development in an optimal or pathological way.

Of course, what Bowlby observed early in his career, was the fact that disturbances or disruptions of the child's attachment to his significant others and family dysfunction often appear in the history of individuals with serious psychological problems. A more sophisticated understanding of these processes only began to emerge many years later.

While working at the school for maladjusted children, Bowlby formed a friendship with a man called John Alford, a volunteer helper who later obtained a Chair in the History of Art at an American university. Alford, who had had psychoanalysis himself, advised John to pursue his medical training and, at the same time, enter psychoanalysis: 'Now what you ought to do is go up to London, complete your medical studies and train at one of two places: one is called the Tavistock Clinic and the other is called the Institute of Psycho-Analysis'. Ursula Bowlby comments: 'I feel sure his advice was an important milestone in John's career. He trusted John Alford's judgement and acted on it'.

In the autumn of 1929, aged 22, John moved to London to pursue his medical career at University College Hospital. Around this time, he also started his psychoanalytic training, with Joan Riviere as his analyst and Melanie Klein as his supervisor.

Colin Murray Parkes (1995) explains:

> It took John Bowlby the usual four more years to qualify as a doctor, but seven to qualify as a psychoanalyst. From the outset he seems to have found it hard to accept the dogmatic beliefs of his supervisors, which failed to satisfy the scientific standards which he had learned at Cambridge or the logical arguments of his new friends. (p.250)

Here, Parkes implicitly refers to Bowlby's new friends of the Labour Party, which he joined with enthusiasm. One of these was Evan Durbin, an economist.

(It may be of interest to note that John Bowlby and Evan Durbin wrote a book together: *Personal Aggressiveness and War* (1939). Their objective was to try to explain the rise of fascism, especially in Germany. Durbin wrote from a socio-economic perspective and Bowlby from the psychological point of view.)

Colin Murray Parkes then proceeds:

Thus, in 1935, while responding to a paper by Melanie Klein, [Bowlby] reported that he had seen several depressed patients who had suffered recent bereavements. This interest in psychological trauma ran counter to the received knowledge of the time that it is unconscious fantasies that are the origin of psychopathology rather than real life events. Consequently, he was soon at odds with Klein, the dominant figure in his school of psychoanalysis. (p.250)

On the tribal area

In 1938, Bowlby married Ursula Longstaff, with whom he lived until his death. They had four children: Mary (born in 1939), Richard (born in 1941), Pia (born in 1945) and Robert (born in 1948). By the time of his marriage, John Bowlby had spent all his capital on his training analysis (a fact about which he used to joke) and his income was low. So he and Ursula went to live with friends in order to share costs but also because of the comradeship. They were all middle-of-the-road socialists who wanted social justice and equality but disliked communism as they thought that a left-wing dictatorship was as bad as a right-wing one.

After the war (in 1946–1947) Bowlby bought the house in Hampstead in which he was to spend the rest of his life and where Ursula and other members of the family still live. He initially shared it with Jock Sutherland, Jock's wife Molly and their baby. Sutherland was a distinguished Scottish psychiatrist who became the first Director of the Tavistock Clinic when it was reshaped and put under the umbrella of the National Health Service. John Bowlby was then the Deputy Director. Mattie Harris, who became Organizing Tutor of the child psychotherapy programme at the Tavistock (and was later going to marry Donald Meltzer, another well-known analyst) lived at the house as well.

John and Ursula liked to live in a community-styled setting and always had friends and relatives living either in their house itself or in its vicinity. Ursula (personal communication) says: 'My sisters call this "the tribal area". So you appreciate our version of the extended family – which I feel sure is repeated countless times all over the world, though less so in Britain'.

Bowlby thought that both one-to-one and group or network attachments are necessary and complementary. Their main biological function is to secure assistance and, therefore, survival in the case of adversity. As the individual grows older, relationships with peers and groups (what he called 'affiliative relationships') become more important. These relationships involve greater reciprocity and a semantic order: they are not 'mechanical', they are not purely based on physical proximity, but are mediated by a complex set of meanings and representations.

The beginnings of Bowlby's professional life

Bowlby qualified in medicine in 1933. Subsequently, he held an appointment for two years at the Maudsley Hospital. Then he moved to the London Child Guidance Clinic, where he worked as a child psychiatrist until the outbreak of war.

Bowlby became an Associate Member of the British Psycho-Analytical Society in 1937 and a full Member in November 1939, at the same time as Ronald Fairbairn and Paula Heimann, just after the beginning of the Second World War.

From 1939 to the early 1960s Bowlby was an active member of the British Psycho-Analytical Society. There, he was a member of various committees. In 1944 he was elected Training Secretary. He was also active in establishing the Benevolent Fund.

One pivotal character in John's career was the late Ronald Hargreaves (whom John called 'my impresario'), the man in charge of Mental Health at the World Health Organization in Geneva. Later Hargreaves was Professor of Psychiatry at Leeds. Regrettably he died young from a brain tumour. John and Ronald had been medical students together at University College Hospital where they became close friends.

The development of Bowlby's ideas

Bowlby's experience in child psychiatry consolidated his belief that psychopathology originated in real experiences of interpersonal life. This contrasted with the Kleinian emphasis on the aetiological prominence of phantasy and purely autogenic and intrapsychic processes.

On the basis of case material that he saw in the course of his work as a child psychiatrist, Bowlby wrote his paper, 'The Influence of Early Environment in the Development of Neurosis and Neurotic Character' (1940). He found that mothers of neurotic children tend to displace hostility originally related to their own parents towards their children and that they also tend to satisfy previously unmet affectional needs by making inordinate and inappropriate demands on them. Here, Bowlby showed his concern with family interaction and intergenerational phenomena. In later papers he showed increasing concern regarding the ill effects of early separation, loss and deprivation of maternal care.

Bowlby's main concern was the study of the nature and vicissitudes of the enduring and powerful bond that develops in early life between the growing individual and his caregivers. Bowlby rooted his approach in psychoanalytic thinking but dismissed traditional metapsychology, which he substituted with a new paradigm based on developmental psychology and ethology. He thought that classical psychoanalysis was ill at ease with this subject and that new organizing principles were necessary to approach it with greater precision.

The 'controversial discussions'

Some years after Bowlby qualified as a psychoanalyst, the British Psycho-Analytical Society went through very stormy times, when the famous 'controversial discussions' took place (see King and Steiner 1991). These discussions were held in the Society between 1941 and 1945, during the Second World War, and mainly concerned questions of theory and technique. These antithetical positions were felt to endanger the future of the British Psycho-Analytical Society and of psychoanalysis in Britain itself.

The main argument was between Anna Freud, Dorothy Burlingham, Edward Glover, Melitta and Walter Schmideberg and others, in opposition to Melanie Klein. On the Kleinian side were Paula Heimann, Susan Isaacs, Joan Riviere, Donald Winnicott and others. In the middle were the participants who were not committed to either point of view but who wanted some compromise to be reached which would maintain the possibility of dialogue and save the Society from a split. Among these were Bowlby, Michael Balint, William Gillespie, Ernest Jones, Sylvia Payne, James Strachey and others.

As an outcome of these discussions, a 'gentlemen's agreement' was informally reached, whereby the Society was divided into three groups: Freudian, Kleinian and the 'middle group' (the later eventually came to call itself 'independent'). According to this agreement there was going to be a fair distribution of committee posts among members of the different groups. Paula Heimann and Donald Winnicott later joined the independent group.

The independent group was born out of the wish to sustain a philosophy whereby its members could give a basic commitment to psychoanalysis while, at the same time, feel free to develop their theoretical and technical approach. It has been said that this group, rather than being an 'independent group', was a 'group of independents'. Bowlby was certainly one of them.

Boundaries between the groups are now, perhaps, blurring. Some independent psychoanalysts have a strong leaning towards Kleinian thinking while analysts of other schools are increasingly interested in knowledge derived from modern attachment research or even actively involved in it. However, it is probably true that one of the original characteristics of the independent group was that many of its members – unlike most Kleinians – tended to see the origins of psychopathology in real interpersonal events. This had been unequivocally so with Balint, Bowlby, Fairbairn and Winnicott.

E. Rayner (1990) points out that independents tend to conceive of the crucial origins of pathology as being, in the first place, in real interpersonal relations. Instead, Melanie Klein saw pathology as rooted in a conflict between impulses, originally between the life and death instincts. The mental representations of these conflicts take the place of phantasies. Relationships with others are seen as epiphenomena of purely autogenerated internal processes rather than as an integral part of interpersonal interaction.

Kleinians today, 50 years or more after the controversial discussions, genuinely say that they do not ignore the environment. The basis of this position can be easily found in Bion's ideas, such as his conception of mother as a 'container'. However, there are considerable differences of emphasis between most Kleinians and many independents in the way they conceptualize the role of interpersonal experience in psychological development and psychological functioning. In many Kleinian and non-Kleinian clinical articles, patients' attachment histories are not ignored or dismissed, although detailed accounts of past events are normally missing.

At the time of the war (and the controversial discussions), Bowlby developed a firm conviction that psychoanalysis was defined by its object of study, not by any particular theory or school of thought, and that the object of study of psychoanalysis was not the intrapsychic life of the individual in isolation but the psychological life of the individual in an interpersonal or social context.

In 1944 he published his paper, 'Forty-four Juvenile Thieves' in which he suggested that antisocial behaviour in young people was rooted in early disorders of attachment. In this way, he began to link in a systematic manner early interpersonal experiences with the development of psychopathology in later life.

The post-war years and the development of attachment theory

After the war, Bowlby was asked to take responsibility for the children's department of the Tavistock Clinic. Between 1946 and 1956 he dedicated a great deal of his time and energy to building what he then re-named 'The Department for Children and Parents'. He divided his time between administrative tasks, research and clinical work. His experience confirmed his idea that continuity of maternal care is essential for the psychological well-being of young children.

Research carried out by his associates, Joyce and James Robertson, since 1948, on psychological reactions of children to separation from their attachment figures, supported Bowlby's view on this matter. The Robertsons were psychoanalytically oriented social workers who joined Anna Freud in the Hampstead Wartime Nurseries in 1941, at the time of their marriage, caring for young children who had lost family life through the bombing of London. In 1948, while Joyce was at home looking after their small children, James Robertson joined Bowlby at the Tavistock Clinic, to make observations on the behaviour of young children who had been separated from their mothers. In 1965, James and Joyce Robertson commenced their research at the Tavistock Clinic on how young children's experiences of brief separation from their mothers affected their mental state and psychological development (for a more detailed account of this topic see Chapter 4). The merit of the Robertsons was that they filmed their observations in a systematic way. They provided clear evidence that experiences of separation between a young child and his mother set in motion a sequence of psychological reactions which are likely to have long-term effects (Robertson and Robertson 1989).

After the war, Hargreaves thought that the World Health Organization should be concerned with the ill-effects on personality development of discontinuities and inconsistencies in the parental care of young children. He invited Bowlby to organize a series of annual discussion groups which took place in Geneva over a period of four years.

Bowlby told Hargreaves: 'You must invite Konrad Lorenz!'. So he did. Lorenz joined the group at its first meeting in 1953. These discussions – involving ethology – undoubtedly had a tremendous influence on John. Bowlby had the opportunity to read Lorenz's *King Solomon's Ring* (1952) and it was then that he became interested in ethology.

Another member of the discussion group was the Swiss psychologist, Jean Piaget, who was concerned with the study of developmental changes in cognitive functioning from birth through adolescence. The discussions in Geneva proved a considerable second education for John Bowlby. He applied concepts taken from ethology to revise instinct theory and from Piaget's thinking to develop the concept of the 'internal working model' (see Chapter 5).

It was Ronald Hargreaves, through the World Health Organization, who commissioned John to carry out the post-war survey of homeless children which resulted in his report entitled 'Maternal Care and Mental Health' (1951). This monograph led to major improvements in the care of young children in hospitals and residential institutions. It was published in a popular edition as 'Child Care and the Growth of Love' (1953), which became a best-seller in English and many other languages.

During the post-war years Bowlby travelled widely, meeting the leading figures in the child development field. He took his appointment with the World Health Organization in January 1950, and during the late winter and early spring he visited several countries in Europe (France, the Netherlands, Sweden, Switzerland and the United Kingdom) as well as the United States. In each country he had meetings with workers concerned with child care and child guidance, saw something of their work and explored the existing literature on this subject.

This study showed that the quality of parental care that a child receives in his earliest years is of vital importance to his future mental health. An infant or young child must experience a warm, intimate and continuous relationship with his parental figures if he is to develop in an optimal way. A 'parental figure' is basically mother, but it could also be father, other members of the family or a parental substitute.

On maternal deprivation

A state of affairs in which a child does not have, or has lost, a secure attachment with mother was originally termed 'maternal deprivation'. This was a general term covering a number of different situations and types of deprivation: perceptual, social, biological or emotional (see Rutter 1981).

Deprivation can occur – it was said – when for any reason the child is removed from his basic caregiver. But it can also occur in his or her presence, if the mother, father or permanent parental substitute is unable to give the child the necessary degree of loving responsiveness, continuous care and support.

According to more recent developments in attachment theory, the term 'deprivation' is now less frequently used. The study of attachment relationships and attachment representations has led to the classification of attachment relationships into two broad categories: 'secure' and 'insecure'. Children who have experienced consistent, reliable and empathic parental care tend to feel securely attached. Children who have experienced various forms and degrees of abandonment, rejection, abuse or inconsistent care are classified as being insecurely attached.

The negative consequences of interruptions in the parent–child relationship and, particularly, of the institutional care of young children was an important subject of study in the post-war years. A number of researchers on both sides of the Atlantic, mostly working independently, had discovered the fundamental importance of the subject and made significant contributions. Dorothy Burlingham and Anna Freud made important observations while running their residential nursery in Hampstead during the war. All these studies showed that children in institutional care experience a number of reactions that can be interpreted as signs of distress, together with the defence mechanisms against such distress, and that they are likely to suffer developmental disturbances if institutional care is prolonged.

The study of defence mechanisms against separation anxiety showed that these mechanisms are not internally generated but are responses to interpersonal events. Phantasies are ways of dealing with experience but do not precede it.

The ill-effects of deprivation vary with its degree. Partial deprivation produces long-lasting anxiety and other painful and disturbing feelings, including anger and depression. Complete deprivation may be even more far-reaching and have permanent effects on personality development and the capacity to form, sustain and enjoy relationships.

Another set of unfavourable conditions that merited exploration were those in which the child lives with his real parents or permanent substitute parents, but lacks sufficient care, support and responsiveness. These deficits are likely to arise in dysfunctional families and influence the child's personality development in a negative way.

Bowlby supplied us with a great deal of trustworthy information about how certain conditions are necessary for the optimal psychological development of children. On this basis, general principles of child care could be formulated and applied to social policy, including the organization of children's in-patient treatment in hospitals, and so on.

A psychoanalytic paradigm

Bowlby's observations led him to question some basic theoretical assumptions in psychoanalysis. Until the mid 1950s, only one view of the nature and origin of affectional bonds was prevalent among psychoanalysts: the attachment between a child and his mother – it was said – develops because the child discovers that in order to reduce instinctual tension, for example his hunger, a maternal figure is necessary. According to this view, the child needs to be fed and gratified orally, but the specificity of his relationship with a single maternal figure is not sufficiently taken into account, let alone explained.

Bowlby, through discussions with Konrad Lorenz, Robert Hinde and Julian Huxley, became interested in the contribution that ethological studies could make to resolve this theoretical problem. Studies on imprinting – and particularly filial imprinting – and its biological function (protection and survival) were relevant. In 1954 the ethologist Robert Hinde began to attend regular meetings convened by Bowlby at the Tavistock Clinic. At some point he drew Bowlby's attention to Harlow's work with rhesus monkeys. Harlow's studies of young monkeys wishing to make contact with a dummy (acting as a mother substitute) showed that proximity-seeking behaviour was independent from the need to be fed (see Harlow et al. 1959; 1966).

Bowlby concluded that the child's tendency to form a strong and fundamental bond with a maternal figure is part of an archaic heritage, the function of which is species survival (protection from predators in the environment of evolutionary adaptedness), and that this tendency is relatively independent of orality or feeding.

Bowlby's interest in ethology was poorly understood by his fellow psychoanalysts, some of whom thought that he was treating humans as though they were animals (see Grosskurth's 1987, p.406) account of her conversation with a senior analyst in London). It is not difficult to understand why Bowlby's attempt to relate psychoanalysis to ethology was found bewildering. In fact, Bowlby tried to use notions drawn from ethology in his efforts to revise traditional metapsychology, but he never attempted to reduce the understanding of human beings to a merely 'animal' dimension.

In the 1960s Bowlby began to convene seminars to study attachment-related issues and form a pluralist study group. Ronald D. Laing was at one point a member of this group and contributed with observations about how certain types of communication in the family tend to generate pathology. Colin Murray Parkes (1995) says:

> Laing was a brilliant young Glaswegian psychiatrist whose ambivalent relationship with his own parents had made him painfully aware of the damage that families can do to their children. It had also made him suspicious of all authority, a revolutionary who was not afraid to take on the psychiatric establishment. In The Divided Self (1960), The Self and Others (1961) and Sanity, Madness and the Family (1964) he formulated a novel view of mental illness, which attributed most forms of it, including schizophrenia, to family pathology. Mental hospitals he saw as an extension of the family system which, far from curing the problem, would often aggravate it. His theories were not popular with the medical establishment. John himself, something of a revolutionary, recognized and helped to channel Laing's maverick genius while subjecting his wilder ideas to critical scrutiny. During his years at the Tavistock Laing carried out his best work and achieved considerable fame. Had he remained, it may be that the decline which took place after he became a 'guru' and surrounded himself with less critical colleagues would have been checked. (p.255–256)

Meanwhile, Bowlby remained active at the British Psycho-Analytical Society and was Deputy President to Donald Winnicott between 1956 and 1961. In 1957 Bowlby presented to the Society his seminal paper, 'The Nature of the Child's Tie to His Mother', which he published the following year. Here a new systematic theory began to coalesce. Bowlby's language was clearly biological and evolutionary. He proposed that several instinctual responses that mature in the course of the first year, namely sucking, clinging, crying, following and smiling, become organized into attachment behaviour related to a specific mother figure during the second half of the first year. Bowlby supported his view in a variety of studies, including those of Piaget and the ethologists he was familiar with at the time. Such papers created a storm in the Psycho-Analytical Society. Joan Riviere, Anna Freud and even Winnicott reacted unfavourably (Bretherton 1991, p.17–18).

In 1956 Bowlby began working on what was to be his fundamental work, *Attachment and Loss*, which appeared in three volumes in 1969, 1973 and 1980.

In 1959, Bowlby presented to the British Psycho-Analytical Society his paper on 'Separation Anxiety' (published in 1960). In this paper, Bowlby pointed out that traditional psychoanalytic theory fails to explain both the intense attachment of infants to a mother figure and young children's dramatic responses to separation. He pointed out that the understanding of separation anxiety will not progress without addressing the specificity of the child's tie to his mother. Unlike other psychoanalysts, Bowlby suggested that excessive separation anxiety is usually facilitated by adverse family experiences and communications that make the child feel insecure in his basic attachments. However, he also explored the significance of those cases in which separation anxiety is unconsciously defended against, so that it appears to be extremely low or altogether absent.

In 1959, at a meeting of the British Psycho-Analytical Society, he read his third major theoretical paper: 'Grief and Mourning in Infancy and Early Childhood' (published a year later, 1960b). Here, in opposition to ideas formulated by Melanie Klein and Anna Freud, he pointed out that if the mother figure continues to be unavailable beyond a certain period of time, significant emotional reactions occur which are essentially related to the specificity of this bond.

Bowlby began to feel alienated from many of his colleagues at the British Psycho-Analytical Society in the 1960s, after he presented 'The Nature of the Child's Tie to His Mother'. Also, his paper 'Ethology and the Development of Object Relations' (1960c) disconcerted many people who were not open to these new ideas. In these papers, Bowlby began to articulate a way of thinking that was incompatible with Freud's and Klein's instinctual theories.

In the course of my supervision sessions, Bowlby was always complimentary of Winnicott's work, which he saw as highly compatible with his own position. However, it seems that Winnicott did not reciprocate in the same way. Jennifer Johns (personal communication) told me that the last time she saw Donald Winnicott was in 1970 at Mansfield House (the London home of the Institute of Psycho-Analysis), when John Bowlby was making a presentation.

Jennifer entered the building and saw Winnicott waiting for the lift, which was stuck on the top floor. She ran up and brought it down. In the lift, she said, 'It's unusual to see you here when John Bowlby is speaking'. Winnicott sighed and responded: 'Look, Jennifer, I thought I'd have one last go at finding out what John is saying!'.

Not long ago, Peter Ellingsen, an Australian journalist, who has developed a deep interest in psychoanalysis, became intrigued by the fact that Bowlby has been so marginalized. In the course of 1997 he began research on this topic and interviewed a large number of psychoanalysts in London. He told me that he was intrigued by the fact that many psychoanalysts have made dismissive comments about Bowlby's work, yet they admit that they have never read it.

Initially, Bowlby's ideas did not have a better reception from academic psychologists. Yet, as Michael Rutter (1995) points out, gradually Bowlby's work began to be understood. Now most of the key components of attachment concepts have received empirical support.

Perhaps the difficulties that Bowlby experienced can be understood in terms of Kuhn's analysis of resistance to conceptual change (Kuhn 1962). Kuhn suggested that in the development of science, the first accepted paradigm is often believed to be the essential explanation. However, the evolution of scientific knowledge requires the periodic renewal of paradigms. Any subsequent attempt to change the original paradigm meets considerable resistance in scientific communities. Furthermore, scientists are political beings and resistance to theoretical and methodological change often takes the form of political action.

For instance, Isaac Newton was the originator of a branch of physics. It has been said that all science depends on physics. Newton certainly built upon other people's work, but it was the publication of his three laws of motion and the theory of gravity that set science off on the road to most contemporary developments. Following his formulation, Newtonian physics (what is now called 'classical physics') reigned supreme for a period of 200 years and the scientific establishment regarded any opposition to Newton's ideas as a serious offence. However, later developments showed that Newton was wrong as far as his theory of light is concerned (Gribbin 1985).

Nevertheless, the degree of hostility that Bowlby received from some of his fellow psychoanalysts cannot simply be explained in terms of differences of opinion. I think there were much deeper issues at stake. Bowlby's uneasy relationship with many of his colleagues could be partly explained on theoretical grounds. He not only challenged traditional psychoanalytic metapsychology, but he also underplayed the role of sexuality and the Oedipus complex, he questioned the notion of unconscious phantasy and he did not deal with symbolism. Furthermore, his colleagues knew that Bowlby's daily work was not mainly centred around five-session-a-week analysis, the context on which many analysts base their clinical observations and professional identity.

Victoria Hamilton (1985) points out that the proportion of practising psychoanalysts who have been able to grasp the picture of human relationships and development outlined by attachment theory remains small. This is due to a complex set of causes. However, one factor that may partially account for this situation is the unconscious resistance to sense fully the painful nature of the material that Bowlby presses upon us: real losses, real deprivation, real trauma.

Bowlby believed that psychoanalysis, as a discipline, is not defined by any particular theory or any specific way of construing it. Bowlby never liked the fact that different trends in psychoanalytic thinking are identified by the name of an author. To fixate the development of scientific knowledge according to one man's paradigm was, in his view, a way of obstructing the development of knowledge. He observed that once a system of ideas becomes identified with a particular name, the writings of such an author tend to acquire a biblical quality. For that reason, Bowlby firmly opposed the emergence of a 'Bowlbian' school.

Attachment and Loss

It took Bowlby 15 years to write his trilogy, published under the general title of *Attachment and Loss*.

The three volumes (which have been translated into many languages and published in many different parts of the world) were brought to light over a period of 11 years. They have a monumental quality and present a coherent account of attachment theory, having been a fundamental source of inspiration for many researchers in the relevant fields. In these books, Bowlby offered a comprehensive account of his thinking and its application to psychoanalytic theory, developmental psychology, psychopathology, psychiatry and psychotherapy.

The last years

In 1972, at the age of 60, Bowlby retired from his Health Service and Medical Research Council posts, but remained an Honorary Member of the Tavistock Clinic and continued his academic work. He also treated some patients and did a great deal of clinical supervision. It was during this period that I met him weekly for supervision.

During the period 1980–1985, I was Chairman of the Scientific Programme Committee of the Institute of Group Analysis. In that capacity I invited Bowlby every year to conduct a series of seminars. Bowlby felt at home there and had the opportunity to exchange ideas actively with a good number of group analysts. Sometimes there were heated arguments, but nonetheless it became clear that attachment theory and group analysis share some fundamental principles. John listened to what people had to say with interest, as though it mattered, and he responded at times with unbending conviction.

In 1984, Earl Hopper presented a paper at the Institute of Group Analysis on 'The Sociocultural School of Psychoanalysis'. The central figures in this school (Erich Fromm, Freida Fromm-Reichman, Karen Horney, Harry Stack-Sullivan, Clare Thomson and others) were interested in social, cultural and interpersonal constraints on the development of personality. In their view, social facts of various kinds, which they would regard as real, affected psychic functioning throughout early development and the life cycle as a whole. Therefore, what is going on inside an individual is primarily a matter of what is represented from an interpersonal and social web. Furthermore, the way individuals can negotiate their circumstances not only depends on their internal endowment but also on the opportunities that are available to them and the ways in which the society construes the situation in which they are acting. In contrast, certain schools of psychoanalysis emphasize projection rather than representation, so that – in their view – perceptions of the world are influenced from the first by projection of intrapsychic elements rather than by the reality of what is already there. Earl Hopper's presentation was partly based on his book, *Social Mobility: A Study of Social Control and Insatiability* (1981).

John Bowlby, who was formally the discussant of Earl Hopper's paper, responded very briefly by drawing areas of coincidence between attachment theory and the socio-cultural school of psychoanalysis. Then, addressing Dr Hopper directly, he said: 'The quality of your paper is such that I have been rendered speechless. I have no more to add. Perhaps we should now invite the audience to speak'. This incident illustrated an interesting aspect of Bowlby's general attitude to knowledge: although he had firm convictions, he was also prepared to listen to other people and accept their contribution as valuable, sometimes without reservation.

During the latter part of his career, Bowlby received many honours from British and American academic bodies. In 1982 he was appointed Freud Memorial Professor of Psychoanalysis at University College, London. In June 1987, the Tavistock Clinic celebrated Bowlby's eightieth birthday by organizing an international conference under the title, 'Fruits of Attachment Theory: Findings and Applications Across the Life Cycle'. The list of topics and contributors was wide and impressive.

A few weeks later, Bowlby collapsed with cardiac arrhythmia and was taken to intensive care. However, he made a good recovery and was able to complete his biography of Charles Darwin, the publication of which was celebrated at the Tavistock Clinic in the spring of 1990. He was just recovering from a new illness and was in a wheelchair. That was the last time I saw him.

John Bowlby died on 2 September 1990, following two strokes in short succession. He was on holiday with his family in Skye, as he had been every summer for many years. His body rests in a beautiful area overlooking the cliffs of Waternish and the Armore Peninsula.

John Bowlby had a secretary, Dorothy Southern, who at the time of his death was still working for him after 39 years of continuous service. Dorothy died in January 1994. Ursula Bowlby (personal communication) comments: 'Dorothy's importance in John's life should be underlined. She was a secure base and typed every word he wrote in an appalling hand-writing!'

CHAPTER 2

Attachment Theory

Introduction

Bowlby (1977) said:

> What for convenience I am terming attachment theory is a way of conceptualizing the propensity of human beings to make strong affectional bonds to particular others and of explaining the many forms of emotional distress and personality disturbance, including anxiety, anger, depression and emotional detachment, to which unwilling separation and loss give rise.

In the above paragraph we can see that Bowlby defined attachment theory as a body of explanations. Furthermore, these explanations are essentially concerned with two issues: (1) explaining why human beings tend to make strong, selective and durable bonds; and (2) explaining how the disruption or threats of disruption of these bonds can cause painful emotions and, ultimately, psychopathology.

Therefore, Bowlby's initial position reflected three main concerns: to amend psychoanalytic theory in the light of new discoveries; to view psychopathology in a developmental context; and to place intimate relationships at the centre of developmental psychology.

Bowlby added: 'Advocates of attachment theory argue that many forms of psychiatric disturbance can be attributed either to deviations in the development of attachment behaviour or, more rarely, to failure of its development; and also that the theory casts light on both the origin and the treatment of these conditions'.

Why a new theory?

Attachment theory was formulated in order to explain observed facts in a way which was more coherent with what was observed. The subjects of observation are the most common features of everyday life: the formation, renewal and loss of emotional ties with specific people and the emotions that emerge in the course of these events.

Although such processes were observed and explained by psychiatrists, psychologists and psychoanalysts, Bowlby came to the conclusion that existing theories did not strike the right chord. More than any other branch of medicine or psychology, psychoanalysis concerned itself with the study of emotional life and relationships. Yet the over-riding importance of primary attachment relationships was overshadowed by theories that put sexuality and a hypothetical 'death instinct' at the very centre of human motivation.

True, a significant number of psychoanalysts discarded the notion of a death instinct and did, indeed, highlight the importance of bonding and relationships, particularly in early development. But none of them said: 'Hold on! Let's revise our basic assumptions about human motivation before we go on with our theorizing!'.

This omission resulted in a certain ambiguity, for people's fundamental need to find security in specific relationships was still explained in terms of feeding or sexuality. Although feeding and sexuality do play an important part in psychosocial life, they cannot easily account for the fact that attachment-related events and emotions play such a central role in human behaviour and early development.

Intimate long-lasting relationships are seen in virtually all human beings, and they are commonly regarded as an integral part of human nature. There is more to it: (1) the strongest emotions, whether associated with joy or pain, emerge in the course of attachment-related events; (2) the quality and vicissitudes of the earliest relationships are determinants of personality development and mental health; and (3) the way people construe and manage relationships is based on previous experiences of relationships.

If attachment is recognized as a primary motivational force with its own dynamics, then it may be easier to comprehend the far-reaching and complex consequences of attachment relationships. Otherwise, the understanding of attachment issues (particularly in their developmental and clinical implications) could only be assumed by making extrapolations from less compatible theoretical schemes.

Bowlby explained that until the mid 1950s only one explicitly formulated view of the nature and origin of affectional bonds was prevalent, and in this matter there was agreement between psychoanalysts and learning theorists. It was assumed that interpersonal bonds develop because the individual discovers that, in order to satisfy certain drives, for example for food in infancy and for sex in adult life, another human being is necessary. This type of theory postulates two kinds of drive, primary and secondary; it categorizes food and sex as 'libidinal' or primary, and other personal relationships as secondary.

The crux of attachment theory is that it assumes that the pains, joys and meaning of attachment cannot be reduced to a secondary drive.

It is true that alternative theories postulated a primitive object relation from the beginning. One of the most prominent versions is that advocated by Melanie Klein. But here mother's breast is seen as the first object and the greatest emphasis – in terms of early development – is placed on food and orality. Furthermore, the death instinct is given an extraordinary significance as the source of primitive envy, projection and early perceptual distortions of the significant other. In this context, most psychic processes are seen as autogenic (mainly coming from inside the individual), and interpersonal life, rather than having its own inherent status, is conceptualized as an epiphenomenon of internally generated psychic events. Again, the primary quality of attachment and its inherent interpersonal context are lost.

Bowlby thought that there was enough clinical and empirical evidence to formulate a new theory. The resulting conceptual framework could easily accommodate all those phenomena to which Freud called attention – for example, love relations, separation anxiety, mourning, defence, anger, guilt, depression, trauma, emotional detachment, sensitive periods in early life, and so on.

Although attachment theory departs radically from certain parts of the Freudian tradition, it also develops many ideas that Freud held to be important. Bowlby was an independent thinker and proposed his paradigm as one that had advantages over preceding conceptualizations. One of his main concerns was that knowledge must be validated.

Bowlby (1982) said:

> Without good theory as a guide, research is likely to be difficult to plan and to be unproductive, and findings are difficult to interpret. Without a reasonably valid theory of psychopathology, therapeutic techniques tend to be blunt and of uncertain benefit. Without a reasonably valid theory of aetiology, systematic and agreed measures of prevention will never be supported. My hope is that, in the long term, the greatest value of the theory proposed may prove to be the light it throws on the conditions most likely to promote healthy personality development. Only when those conditions are clear beyond doubt will parents know what is best for their children and will communities be willing to help them provide it.

On psychoanalytic metapsychology

Metapsychology is a term coined by Freud to refer to a core of conceptual formulations to clarify and define the theoretical assumptions on which psychoanalysis is founded. In Chapter 1 of *Attachment and Loss* (Volume 1), Bowlby (1969) tried to locate attachment theory in the context of psychoanalytic metapsychology. In my view, this should always be the starting point in the process of learning the basics of attachment theory.

Here, Bowlby classified the assumptions which constitute psychoanalytic metapsychology in accordance with Rapaport (1960). The five viewpoints and the types of proposition each demands are held to be the following:

- *The dynamic*: This point of view demands propositions concerning the psychological forces involved in a phenomenon.

- *The economic*: This demands propositions concerning the psychological energy involved in a phenomenon.

- *The structural*: This demands propositions concerning the abiding psychological configurations (structures) involved in a phenomenon.

- *The genetic*: This demands propositions concerning the psychological origin and development of a phenomenon.

- *The adaptive*: This demands propositions concerning the relationship of a phenomenon to the environment.

Bowlby stated clearly that he had no difficulty in accepting the structural, the genetic and the adaptive points of view. Propositions of this sort are to be found throughout his writings. However, he did not adopt the dynamic or the economic viewpoint. He dispensed of any concept related to these propositions.

The main variants are: (1) to postulate a new concept of instinct behaviour within which the need to form and sustain attachment relationships is primary and distinct from feeding and sexual needs; and (2) to borrow from modern biology a control theory or cybernetic model to understand psychic organization.

On instinct

As Hamilton (1985) explains, all studies of human behaviour (except those based on the most extreme theories of learning and conditioning) posit certain basic behavioural patterns, which are described as 'instincts'. Although there is disagreement about the nature of these basic patterns, all agree that the term 'instinctive' denotes those behaviours that are common to the members of a species and that are more or less resistant to environmental influences.

In psychoanalysis, the concept of instinct is derived from Strachey's translation of Freud's '*trieb*'. Some psychoanalysts have regarded the term 'drive' as a more suitable translation of the German word *trieb*, which is different from '*instinkt*'.

Freud himself used the term '*instinkt*' quite selectively. This referred more to a precisely determined activity. *Trieb*, on the other hand, was used to designate a surging and rather undifferentiated need. Thus, as Victoria Hamilton rightly points out, problems of translation have compounded the confusions arising out of the psychoanalytic view of instincts and of behaviours and the emotions to which they supposedly give rise.

Like Freud, Bowlby defined the concept of instinct precisely, adopting its definition from modern biology. It is an observable pattern of behaviour which follows a recognizably similar and predictable pattern in almost all members of a species (or all members of one sex). It is activated by specific conditions and terminated by others. It involves a sequence that usually runs a predictable course. It serves a fundamental function which has obvious value in contributing to the preservation of an individual or the continuity of a species. It tends to develop without recourse to learning.

Moreover, this model of instinct has an adaptive quality. This means that it leaves open the possibility that an instinct – having a strong adaptive component – can be in mutual interaction with environmental factors.

The idea of attachment as a form of instinctive behaviour fits the following conceptual requirements:

1. Attachment behaviour follows a recognizable pattern and predictable course in all human beings.

2. Attachment behaviour is usually activated by specific conditions and terminated by others. For instance, attachment behaviour in a child is readily activated by the appearance of something strange, by sudden separation from an attachment figure, by sudden darkness, by a loud noise and so on, and under certain internal conditions such as fatigue, hunger, ill-health and pain.

3. Attachment behaviour serves a survival function: an individual is more likely to survive adverse conditions if assisted by another human being, especially if the latter is stronger, wiser and more able to cope with the world (as happens with the child in relation to his parent).

4. Attachment behaviour, because of its adaptive nature, can only function effectively within a social system and is part of it.

Another characteristic of instinctive patterns is that they are usually linked together, so that co-ordination results in one form of behaviour. This is the case, for instance, with sex and attachment going together in mutual co-ordination.

An important reference framework in Bowlby's development of an instinct theory is the 'theory of primary object clinging', which proposed that there exists an inbuilt need to touch and cling to a human being, and that this need is on a par with the need for food and warmth. This view was proposed by Imre Herman in Budapest and adopted by Alice and Michael Balint (Hamilton 1985). Bowlby (1958) listed five responses which in infancy serve the function of: (1) binding the child to the mother; and (2) contributing to the reciprocal dynamic of binding the mother to the child: sucking, clinging, following, crying and smiling.

Behavioural systems

Attachment theory assumes that the organism organizes behavioural systems or 'effector equipments'. Among these systems we can list the attachment system, the affiliative system (affiliation to groups) and the feeding, sexual and exploratory systems. Each one of these serves a particular biological function. The attachment system is basic because it secures survival.

Bowlby's model differs from Freud's in three ways:

1. In Freud's model, attachment is secondary to oral and libidinal gratification. In Bowlby's model, attachment is primary and has a status of its own.

2. In Freud's model the child is enclosed in a state of primary narcissism, 'shut off from the stimuli of the external world like a bird in an egg' (Freud 1911). In Bowlby's model, the individual is actively involved from the first in an intersubjective context which requires reciprocal responses.

3. In Freud's model, instinctive behaviour is activated by a load of energy which – once built up to a certain level – requires discharge. In Bowlby's model, instinctive behaviour is activated by both internal and external conditions when the function it serves is called upon.

A young child may be playing away from his mother in a park, while his mother is sitting and reading a magazine. He is acting under the predominant influence of his exploratory system. Suddenly, he falls and hurts himself. As a consequence of the pain and fright, the attachment system is reactivated and consequently he goes to his mother, crying and seeking comfort and assistance. We can then say that the accident has de-activated the child's exploratory behaviour and activated his attachment behaviour.

In a case like this, behavioural systems serve 'set goals'. This denotes a time-limited event or an on-going condition, either of which is brought about by specific and relevant conditions.

As Bowlby (1969) put it, past discussions of instinctive behaviour have tended to concentrate on sequences that have a dramatic and time-limited outcome, such as orgasm, and to neglect behaviour the outcome of which is an on-going relationship, such as maintenance of a specified distance over a long period. A main reason for past neglect of this sort of behaviour is that it cannot be readily understood in terms of such concepts as drive or energy discharge. Behavioural systems resulting in the maintenance of specified distance over time could be organized on less or more sophisticated lines. It follows that the attachment system may be an integration of at least two sub-systems: one aimed at maintaining the relationship as such over time; and the other at seeking immediate proximity under temporary circumstances. An example of the first in adult behaviour is the need to keep in contact with the attachment figure through regular visits, telephone calls, and so on. An instance of the latter is the sudden search for proximity with, and assistance from, the other when a sudden adverse situation arises.

Just as there are many different types of behavioural system, there are a number of different ways in which their activities can be co-ordinated. Often a behavioural organization is made up of subordinate or complementary parts.

Attachment behaviour is organized around the mental representation of a relationship. This relationship is *specific* – it is formed in relation to a specific person. The representation of this relationship is *durable* – it usually endures either indefinitely or for a large part of the life cycle, even after the relationship has ended. It has inherent emotional components. It can be expressed through symbolism. It also has a semantic component: the representation of a relationship has particular meanings.

Attachment theorists have focused on the study of the *child–parent relationship* because it is the most important in terms of its influence on early personality development. This is a relationship that a young person has with someone seen as stronger, wiser and more able to cope with the world.

However, other relationships are important as the individual grows older, such as relationships between siblings. The child's relationship with influential teachers and peers should not be neglected. In adulthood, the individual's relationship with his parents continues to be important, but relationships with peers (particularly the sexual partnership) and parental attachment to offspring acquire a predominant value. At any given time, the subject's relationships are organized hierarchically, so that some relationships are more valued and influential with respect to the subject's emotional life than others.

Attachment and ethology

Bowlby developed a marked interest in ethology because he discovered that this discipline could provide some important clues to understanding instinctive behaviour. Lorenz's work on imprinting (which first appeared in 1935 and became more generally known in the 1950s), offered a useful model. At least in some species of bird, he had found, strong bonds to a mother figure develop during the early days of life without any reference to food and simply through the young being exposed to, and becoming familiar with, this figure.

This picture was confirmed when Harry Harlow (1958) published the results of his first studies of infant rhesus monkeys reared with inanimate mothers.

Harlow's ethological work was inspired by the pioneering work of the psychoanalyst, Rene Spitz. Spitz (1950) found that infants in conditions of maternal deprivation experienced anxiety and risked developing psychopathology. Harlow took infant monkeys from their mothers soon after birth and raised them with two surrogate 'mothers', one made of bale-wire mesh, the other covered with terry cloth. Either dummy could be equipped with a feeding nipple which provided milk. In one setting, the bale-wire 'mother' was equipped with a feeding nipple while the terry-cloth 'mother' was not. Under these conditions, the infant repeatedly clung to the terry-cloth dummy, cuddling it, running to it when frightened and using it as a base for explorations. The monkey only went to the feeding bale-wire 'mother' when hungry. These experiments seemed to disconfirm the hypothesis that orality and feeding were at the origin of attachment behaviour. To rhesus monkeys, at least, warm contact seemed more important.

In 1966 Harry and Margaret Harlow published a paper under the title of 'Learning to Love'. In this paper they pointed out that they did not believe that monkey research will give us total understanding of human behaviour. However, some salient developmental variables – presumably characteristic of all the Anthropoidea: monkeys, apes and men – may be brought into clear relief.

These experiments caused animal suffering and may consequently evoke strong reactions from many people. Nevertheless, what we have learned from them is based on the fact that with monkey subjects it is possible experimentally to disrupt any or all of the normal developmental stages and study the consequences of such disruptions.

The Harlows observed that the infant monkey becomes selectively attached to its mother. The mother's function is to handle the baby's nutritional, temperature and eliminative needs; provide it with physical support and intimate physical contact (which seem to be important in the development of the child's sense of security); and protect it from external threats or dangers (including the dangers to which the unknowledgeable infant inadvertently exposes itself as it begins to explore the physical world that surrounds it).

These studies have demonstrated that the primate child–mother relationship has a lasting quality and that disruption of this tie causes psychological distress in the child and serious damage if perpetuated. Attachment behaviour on the part of the child is manifested through proximity-seeking attempts such as sucking, clinging and imitation, as well as through visual and locomotor following behaviour. Out of adequate maternal responses the child develops strong feelings of safety and security.

Monkey children achieve a strong and socially useful sense of security when raised by their real mothers. In their absence, surrogate monkey mothers will do better than a dummy or no mother at all. In the presence of the mother, surrogate or real, the infant shows a growing capacity to go out and explore the inanimate world, returning from time to time to the mother's body for comfort and reassurance. The sense of curiosity only seems to be present when there is a secure attachment to a maternal figure. As the securely attached child monkey grows older, he becomes more autonomous and independent from mother, while at the same time developing peer relationships.

Deprivation of maternal care produces dramatic and pervasive effects. Infants raised in groups without mothers tend to seek physical contact with each other and they show little activity other than clinging. A monkey placed in total isolation, yet fed, will respond with self-clutching and crouching.

The immediate response of infant monkeys to maternal separation turned out to be similar to that of human children. There was an initial phase of protest with searching behaviour and vocalization, followed by a phase of despair (sitting in a hunched, depressed posture, and so on).

Subsequent studies (Hinde 1982) indicated that the application of ethological studies to understanding human behaviour has limitations. However, ethological studies had an important role in the development of attachment theory, particularly because they were useful to substantiate the need to find a model of understanding motivation different from the traditional psychoanalytic view of instinctual behaviour.

As Hinde (1982) pointed out, Bowlby deliberately played down the importance of oral or nutritive responses in the attachment of infants to their mothers. However, he said:

> There was no suggestion that the early development of the mother–baby relationship was just like the parent–offspring relationship in other species. Rather Bowlby made use of aspects of parent–offspring relationships that were common to a wide range of species, and suggested that they were likely to be important also in man. In particular he pointed out that natural selection must have favoured mechanisms that promoted parent–offspring proximity in our 'environment of evolutionary adaptedness' – that is, the environment in which the relevant characteristics of the human species evolved: infant survival would have depended on it.

Bowlby clarified his point of view in this respect in Part II of *Attachment and Loss*, Volume 1 (1969). He said: '...the basic structure of man's behavioural equipment resembles that of infra-human species but has in the course of evolution undergone special modifications that permit the same end to be reached by a much greater diversity of means'.

On control theory

Another implication of Bowlby's use of ethological concepts was that he began to conceptualize psychic processes according to 'control theory', that is to say, according to a cybernetic model. This is the model we use to study biological organisms, the organization of the brain and the computer.

The way a computer or a biological organism can behave in a purposive way, in the sense of achieving a predetermined goal by versatile means, is feedback. This is simply a process whereby the actual effects of performance are continuously reported back to a central apparatus for the purpose of maintaining the initial goal in variable conditions through interactive regulation.

These interactions take place between parts of the organism and between the organism and its environment. Through these interactions structures are organized and homeostasis established and maintained. Structures take a form that is determined by the kind of environment in which each system has been operating during its evolution. This is what Bowlby called the 'environment of adaptedness'.

In summary, attachment theory emphasizes:

1. The primary status and biological function of intimate emotional bonds between individuals (particularly in the parent–child relationship but also throughout the life cycle), the making and maintaining of which is achieved and controlled by a cybernetic system situated within the central nervous system.

2. The powerful influence that early attachment relationships have in personality development and – in some cases – in the origins of psychopathology.

Other aspects of attachment theory

Attachment theory also involves: (1) a developmental theory (concerned with both normal and pathological development); (2) a theory of sensitive responsiveness as psychic organizer; (3) a theory of internalization and representation; and (4) a theory of anxiety. In the following paragraphs I shall explain these points.

A developmental theory

In the course of his studies, Bowlby realized that a new developmental model was necessary. Existing developmental theories included Freud's notion of libidinal phases, whereby an energy rooted in the sexual instinct changed the source of sexual excitation (the erotogenic zone) and its object (cathexes) along a line of progression. This progression could be halted (fixation) or reversed (regression), and by virtue of these processes psychopathology emerged.

Another influential theory of development was the one proposed by Melanie Klein, whereby early psychic life was seen as dominated by either a paranoid or a depressive position, alternating sequentially. The paranoid position was a mode of object-relating which was specific to the first four months of life but could re-occur later. It was characterized as the expression of aggressive instincts which carried a threat – via projection – of persecution by the 'bad object'. The bad object was the result of splitting the 'part object' (chiefly the mother's breast) into two: the 'good' and the 'bad' object. The 'depressive position' was, instead, a modality of object relation which was established sequentially after the paranoid position had been resolved. It was characterized as the child's capacity to apprehend the mother as a whole object, with both good and bad aspects. Klein's model has several problems: (1) it is based on the assumption of the predominance of aggressive impulses, linked with a notion of a hypothetical 'death instinct', which is scientifically untestable; (2) it uses terms derived from psychopathology to describe normal processes; (3) it assumes that the infant is unable to see mother as a total object and relate to her accordingly, an assumption which has been disconfirmed by modern developmental research; and (4) it confuses defence mechanisms against pain and anxiety (such as splitting and projection, which more often arise in conditions of deprivation, trauma or insecurity) with normal stages of development.

ON DEVELOPMENTAL PATHWAYS

Bowlby used the concept of 'developmental pathways' proposed by the biologist, C.H. Waddington (1957). Within this framework, human personality is conceived of as a structure that develops unceasingly along one or another of an array of possible and discrete pathways. All pathways are thought to start close together so that, at conception, an individual has access to a large range of potential pathways along any one of which he might travel. The choice of pathway is determined by the interaction between the individual and his environment. Thus this conception of development is based on an interactive model.

Since birth, the main context of interaction is the way a child is treated by his parents. In this interaction, the child's temperament plays an important role. In other words, the child brings into the interaction his own personal responses. However, for Bowlby, what determines health or pathology is fundamentally the parental style (which is normally based on an intergenerational line of causality). A child who grows in conditions of emotional security and stability is likely to follow an optimal pathway, whereas another child – whose social environment does not provide such conditions – is likely to follow a sub-optimal pathway. In other words, as Bowlby (1985a) put it, the pathway along which the individual is going to develop is largely determined by the way his caregivers treat him, not only during infancy but throughout his childhood and adolescence as well.

Some individuals may show resilience to adverse conditions, but such resilience may be due to one or both of the following conditions: (1) having had a solid and satisfactory foundation in earlier life; or (2) having secondary attachment figures that provide – from the background, as it were – some support and stability.

In this context, psychopathology is seen not as the result of fixations or regressions, but as the result of the individual having taken a sub-optimal developmental pathway either right from the start or at some point in the course of childhood or adolescence (as the consequence of deprivation, ill-treatment, trauma or loss).

Change towards either a more optimal or less serviceable pathway is possible at any point in the course of development (from infancy to late adolescence), according to changes in environmental conditions. However, change is constrained by prior development. This implies that the longer a maladaptive pathway has been followed, the less likely it is that favourable conditions will bring development to a near-optimal course.

A theory of sensitive responsiveness as psychic organizer

An important notion in attachment theory is that 'sensitive responsiveness' is a major psychic organizer. Mary Ainsworth (a close associate of John Bowlby, see Chapter 4) inferred through her research work that what matters most in determining a developmental pathway is the caregiver's sensitive responsiveness. In infancy, the parent's sensitive responsiveness includes noticing signals from the baby, interpreting them accurately, and responding appropriately and fairly promptly. Insensitivity, on the other hand, may or may not entail hostile or actively unpleasant behaviour on the part of the caregiver. It exists when the caregiver fails to read the baby's mental states or goals or fails to support the baby in achieving his positive states or goals.

Later, throughout life, sensitive responsiveness plays an important role in evoking a sense of self-integration and self-worth as well as in eliciting loving, co-operative and reciprocal responses. In childhood and adolescence, one major characteristic of sensitive responsiveness is the parent's capacity to see the child as a separate human being, with his own needs as separate from those of others. In this context the child is welcome when his attachment behaviour is activated and – conversely – is allowed freedom and support when his exploratory behaviour is activated.

The insensitive caregiver thus teaches the child that his care-eliciting signals are ineffective – or even counter-productive, for example by making the child feel bad about himself when he is in greatest need of support and emotional soothing (see Chapter 7).

Sensitive responsiveness involves at least two operations: the first is gaining access to the mental state of the child, and the second is attributing meaning to the mental state. The latter involves complex cognitive-affective processes, based on the parent's own internal working models and capacity to understand mental states and reflect upon them.

The notion of 'sensitive responsiveness' is similar to that of 'empathy'. However, the word 'empathy' implies identification with the other's mental state. Sensitive responsiveness, instead, involves some internal negotiation between the momentary state of feeling like the other and the ability to react as a separate being.

A theory of internalization and representation

Attachment theory recognizes the fact that the pattern of parent–child interaction (which takes place in a social context) tends to become a property of the child himself. This is not a novel idea in psychoanalysis, but the merit of attachment theory is to present it as part and parcel of a new metapsychology. In order to account for such a tendency, attachment theory contains a notion of representation defined by the term 'internal working model' of self and other. The working models that a child builds of his main caregivers (in usual circumstances mother and father) and their ways of communicating and behaving towards him, together with the complementary model of himself in interaction with each one of them, are built by the child during the first few years of his life, continue to be built during the years of immaturity and, during this long period, become firmly established as influential cognitive structures (for a detailed exploration of this topic, see Chapter 5).

Bowlby (1988a) said that there is strong evidence that the form these internal working models take is based on the child's real-life experience of day-to-day interactions with his parents:

> Subsequently the model of himself that he builds reflects also the images that his parents have of him, images that are communicated not only by how each treats him but by what each says to him. These models then govern how he feels towards each parent and about himself, how he expects each of them to treat him, and how he plans his own behaviour towards them. They govern too both the fears and wishes expressed in his day dreams.

In this context, internal working models are formed through a process that in psychoanalysis has been called 'internalization'. Let me now use this term as a temporarily useful concept, to refer to a 'transposition' into the representational world of a relationship that has existed before in the interpersonal world. While attachment theory starts with an idea of such 'internalization', Kleinian theory starts with projection. Klein placed much emphasis on destructive impulses (generated from inside the individual and primarily inwardly directed), these being seen as derivatives of the death instinct. In this scheme, the individual, from the first, defensively turns the destructive impulse outward, against an external object. The projection distorts the perception of reality. Therefore, an individual's account of his interactions with others is rendered invalid by virtue of the fact that – in this view – the whole process starts as projection. This point of conflict between attachment theory and Kleinian thinking is crucial.

Bowlby (1988b) once referred to the understanding of the process of forming internal working models of a relationship as 'a theory of internalization' (p.129–133). However, he did not use this concept frequently and I am glad that he did not, because it is an inadequate concept. 'Internalization' indicates something of a mechanical nature, which consists of making internal what has been external. Here, instead, we are talking about representing in the person's mind something that has been neither entirely outside the person nor entirely inside. What the individual represents is basically a relationship – as Stern (1995) puts it, an 'experience-of-being-with'. A dominant feature of the child–parent relationship is the way the parent treats the child, but (and I really want to underline this fact) what is represented in the person's mind is the relationship and not the parent as a separate entity. As Nicola Diamond (personal communication) says, 'this representation is not a simple transposition but a process mediated by language and a system of meanings'.

Therefore, after all, we can do better with the concept of representation rather than internalization. Ruth Robinson (personal communication) says: 'This is a very important point because it shows how attachment theory has moved away from the rather simplistic notion of things coming from the "inside" or the "outside"'.

Attachment theorists have been fundamentally concerned with the representation of primary attachment relationships since they are held to be highly influential in personality development. However, it would be wrong to believe that a concern with representations of social relationships within a certain culture and socio-political structure falls outside the realm of attachment theory. In Chapter 1 I referred to the way in which John Bowlby agreed with Earl Hopper's endorsement of the contribution made by the socio-cultural school of psychoanalysis to the understanding of socio-representational processes.

A theory of anxiety

The psychoanalytic literature is full of references to concepts such as anxiety, separation anxiety, signal anxiety and anxiety neurosis, and inferences about their origins. I do not propose to revise these concepts here but to summarize some of the relevant points.

In 1926, (in *Inhibitions, Symptoms and Anxiety*) Freud wrote:

> We can at any rate note one or two things about the feeling of anxiety. Its unpleasurable character seems to have a note of its own – something not very obvious, whose presence is difficult to prove yet which is in all likelihood there.

But besides having this special feature which is difficult to isolate, we notice that anxiety is accompanied by fairly definite physical sensations which can be referred to particular organs of the body. (SE, p.132)

Freud went on to say: 'In accordance with our general views we should be inclined to think that anxiety is based upon an increase of excitation which on the one hand produces the character of unpleasure and on the other finds relief through the acts of discharge already mentioned' (SE, p.133).

Here Freud, as he repeatedly did, placed the roots of anxiety in a metapsychological context, in which the notions of energy, excitation and discharge were fundamental. This was in line with his earlier assumption that anxiety was the result of repressed libido. This position is, of course, foreign to attachment theory and one to which few contemporary psychoanalysts subscribe.

However, a few paragraphs later, Freud stated:

Only a few of the manifestations of anxiety in children are comprehensible to us, and we must confine our attention to them. They occur, for instance, when a child is alone, or in the dark, or when it finds itself with an unknown person instead of one to whom it is used – such as its mother. These three instances can be reduced to a single condition – namely, that of missing someone who is loved and longed for. (SE, p.136)

Further on, Freud suggested that the function of anxiety is to produce a rescuing signal, in the face of anticipated danger, for the avoidance of the dangerous situation. This is the 'alarm bell' model of anxiety. The dangerous situations were – in Freud's view – loss of object in early childhood, castration in the phallic phase and threats from the super-ego during the latency period. He also added loss of the object's love to the list of potential dangers. However, he also indicated that anxiety may be the result of sadistic phantasies and the retaliation expected because of them.

Bowlby endorsed the idea that anxiety is mainly based on the threat of possibly losing the object. He distinguished the emotional consequences of an actual present loss from the danger or threat of a possible future loss. He explained that Freud wrestled with the problem and advanced a number of hypotheses. Every other leading analyst has done the same. With poor means of evaluating these ideas, many divergent schools of thought have proliferated. However, these difficulties disappear when an ethological approach is adopted, for it then becomes evident that man, like other animals, responds with anxiety to situations which carry an increased risk to biological survival. In other words, by implication, Bowlby saw anxiety as a reaction to threats of loss and insecurity in attachment relationships. This psychoanalysis indicates that often the source of anxiety is not a concrete threat to the person's biological survival but to his/her psychological survival (to the 'self'). This often occurs when the subject is implicitly or explicitly led to believe that he is nothing in the eyes of the significant other.

CHAPTER 3

Empirical Research
and Clinical Observations
Intersecting Points

Attachment theory and empirical research

Bowlby's work was characterized by a sustained and productive tension between the clinical and the research domains. He was unashamed at declaring that psychoanalysis could greatly benefit from laboratory experiments. He felt free to use, combine and integrate data provided by clinical evidence, developmental research and ethological studies. He was very interested in studies of family interaction and thought that sociology and social anthropology had much to contribute to psychoanalysis. As a result, his thinking moved from one perspective to another, yet always keeping track of how knowledge was being interwoven in a logical and coherent manner. He kept clearly in mind the links between clinical and empirical observations and how the interaction between these two fields could be articulated in a methodological way. However, he did emphasize the importance of empirical research, even more so in later life.

However, quantitative reviews based on the study of a particular phenomenon as it occurs in a large sample of individuals can complement, but not replace, the study of a person's subjective life in the psychoanalytic situation.

There is something unique about the psychoanalytic situation: the privileged access to the patient's mind. This is related to the possibility of seeing the patient continuously, regularly and frequently in a private situation; the openness of the patient's free associations without thematic restrictions; the confidentiality which allows for frankness; the use of countertransference in understanding the material, and so on. There is no other method which makes possible such privilege. As Peter Fonagy – who is both a clinician and a researcher – explains (Fonagy 1996), psychoanalytic insights are hard-won and cannot be regarded as trivial or arbitrary. They are the result of many millions of hours of careful listening, sometimes immensely painful. Therefore, we need to develop a clearer understanding of how we can convincingly reconcile empirical findings with the larger mosaic constituted by patients' subjective experiences.

Bowlby (1988) argued that psychoanalysis is an art and a natural science. The art is the clinical practice of psychoanalytic psychotherapy. The science is the body of knowledge and the methodology to create it. Bowlby said:

> The distinction I am drawing, of course, is not confined to psychoanalysis. It applies in every field in which the practice of a profession or a craft gives birth to a body of scientific knowledge – the blacksmith to metallurgy, the civil engineer to soil mechanics, the farmer to plant physiology, and the physician to the medical sciences. In each of these fields the role differentiates. On the one hand are the practitioners, on the other the scientists, with a limited number of individuals attempting to combine both roles. As history shows, this process of differentiation often proves painful and misunderstandings are frequent. (pp.39–40)

He went on to say:

> The aim of the practitioner is to take into account as many aspects as he can of each and every clinical problem with which he is called upon to deal. This requires him not only to apply any scientific principle that appears relevant but also to draw on such personal experience of the condition as he may have acquired and, especially, to attend to that unique combination of features met with in each patient. (p.40)

In this context, he affirmed: 'Taking all factors into account and giving each its due weight is the art of clinical judgement'.

However, he added:

> The outlook of the research scientist is quite different. In his efforts to discern general patterns underlying individual variety he ignores the particular and strives to simplify, risking thereby over-simplification. If he is wise he will probably concentrate attention on a limited aspect of a limited problem. If in making his selection he proves sagacious, or simply lucky, he may not only elucidate the problem selected but also develop ideas applicable to a broader range. (p.40)

Next, Bowlby pointed out that research has to do with selecting a limited manageable problem and the methods that will best help to solve it. No science can prosper for long without enlisting new methods to cross-check observations made by means of, and on hypotheses born of, older methods. Here the research scientist is likely to make important contributions.

When Bowlby talked about empirical research, he mostly referred to developmental and socio-psychological studies concerned with mental representations of attachment relationships and their effects on behaviour and mental health. These include experiences of our ties with significant others, developmental issues, memories of our past relationships, the expectations and forecasts engendered both by previous experience and by what we need from the others, and the way we organize our perception of their reactions and responses. All these themes concern psychoanalysis too, as fundamental issues.

Although Bowlby's studies focused on infancy and early development, he thought that all the years of immaturity, from infancy to late adolescence, are important in personality formation. Furthermore, the term 'development' applies to the entire life cycle. This needs to be said since some poorly informed people believe that attachment theory is only concerned with infancy and early development.

Some characteristics of attachment research

Attachment research evolves according to a certain framework, which can be defined in the following way: it brings some issues or questions into focus while leaving many others outside the central interest. The focus of attachment research is the study of relationship factors that lead human beings (particularly during their formative years) into an optimal or sub-optimal developmental pathway. Organism and context are viewed as inseparable. Attachment is a relationship construct, not an intrapsychic construct.

Established assessments of infant–caregiver attachment, like the Strange Situation procedure (see Chapter 4), are basically assessments of relationships, not individuals. It is now well known that: (1) the attachment pattern with each parent is often different from that with the other; and (2) the pattern a child has with one parent may change as the result of changing life circumstances.

Attachment research is also concerned with security and insecurity. Anxious or insecure attachment in childhood is proposed to be a risk factor for psychopathology but not necessarily psychopathological itself. When the caregiver is consistently responsive to the child's care-eliciting communications, the child develops a basic sense of trust that help, support and care will be available when needed. Such trust is precisely what is meant by 'secure attachment'. It is normally accompanied by a sense of self-worth and self-integration. In contrast, routinely unresponsive or inconsistent care undermines security.

Within this framework, psychopathology is seen as the outcome of a successive combination of liabilities. Of course, one of the liabilities is always likely to be early attachment insecurity. But attachment insecurity involves anxieties, these anxieties require the use of defence mechanisms, and the persistent use of these mechanisms can shape character pathology. The study of the relationship between attachment insecurity and later mental disorder is likely to become an area of foremost importance.

A brief note on psychoanalytic epistemology

The attempt to link development and psychopathology together in a definition appropriate for psychotherapy has always been inherent in psychoanalysis. However, psychoanalysis has been constrained by the fact that it has basically relied on clinical data from actual patients to study development and aetiology. Patients who come to analysis are more likely to be those who have followed the aetiological trajectory from early insecure attachment to adult psychopathology. But, as clinicians, we are less able to assess factors that may contribute to resilience or healthy development in spite of adversity. There are many situations which fall outside what psychoanalysis is good at. Clinical psychoanalysis has poor resources to draw data from wider samples of the population and make predictions on the basis of such data.

I believe that Bowlby was extreme in saying: 'On the one hand are the practitioners, on the other the scientists' (see p.??), because this may be interpreted as an invalidation of the contribution that clinicians can make to psychoanalytic theory. It would probably be fairer to say that this contribution has constraints. Late in his career Bowlby emphasized more and more the importance of empirical research. This is not difficult to understand. While Bowlby's position was ignored by psychoanalysts, it was adopted by many empirical researchers as their central paradigm. Among these, his friend Mary Ainsworth (see Chapter 4) gave him not only a great deal of support but, in fact, the chance to keep attachment theory on the map: it is possible to imagine that attachment theory would not have achieved its present popularity without her pioneering work.

How can we link an exploration of the relationship between empirical research and clinical psychoanalysis with current debates on the epistemology of psychoanalysis? This is such a complex matter that it may be unrealistic to consider it in depth in this book. However, we must be aware that there are major dilemmas in this area.

For many 'hard-liners' of science, standardized research methods and procedures are indispensable if a discipline or paradigm is to attain scientific status. From this standpoint, psychoanalysis should either develop tools to give evidence of its explanatory powers and ability to make predictions or relinquish its claims to be a scientific discipline.

On the other hand, it has been held that psychoanalysis, like law or history, is inherently interpretative rather than empirical. From this point of view, any attempt to bring psychoanalysis close to an empirical approach is seen as a distortion, if not an impossibility. The problem with this is that it gives justification to making assumptions whose validity is only supported by their axiomatic character. Unfortunately, the psychoanalytic literature is full of examples of this sort. Such a horrendous way of theorizing largely accounts for the poor reputation that psychoanalysis has regarding rigorous academic debates and standards.

What is characteristic of the analytic method is that both analyst and analysand make inductions in mutual exchange. Perhaps it may be more appropriate to say that the analytic method is 'inter-inductive'. In optimal circumstances, during the course of an analysis, analyst and analysand explore, elicit, identify, compare, refute and re-organize knowledge as part of an interpersonal and continuous process. Here, I am careful to say 'in optimal circumstances' because I am aware (as we shall explore in Chapter 12) that some analysts impose their interpretations on their patients rather than involving themselves in a process of joint discovery. Validation in psychoanalysis is (or should be) interpersonal and highly specific to this context and discipline.

The empirical researcher, instead, comes along, involves the subject in a particular procedure, makes observations and then retreats into his office to process them. The subject is not involved in interpreting and organizing what has been observed.

Bowlby's extreme position (his emphasis on the way psychoanalysis should rely on empirical research to validate its points) can be explained as a reaction against the lack of rigour in psychoanalytic writings. However, he rendered himself unnecessarily vulnerable to the critiques that his fellow analysts made of his epistemological stance.

If the validity of the clinical method and its inherent ability to achieve rigour are not preserved, we may end up with a situation whereby empirical researchers will dismiss with contempt the contribution that clinicians make. This contribution is essential to: (1) provide a more solid and wider theoretical framework to empirical work (the presentation of which can easily be limited to mere descriptions of research tools, specific findings, classifications, tables and numbers); and (2) to build better bridges between pure research and clinical applications. I would like to argue for a meeting of these different but complementary methods of acquiring knowledge. Both have strengths and limitations.

CHAPTER 4

The Evolution of Attachment Theory

Introductory Remarks

The importance of attachment theory is that it has given scientific authority to the study of the bond that children and their parents (or main caregivers) establish from the early stages of development. Furthermore, attachment theory has clarified (and is still exploring) issues regarding how disturbances in this primary bond may explain psychopathology.

The fact that certain conditions are necessary for children to feel that the human world – however difficult it may be – is a place where one can be relatively secure, trustful and self-confident, has been formulated by many psychologists and psychoanalysts over the years. Benedek (1938) talked about the notion of 'confident expectation', and many other analysts of the earlier generations (including Anna Freud) coined similar terms.

For many years, psychoanalysts have been interested in studying those experiences that make it possible for a child to feel a sense of basic trust in the world and also to recognize and avert danger, so that it becomes possible to make predictions and discriminate between potentially safe and potentially unsafe situations.

Psychoanalysts interested in early developmental issues studied the function of the maternal role; the child's symbolic use of inanimate objects as representatives of attachment figures; the significance and effect of the child's contact with the maternal body and responses to her facial expressions; and the interpersonal experiences that favour states of inner stability and integration, and so on. These studies are not new.

However, contemporary and leading psychoanalytically oriented developmental psychologists (see Eagle 1984, 1995; Stern 1985) acknowledge that attachment theory has provided a more solid framework to understand how conditions of emotional safety in the child's social context, together with adequate quality of parenting, contribute in a fundamental way to the individual's optimal development.

Bowlby and the Robertsons

As mentioned briefly in Chapter 1, in 1948, Bowlby, working at the Tavistock Clinic, hired James Robertson to observe children who were admitted into hospital. Robertson had worked with Anna Freud and Dorothy Burlingham at the Hampstead wartime nursery and already had a good understanding of the problem to be examined. At the time, Robertson was a qualified social worker and training in psychoanalysis.

Robertson's job was to observe young children in hospital. At the time, visiting hours were restricted and parents were given little opportunity to gain access to their children. At the Central Middlesex Hospital, Robertson saw children in states of severe distress. The hospital staff were unaware of the damage being done and resistant to taking responsibility for what was happening. Robertson, a man with a profound sense of social and political responsibility, tried to denounce publicly what he was observing. Yet, outside Bowlby's team at the Tavistock, most professionals were unwilling to hear what he had to say. Consequently, Robertson decided to get hold of a 16mm camera and make a film.

This film, 'A Two-Year-Old Goes to Hospital' (1953) records the plight of a young girl, Laura, who was in hospital for eight days to have a minor operation. Because her mother was not allowed to be there and nurses were changing frequently, she had no familiar person to soothe her and give her reassurance and support during this difficult period. On the first day, after the routine bath, Laura runs naked to the door and tries to escape. She is frightened, hurt and reacts badly to a rectal anaesthetic. Her expression, normally bright, becomes dull, sad, she holds on to her teddy. Eventually, she becomes quiet and shows a mixture of submissiveness and resentment. At the end of her stay she is withdrawn from her mother, shaken in her trust, sleeping poorly, soiling herself and having temper tantrums. The film shows a typical sequence of emotional deterioration experienced by a child admitted into hospital and separated from her familiar figures. It also highlights the risks that situations like this imply in terms of the child's future mental health (Quinton and Rutter 1976).

When Robertson's film was shown to an audience of psychoanalysts, responses were mixed. Anna Freud was supportive but the Kleinians rejected the idea that the child's distress had anything to do with separation from her mother. Bion argued that Laura was probably upset because her mother was pregnant (Grosskurth 1987; Karen 1994). This would be considered incredible today.

In 1953 Robertson took a short-term appointment with the World Health Organization and toured the United States showing his film. Although he had a positive response, he felt impotent in achieving what was imperative: a widely held recognition that parents should be allowed on to hospital wards.

Between 1967 and 1971, James and Joyce Robertson made five complementary films, usually called 'the young children in brief separation series'. They observed children aged between 18 and 30 months whose mothers were in hospital for the birth of their second babies. Four of the children were fostered in the Robertson family, where every effort was made to compensate for the parental absence; the fifth child went into a residential nursery. The children's names were John (17 months old), Jane (17 months), Lucy (21 months), Thomas (28 months) and Kate (29 months). In each case the children were securely attached to their parents, with no previous experience of separation.

These films show how the child's ability to cope with the absence of mother is affected by length of separation, stage of development and the quality of substitute care that is given. Defence mechanisms against separation anxiety are evident; often, at certain stage, the child's emotional neediness gives way to a state of 'freeze', when the child gives up his efforts to regain access to his attachment figures, withdraws and stops making demands. This state of withdrawal is what uneducated staff in institutions celebrate when they say 'the child is now settled'. Angry responses upon reunion with mother and conflicts of feelings in relation to her are also well illustrated, and stages of protest, despair and detachment as a sequence to be expected during periods of separation are documented.

The Robertsons concluded that no matter how good substitute mothering is, separation is always hazardous and problematic. However, when separation is inevitable, good quality of foster care is likely to ameliorate the effects of the separation.

Eventually, Bowlby and the Robertsons became distant from each other. However, Bowlby always included the Robertsons' contributions in his writings and credited them unreservedly.

Bowlby and Ainsworth

The association between John Bowlby and Mary Ainsworth was a very important and fruitful one. Some of the important elements of contemporary attachment theory were formulated by Ainsworth rather than by Bowlby himself. Ainsworth has been, respectively, the mother and grandmother of two generations of attachment researchers in the United States.

Seven years younger than Bowlby, Mary Ainsworth (formerly Mary Salter) entered the University of Toronto in 1929 at the age of 16. There, she met her first professional mentor, William Blatz. Blatz was a psychologist whose studies were mostly concerned with human beings' sense of security. He was the man who suggested that a child derives a sense of security in his being in the world by means of having a satisfactory attachment to his parents (Karen 1994, pp.131–132). Many years later, in 1966, Blatz published his book, *Human Security: Some Reflections.*

Blatz said that it is this sense of security that enables the child to move out, to explore his world, and to learn and develop a basic sense of mastery over the problems he may encounter in it. This is historically important, because it was Blatz who gave Mary Ainsworth the idea that when the attachment behaviour system is activated at low intensity, the situation is open for the exploratory system to be activated at a higher level by novel features of the environment. This is the phenomenon that Mary Ainsworth and colleagues (1978) termed 'using the mother as a secure base from which to explore'. In other words, if we are confident that our attachment figures are reliable and consistently available, we are more likely to venture into the world because we assume that the attachment figures will be there when we decide to return (especially at times of uncertainty, stress or fatigue). In psychopathology, agoraphobia can be explained as an anxious inhibition of exploratory behaviour due to lack of security in the attachment relationship.

In toddlers, the almost simultaneous onset of autonomous locomotion and symbolic representation (including language) offers them new possibilities of exploration. This brings about a major restructuring of the relationship between two primary motivational systems: *attachment* and *exploration.* The interaction between these two systems continues for the rest of a person's life.

The situational balance between the two systems in toddlerhood is going to be a fundamental determinant of secure attachment. The parent must learn to provide a balanced set of complementary caregiving behaviours: *protective behaviour* (which provides support and safety) and *letting go* (which encourages the child to explore and learn without fear).

These are notions originally suggested by Blatz, developed by Bowlby and systematically studied by Ainsworth. As we shall see, these ideas developed in the historical context of the relationship that Ainsworth and Bowlby were to form (Karen 1990). Mary Salter did her doctoral dissertation on Blatz's security theory and in 1939 became a lecturer at the same university. In 1946 she and Blatz co-directed a research project, studying security in adult life. In 1950 she married Len Ainsworth, he himself a psychologist. Around that time, Len decided to do his PhD at University College London, and the couple came to live in England.

Mary Ainsworth joined Bowlby at the Tavistock. During their first meeting, they discovered that they shared many interests and ideas. Subsequently, they worked together for four years. During that time, they studied separations and disruptions in the parent–child relationship in the first five years of life. They also ran multidisciplinary study groups on attachment issues.

In 1954, Ainsworth and her husband went to live in Uganda (apparently at her husband's initiative). There, Mary took the opportunity to start some research work with little methodological and institutional support. She observed 28 unweaned babies from several villages near Kampala in their homes. She came to the conclusion that mother–child pairs differ in the quality of their attachment relationship and that it is possible to measure and classify these differences. She also began to realize that the mother's behaviour in the early months of the child's life is a predictor of the classification of the relationship between mother and child. Ainsworth classified these 28 babies as secure, insecure and non-attached (a category that she would later discard). She published her findings many years later (in 1967) under the title *Infancy in Uganda: Infant Care and the Growth of Love*.

Some time later the Ainsworths moved to Baltimore. At some point their marriage dissolved. Meanwhile, Mary obtained an academic appointment at Johns Hopkins University. She also started her own personal analysis. She and Bowlby remained in contact. In Baltimore, with greater manpower, technical and financial resources, she started a research project aimed at replicating her Uganda studies.

Mary Ainsworth was able to classify the usual patterns of mother–child relationship into two broad categories: *securely attached* and *insecurely (or anxiously) attached*. This classification is now central to attachment theory.

The concepts of secure and insecure attachment not only relate to what is going on in the mother–child relationship, but also (and more fundamentally) to the *internal working models* or *representations* that the child builds of this relationship. As we shall see later, this classification also applies to the father–child relationship.

The Strange Situation

The 'Strange Situation' is a standardized laboratory procedure, devised by Ainsworth and members of her team at Baltimore. It was originally devised in 1964 for use in conjunction with an intensive longitudinal study of the development of infant–mother attachments throughout the first year of life. The procedure consists of several episodes, involving the child, his mother and a 'stranger' (a member of the research team), which evolve in a particular room where there are two chairs and some toys to which the child has access. These episodes are intended to activate and/or intensify the infant's attachment behaviour by means of introducing an 'unfamiliar situation' (the adjective 'strange' denotes 'unfamiliar').

The child enters the room with his mother. A massive instigation to exploratory behaviour is provided by a large array of toys. Next, an adult who is friendly but unfamiliar enters the room. Then the mother leaves the room and leaves the child with the stranger. The mother returns within three minutes or so and there is an episode of reunion between mother and child.

Next, the mother leaves the room again and so does the stranger. Therefore the child is left alone in the room. The stranger returns before the mother does. After the second reunion between mother and child, the procedure comes to an end. After the Strange Situation is over, the researchers spend some time with the mother and baby in pleasant interaction, offering the opportunity to discuss what happened.

Every aspect of the participants' reactions is observed and video recorded. But what is noted with greatest attention is the child's response upon reunion with mother. The entire attachment literature suggests that the child's response upon reunion yields a clearer picture of the state of attachment than the mere response of the child to separation itself. It is proposed that different patterns of behaviour during the Strange Situation indicate differences in the way the mother–child attachment has been organized. Although the Strange Situation procedure has been criticized for the fact that it is stressful for the child, it has also been argued that it is modelled on common everyday experiences. Mothers do leave their children for brief periods of time in different settings, often with strangers such as baby-sitters.

A securely attached child plays with the toys, shows signs of being upset when the mother leaves the room, interrupts his playful or exploratory behaviour and somehow demands reunion. When the mother returns, he is easily comforted, settles and returns to play. Statistically, approximately half of the infants observed react in this way. The chief characteristics of their reactions include: greater ability to play and explore the environment with enjoyment, confidence and curiosity; greater ability to show distress as an appropriate reaction to separation and, finally, greater ability to be soothed. It is assumed that children who have built an internal working model of their relationship with their mother as secure are more likely to respond in this way.

In Mary Ainsworth's samples, some children did not behave in that way. Roughly a quarter of the infants observed avoided close proximity with the mother and failed to cry or to be overtly upset when she left the room. When the mother returned, these young children actively avoided contact with her. Throughout the procedure, the children seemed to be more attentive to inanimate objects than to interpersonal events. This type of behaviour is interpreted as the result of defence mechanisms: the child turns to objects instead of human beings, hides his distress and avoids proximity in order to keep under control feelings of neediness which he predicts may not be adequately satisfied. These children are classified as *insecure-avoidant*.

A third group, roughly 10 per cent of infants, reacts strongly to separation. When mother returns they seek reunion and comfort but they may also show anger or passivity. They do not settle easily, tend to cry in an inconsolable way and fail to return to exploration. These children are classified as *insecure-ambivalent* or *ambivalent-preoccupied*.

Each pattern has distinct precursors in the mother–child everyday interaction. This has been observed in the families' homes on a regular basis during extended periods of time. More specifically, the mother's style of behaviour is the most clear factor that predicts the child's reactions in the Strange Situation. A mother's 'sensitive responsiveness', offered in a predominantly continuous way across the child's first year of life, is the best predictor of infant security of attachment at one year of age (Bretherton 1985; Smith and Pederson 1988).

A caretaker's distant attitude and rejecting behaviour (particularly of physical contact with the infant), predicts an avoidant pattern in the child (Ainsworth et al. 1978; Main and Stadtman 1981).

There seems to be clear evidence that ambivalent children have inconsistent mothers who also tend to discourage autonomy and independence. Ambivalence in these infants seems to be the result of contradictory internal models of the parental figure. The whole question of dysfunctional parental styles as determinants of insecure attachment and psychopathology deserves careful study. We shall have a closer look at this in Chapter 7.

After Mary Ainsworth made her original description of three patterns of attachment (secure, insecure-avoidant and insecure-ambivalent), a Berkeley research team formed by Mary Main, Judith Solomon and Donna Weston found a fourth pattern, which they called 'disorganized-disoriented' (Main and Weston 1981; Main and Solomon 1990). The infants who fall into this category react to reunion with mother in a confused and disorganized way.

Evidence began to emerge, indicating that parents of disorganized-disoriented children frighten them through direct experience of abuse or in some other way (Carlson et al. 1989; Lyons et al. 1987; O'Connor, Sigman and Brill 1987; Spreker and Booth 1988). Main and Hesse (1990) postulated that the mother of the disorganized infant is unpredictably frightening to her child and that disorganization is a response to this fear and inconsistency. One important parental role is that of soothing the child when he is frightened or alarmed. It is a tragedy that the same person who is supposed to provide this supportive function may be the person who is frightening and alarming.

A modified version of the Strange Situation has been applied to fathers and children and to older children. The pattern of attachment elicited by this test predicts subsequent development, including quality of peer relationships in later life, adaptation to new social situations and ego-resiliency (Sroufe 1988).

Secure and Insecure Attachments: A review of the classification

The Strange Situation is a semi-standardized laboratory procedure for examining attachment behaviour, exploratory behaviour and affiliative behaviour. Ultimately it allow us to make inferences about a young child's representational world. The observed pattern is assigned to one of the categories defined by Ainsworth *et al.* (1978) and by Main and Solomon (1986, 1990):

- the 'A' category: avoidant attachment
- the 'B' category: secure attachment
- the 'C' category: ambivalent attachment (this category has also been called 'resistant' (see Colin 1996)
- the 'D' category: disorganized-disoriented.

Categories A, B and C have been divided into sub-groups (see Colin 1996). However, a detailed description of these sub-groups falls outside the scope of this book.

The Minnesota Studies and other developments

Mary Ainsworth, at Johns Hopkins, created a great deal of interest in her work among colleagues and undergraduates. Some of these people were to become important figures in the field of attachment research, such as Inge Bretherton (now a leading scholar at the University of Wisconsin) and Everett Waters (now based at the State University of New York at Stonybrook). Waters met Alan Sroufe in Minnesota in around 1972 and communicated to him his enthusiasm about Ainsworth's work. Sroufe was to become a well-known researcher in the field. His 1977 article, 'Attachment as an Organizational Construct', written with Waters, created a great deal of interest among developmental psychologists in North America. Mary Main, a former student of Mary Ainsworth, has become an internationally known attachment theorist. This list is not comprehensive. The majority of these people are not psychoanalysts or psychotherapists. Many of them were in contact with John Bowlby, who visited the United States from time to time.

The findings of the Baltimore study, conducted from 1963 onwards, did not begin to be published until 1969. Ainsworth's book, *Patterns of Attachment*, written with Mary C. Blehar, Everett Waters and Sally Wall, was not published until 1978.

As these studies unfolded, it became clear that it was wrong to believe that a strict and relatively ungiving style of parenting could help a child to develop a satisfactory sense of autonomy and self-confidence. In fact, quite the contrary seems to happen. Children who receive consistent and reliable care, who are treated with warmth, empathy and respect, tend to become self-reliant and competent. However, the term 'self-reliance' is not used here to denote lack of emotional response to separation or sudden emotional deprivation, because one of the interesting aspects of securely attached children is that they are very able to show distress (without falling apart) and make strong care-eliciting emotional communications. Securely attached children seem to be more resourceful, more flexible and display greater tolerance to frustration. They are more able to use the assistance of their mothers without becoming unduly dependent on it. Alan Sroufe's studies in Minnesota, provided the empirical evidence for this (Karen 1994). His findings have been consistently replicated by other research teams in the United States and other countries.

Numerous empirical findings indicate that secure attachment in the first two years of life is related to sociability with other adults and children and more effective internal regulation of emotional states during pre-school years. Securely attached children are more able to engage in symbolic play, especially when it represents co-operative interpersonal interactions. Insecurely attached infants tend to show lower sociability, greater manifestations of anger, poorer peer relations and poorer control of impulses in later life.

Studies carried out at the University of Minnesota by Alan Sroufe and members of his team confirmed the conclusions previously drawn by Margaret Mahler, the well-known psychoanalyst who had independently done a great deal of developmental research. Mahler, Pine and Bergman (1975) indicated that some mothers cannot tolerate the child's growing sense of separateness, while others cannot maintain emotional availability in the face of the child's demands. Some of these mothers are intrusive, others are distant or ineffectual in offering support and assistance.

Mothers of securely attached children, instead, have a satisfactory degree of resourcefulness to negotiate with the child his demands for care and attention as well as his need to become increasingly independent.

The nature of the parent–child interaction during infancy and toddlerhood is then a central causal factor in the child's personality development and behavioural adjustment. It determines whether a child is going to be securely or insecurely attached.

One of the most striking aspects of the Minnesota studies is that some subjects have been followed up for many years, initially from infancy to the pre-school years. Some of them were observed in a specially created nursery school on the Minnesota campus (Sroufe 1997; see also Karen 1994, pp.181–194).

A sequence of studies, initiated by Byron Egeland and Sroufe, show that children identified as securely attached at one year of age are more likely to function well with peers 5, 9 and even 14 years later (Urban et al. 1991).

A very interesting aspect of these studies is that they show a correlation between patterns of parent–child interaction and the child's later behavioural tendencies in peer interactions (Troy and Sroufe 1987).

Securely attached children appear to evoke respect and have empathy for children in distress. Therefore the capacity to have concern and empathy for others without over-identifying with the other seems to be closely associated with attachment security.

Children judged avoidant at one year are likely to victimize others when they reach school age. In my view, a possible interpretation of this behaviour is that these children cannot acknowledge their own vulnerability and therefore they project it on to others and then poor scorn on the other person's vulnerable response. Another possibility is that some of these children have been frequently subjected to hostility by one or both parents and then identify with the aggressor, treating others as they have been treated.

Children judged ambivalent are more likely to be victimized. These children have a tendency to show lack of emotional stability, to be irritating and to break down easily. They tend to be 'psychic haemophiliacs': when they get hurt emotionally, they cannot stop bleeding. Therefore they become easy targets for bullies.

Sroufe identified three types of avoidant children at pre-school age: the lying bully who blames others; the shy loner who seems emotionally flat; and the obviously disturbed child, with repetitive twitches and tics who daydreams and shows little interest in his environment. The latter group would probably be classified as 'disorganized-disoriented' by other research workers (Karen 1994).

At school age, avoidant children seem least likely to show distress and dependency when hurt or disappointed. These characteristics make them similar to the character configuration described by Winnicott (1965a) as 'false self'. These children have been pushed towards premature independence, compliance and denial of their needs by their parental figures. They often come across as arrogant, oppositional, self-righteous and – because of the nature of their rigid and stable defences – they may give the false impression of being emotionally mature and stable. They seem to be less able to enjoy closeness and intimacy than securely attached children. As they reach pre-adolescence, these patterns seem to continue in some way. Securely attached children are less affected by rebuffs and maintain loyalty and trust to their closer friends in larger groups. My impression, based on clinical observations, is that these patterns persist throughout life and underlie the complexity of adult behaviour.

The role of father

Bowlby's and Ainsworth's initial work emphasized the role of mother. However, in the mid 1970s, attachment workers began to show an increased interest in the child's relationship with his father. One of the first efforts to fill this gap was made by Michael Lamb, a former student of Ainsworth. Observing young children at home, Lamb found that they gave care-eliciting communications to fathers in the same way as they did to mothers (Karen 1994). That this is so is obvious to all of us who live in or work with families with young children. The first study to assess quality of attachment to father was presented by Mary Main and Donna Weston (1981). They found that the quality of a child's relationship with mother may differ from the quality of the child's relationship with father. Thus a child could be securely attached to both, securely attached to one and insecurely attached to the other, or insecurely attached to both parents. Children who are securely attached to both parents score higher in terms of self-confidence and empathy towards others, and so on.

These findings are not surprising to psychoanalysts, who know very well how some patients spend a great deal of analytic time exploring their relationships (past and present) with their fathers. This experience is consistent with Bowlby's assumption that human beings (from infancy to the end of their lives) have attachments with multiple figures, but that their desire for proximity to any one of these figures is organized according to a hierarchical order of preference.

The family as a secure base

Beyond the parent–child dyad or the mother–father–child triad, infants, children and adolescents normally live in families, groups or interpersonal systems. Whatever goes on in these systems must necessarily affect any one of the members. Attachment theory must take into account the complexity of the family context in which early development takes place.

John Byng-Hall, a family therapist at the Tavistock Clinic who was close to John Bowlby, has made interesting contributions to the field. He formulated the concept of 'family scripts' (Byng-Hall 1985, 1986, 1988, 1991, 1995). These are manifest in interaction patterns which are evoked in particular situations. Such scripts are usually constructed through repeated experiences of similar scenarios and can be interpreted as representations of multi-person interactions. On the basis of these representations, any individual in the family can predict the next sequence in a series of interactions. Of course, each member of the family, depending on his developmental stage, may give personal significance to these scenarios. However, there is a shared construction of working models or mental representations of the patterns of attachments characteristic of this particular group setting.

Some studies seem to indicate that the quality of the parents' marriage predicts the security of the child's attachment to either parent; however, findings are not conclusive. Clinical experience does give the impression that absence of violence in the family, father's presence in the home, mutual support between parents and low conflict in the marriage are important contributors to children's security of attachment. Children of single mothers may or may not be at risk of insecurity of attachment.

Relationships with peers and siblings

It is an established fact that conflict with, and rejection by, siblings and peers in childhood may have adverse effects, sometimes long-lasting. The frequent observation that there is a relationship between children's experiences with their agemates and social adjustment has been a central motivator for the extensive attention that attachment researchers have recently directed towards peer relationships (Cicchetti and Bukowski 1995). For instance, rejection by peers in childhood has been found to predict aggressive behaviour in adolescence (Coie *et al*. 1995). In the analytic treatment of a young woman, whom I saw five times a week for five years, I found a clear association between memories of rejection by neighbours of her age during childhood and low self-esteem in adulthood.

Luisa Brunori (personal communication) suggests that the arrival of a new baby activates attachment behaviour, because the older child feels displaced. This activation shows the degree of security or insecurity that the child has already established. Moreover, the newborn is a stranger intervening in the parent–child couple. Also, both siblings become objects of attachment to each other. However, this occurs in different ways for each, because the older sibling is already part of the landscape into which the newborn arrives. This relationship has inherent conflicts for both the older and the newborn child. The older child wants to form a relationship with the newborn but fears displacement. The newborn immediately becomes an object of ambivalence both to the older child and to mother (who wants to establish a relationship with her younger child but feels guilty about displacing the older one). In terms of attachment theory, one important point is how family dynamics may increase or contain these conflicts. In addition, it is interesting to explore how the vicissitudes of sibling relationships affect the relationship that each child has with each parent. The way the mother reacts to her children also depends on the position she had in her original family and how her parents managed these conflicts.

Another point to be remembered is that in the history of families where abuse takes place, the victim and the victimizer may be siblings.

Earned security

Some attachment theorists have identified a group of individuals who have been classified as secure in spite of the fact that they report adverse early relationships with parents. It is assumed here that these individuals have obtained their source of security from secondary attachment relationships (other relatives, teachers, peers) in the course of their lives. Lisa Crandell (personal communication) has some preliminary evidence that mothers who had experienced painful and unloving relationships with their parents in childhood but who were securely attached as adults, had experienced a secure attachment with an alternative attachment figure in childhood. These mothers were also more likely to have engaged in individual psychotherapy in adulthood.

Studies on bereavement

Grief and bereavement result from the severance of bonds. Hence it is not surprising that studies on normal and pathological grief are intimately related with attachment theory. A pioneer in this field has been Colin Murray Parkes, a British psychiatrist who was a close associate of John Bowlby. Parkes' studies have several important aspects. First, they draw conclusions which support the notion that attachment relationships have a primary role in motivation and psychic functioning. Second, they explain how bereavement is a process that evolves sequentially, according to certain phases. Third, they give essential clues to understanding atypical bereavement and psychiatric as well as medical syndromes related to it.

Colin Murray Parkes joined Bowlby's research team at the Tavistock in 1962. From that time until Bowlby's death in 1990 their collaboration was close. Many aspects of attachment theory are the result of this association.

Parkes' ideas have generated a great deal of research, and the literature on bereavement that has emanated from this work is now vast. What now seems clear is that the course of an adult's state of bereavement depends on several factors: (1) the nature and quality of the relationship the subject had with the lost person; (2) the quality and fate of the subject's earlier attachments; (3) the defence mechanisms that the subject may use against loss and deprivation; and (4) the existence or otherwise of current social support for the bereaved subject.

The existence of vulnerability factors preceding the loss determines the extent to which a bereaved person may need psychiatric or psychotherapeutic help. Research findings strongly suggest that the patterns of attachment formed in childhood colour the bonds of adult life and that these, in turn, influence reactions to loss and the pattern of bereavement in a distinct and logically comprehensive way (Parkes 1991).

It is now widely accepted that loss of a parent in childhood through death or divorce is a contributing factor to explain adult psychiatric disorder (Harris, Brown and Bifulco 1990). However, this has a much greater impact through the inadequacy of the replacement care such children may receive.

Studies on failing marriages, emotional reactions to marital break-up and the effects of parents' separation on their children have been conducted using attachment theory as a reference framework (Weiss 1975).

Studies on supportive behaviour

Tirril Harris, a psychotherapist and researcher in medical sociology who was a member of John Bowlby's multidisciplinary study group in London, has studied the nature of supportive behaviours, their complexity and their role in preventing psychological breakdown in times of crisis in adulthood.

Following a lifespan model of such unsupportive relationships from neglect and abuse in childhood (Bifulco *et al.* 1994) to lack of intimacy in adulthood, Harris and colleagues have built up a complex perspective on clinical depression. Adversity in childhood not only promotes chronicity of depression (Brown and Moran 1994; Brown *et al.* 1994) but also co-morbidity with anxiety (Brown and Harris 1993).

I believe that the subject of social support is an important topic for psychoanalytic technique, since the idea of giving support is often dismissed as irrelevant, if not antithetical, to in-depth psychotherapy. Often, the notion of 'supportive psychotherapy' has been treated in a pejorative way and the patient's requests for support or reassurance have been interpreted as resistance. Yet in my opinion, providing support is a necessary part of the therapeutic situation. However, having said that, I am not entirely convinced that the word 'support' is a good one, for it does not explain how the support is given and taken. This concept seems a bit mechanistic. It is probably better to use the term 'empathy'.

It is clear that a person (not only a child but an adult as well) may encounter major difficulties in life, such as unwanted changes in lifestyle, stress at work, financial hardship, losses, injuries to self-esteem, illnesses, and so on. A person's capacity to deal with adversity usually depends on a combination of factors, including internal and external vulnerability. Under a certain set of unfavourable conditions, the person may become a psychiatric casualty. Depression, generalized hopelessness and so on, may be the main aspects of the clinical picture.

Feelings of hopelessness in relation to the specific life event that created them, may – under certain conditions – become generalized, so that the person cannot make positive predictions about any area of his future life. This notion of generalization is crucial. It is often associated with a crisis of self-esteem. However, the problem is more complex than this description seems to propose. No life event is experienced in isolation; it is experienced in the context of one's own personal struggles to deal with rivalry, ambivalence, jealousy, shame, guilt, and so on, and these struggles may also account for the way one responds to life events.

Studies carried out by Tirril Harris and other members of her team, show that supportive or unsupportive behaviour by a significant other in close contact is a fundamental factor in determining the psychological course of a crisis. What I find interesting in these studies is that 'unsupportive behaviour' is not defined as absence of support but as something that goes against it, a way of relating with the person in crisis that undermines his own sense of sensitivity and/or mastery over the situation and, more specifically, his self-esteem. For instance, one of the most negative responses is to convey to the sufferer that he only has himself to blame for the crisis (i.e. 'you made your bed, now you lie in it'). Another form of unsupportive communication is to minimize the significance of the event and suggest that the sufferer is emotionally over-reacting.

In my opinion, the study of unsupportive behaviour is important for psychotherapists, as it may help to avoid giving unsupportive communications in the form of 'interpretations'. For instance, a psychotherapist may affirm that the patient has himself, consciously or unconsciously, engineered an adverse situation. Although sometimes there may be a strong element of truth in such an interpretation, the explanations of emotional reactions to life events are always multifactorial. In this context, it may be appropriate to analyse the patient's contribution to his difficulties. If the patient feels critized or persecuted by the analyst, this can be explored. It could be a transference reaction. Ruth Robinson (personal communication) comments: 'I think that one of the outcomes of a difficult attachment history is either to defensively deny the need for support or to blame external events for one's feelings of being unsupported'. Nevertheless, here I am reacting to a style of interpretation that is always implicitly blaming the patient for all ills.

In situations of crisis, the most effective help is provided by attachment figures or 'core contacts', by someone defined as a 'very close other'. Continuity of contact and nourishing empathy are essential. Tirril Harris (1992, p.171–189) describes such support using as a metaphor the notion of 'milk-van support'. In Britain, milk is traditionally delivered in slow-moving electric vans that come every day to the household doorstep. A different type of support is that given according to the 'fire-engine' model, where a competent stranger comes in specially to deal with the crisis. Fire-engine support is often necessary in the form of crisis intervention but may not be as effective as milk-van support.

Social support in a wider context

Attachment theory and research are also concerned with social policies and socio-political structures through linking the social and psychological aspects of human behaviour. One of the important contributors to this area is Peter Marris, Professor of Social Planning at the Graduate School of Architecture and Urban Planning of the University of California.

As a result of Marris' studies, a notion of a good enough society emerges. This is a society which, as far as is humanly possible, minimizes disruptive events and protects its members from various forms of hardship through mutual support. As Marris (1991) puts it:

The qualities of good social relationships and good experiences of attachment are essentially the same: predictability, responsiveness, intelligibility, supportiveness, reciprocity of commitment. To achieve this we have to struggle constantly against the tendency of the powerful to subordinate and marginalize others in the interest of their own greater security. (p.89)

It seems clear that the political meaning of attachment theory is basically one of promoting social justice and reciprocal support. This is far removed from the poor understanding represented by the position of many feminists who criticized Bowlby because they felt he was opposed to women's rights by trying to make mothers prisoners of their own children. Patrick de Maré (personal communication) suggests that his concept of 'Koinonia' (fellowship, communion and dialogue in large groups) is congenial with the social implications of attachment theory (see de Maré *et al.* 1991).

On the intergenerational transmission of disturbed patterns of attachment

Bowlby's attachment theory has provided a theoretical and methodological framework for transgenerational studies. These have demonstrated a strong association between the child's security of attachment and his parents' internal working models which can be assessed using specific diagnostic tools. This work has been facilitated using the Adult Attachment Interview, a structured assessment instrument devised by Mary Main and colleagues at Berkeley University (see Chapter 6).

The transmission of insecurity of attachment evolves in the following way:

1. Each parent's attachment-related experiences in childhood and adolescence are represented in the form of 'internal working models'.

2. These parental internal working models influence the children's representational organization.

3. Each parent's representation of the child influences the way he/she treats the child and the quality of his/her sensitive responsiveness to the child's care-eliciting communications.

4. The quality and degree of sensitive responsiveness constitute the primary determinants of the child's quality of attachment to each parent.

A survey of the existing literature and my own clinical experience indicate that the two most important factors that determine parents' contribution to their children's sense of security are: (1) their capacity to offer empathy or sensitive responsiveness; and (2) their ability to engage their children in meaningful conversations where the capacity to reflect upon interpersonal issues is shown.

It seems that a crucial factor that impairs caregiving sensitivity is the extent to which parents use defence mechanisms in respect of their own negative emotional experiences and sense of vulnerability.

Parents who are high in reflective capacity are more likely to promote secure attachment in the child, notwithstanding adverse experiences. An important aspect of the child's acquisition of reflective capacity through thoughtful interaction with parents is the development of the notion that other people have a mind of their own and, consequently, mental states. Individuals' resilience to unfavourable conditions can be explained in terms of their capacity to reflect, which – if present – becomes a form of mental immunological system.

Other studies

Studies on the sequelae of child maltreatment ('battered child syndrome') and abuse are progressing. The effect of maltreatment and abuse on the victims' social, cognitive, affective and sexual adjustment has been investigated (see Cicchetti 1994).

The physiological and psychosomatic component of attachment

It is now well recognized that attachment-related events have neurochemical, physiological and psychosomatic components (Hoffer 1984; Weiner 1984). The literature is vast and I do not propose to review it here. However, studies have focused on the following areas:

Studies concerning physiological and psychosomatic responses to bereavement

Loss and bereavement affect the regulation of sleep and arousal, appetite and sexuality. The immune response system is also reflected (Bartrop *et al.* 1977; Pettingale, Hussein and Tee 1994; Schleifer *et al.* 1983; Spratt and Denney 1991). Older bereaved people seem more prone to infections, especially viral ones, and also to malignancy. This vulnerability increases in elderly people in institutional care who lack frequent contact with relatives and friends. Reversing their social isolation may also reverse the psychosomatic manifestations.

Pathological mourning in adults seems to be significantly correlated with the development of a variety of autoimmune diseases: rheumatoid arthritis, giant cell arteritis, systemic lupus erythematousus, polymalgia, Sjogren's syndrome and autoimmune thyroid disease (Paulley 1982).

Experimental studies with animals

Studies of physiological reactions to disruptions of relationships in young animals (Weiner 1984) show that stable relationships with mothers lead to stabile body functions. Early disruptions of these functions, however, produce neurochemical alterations in the central nervous system and predispose the young individual to later diseases (Kraemer 1985).

There is a great deal of experimental evidence to indicate that separation and insecurity of attachment in infant animals have physiological effects and place them at risk. This is true of every organ system studied: blood pressure, pulse rate, sleep, body temperature regulation, gastric function and histology, immune function, height and regulation of enzyme levels (which is crucial to proper growth and development of organs such as the heart and brain) (Weiner 1984).

Clinical studies on the psychosomatic manifestations of avoidant strategies

There is clinical evidence that subjects who conceal their feelings and thoughts because they do not believe that there are people available to listen to them with empathy, tend to develop specific psychosomatic manifestations. Patterns of intimacy avoidance, conflict avoidance and self-restraint in expressing feelings seem to be significantly higher for cancer patients than for those with no cancer.

Some clinical observations (which have not been confirmed by research findings) suggest that patients with hypertension in group therapy tend to react with minimal emotion and sudden increase of blood pressure when attachment-related emotions are reactivated. Patients who can express their feelings openly do not show an increase in blood pressure (Isaac Abecasis, personal communication).

Subjects who responded to attachment-related questions in a dismissive way showed increases in skin conductance level (Dozier and Kobak 1992).

CHAPTER 5

On Representational Models

Introductory Remarks

A central point in attachment theory is the concept of *working models* (or 'internal working models'), developed by Bowlby (1969) and clinically applied by Peterfreund (1983). Working models are cognitive maps, representations, schemes or scripts that an individual has about himself (as a unique bodily and psychic entity) and his environment. Such maps can be of all degrees of sophistication, from elementary constructs to complex ones. A working model is a selected representation of whatever is mapped – aspects of a person, aspects of the world – anything that may be the object of knowledge or psychic representation.

Working models make the organization of subjective and cognitive experience, as well as adaptive behaviour, possible. One function of these models is filterability of information about oneself or the external world. As a result of the activity of existing working models, information is highlighted; information is selected for different purposes.

Several working models of the same thing (particularly of oneself and other people) can co-exist. They can remain split off from each other or can be put together through integrative and synthetic processes.

Bowlby's notion of internal working models is compatible with Piaget's (1954) theory of representation. It is also influenced by the work of Craik (1943), who showed that organization of adaptive behaviour is not possible without using knowledge derived from past experiences.

As Bretherton (1985) puts it, as a conceptual metaphor the term 'internal working model' has several advantages. First, the adjective 'working' refers to the dynamic aspects of psychic representation. By operating on mental models, an individual can generate interpretations of the present and evaluate alternative courses of future action. Second, the word 'model' implies construction and hence development, with later, more complex, working models forming to replace earlier and simpler versions.

Peterfreund (1983) explains that internal working models represent a variety of experiences in life and their environment. However, in attachment theory, the term is more specifically used to refer to a representational system of oneself in relation to significant others. In this context, the defining qualities of the working model are based on at least two judgements: (1) whether or not the attachment figure is assumed to be a person who in general will respond to requests for support and protection; and (2) whether or not the child judges himself or herself as a person to whom anyone, particularly an attachment figure, is likely to respond in a supportive way. Although these two judgements may appear to be independent, in practice they are mutually confirming (Pearson *et al.* 1994).

Definition of concepts

The concepts of 'internal working model' and 'self- and object representations' are almost synonymous. Attachment theorists tend not to use the word 'object' since it offers a poor metaphor for what it is trying to describe.

The psychoanalytic literature on self- and object representations is so extensive that any attempt to review it in this book would be unrealistic. However, it should be pointed out that the notion of an 'internal object' is being replaced here.

The term 'working model' can be used to denote all the representations about the world and ourselves in it that we build in the course of experience, including people, places, ideas, cultural patterns, social structures, and so on. However, as I have already explained, there are specialized forms of working models which can be defined as a set of conscious and unconscious notions about oneself as a person and the other as a significant figure in one's life.

Working models of oneself contain a notion of being the object of love and appreciation, which we normally call 'self-esteem'. There is also a sense of separateness from the environment, of 'self-sameness' and continuity in relation to time, and of self-knowledge.

Internal working models of oneself and others are formed in the course of attachment-relevant events and reflect the outcome of the individual's care-eliciting communications. These models do not depend solely on events experienced in the attachment figure's presence. They may also include the outcome of, for example, the subject's efforts to seek reunion with the other in the other's absence.

Internal working models begin to be formed in the earlier months of life. However, working models continue to be construed and reshaped in later life. The importance of the earliest models is that they are likely to influence the way the child will subsequently experience the world. Hence these earliest models may influence the construction of later models.

Although attachment-oriented developmental researchers emphasize the importance of studying the earliest formation and organization of internal working models (for instance, through the extensive use of the Strange Situation), Bowlby (personal communication) said that – in his view – all working models construed during the many years of immaturity (infancy, childhood and adolescence) are clinically relevant.

Working models as dynamic structures

Working models are not static structures. They are very stable, yet they can change and be activated or inactivated in any particular situation. The understanding of working models as dynamic structures can best be done in the context of a cybernetic model of psychic functioning. This model may appear to be mechanistic, but is, in fact, a biological model which does not exclude the notion of higher levels of symbolic representation.

A working model of something that was experienced in the past may not match the perception of current reality. Then, the working model may be modified in order to take into account the new perception, otherwise the current reality may be perceived with distortions.

For instance, a child may form a working model of the house in which he lives at the age of seven. If subsequently he does not see this house for 20 years and then comes back to see it, he may find that the house looks smaller than in his original conception. Consequently, he may update his working model of the house.

As Peterfreund puts it, from childhood to adulthood we understand the world through our constantly changing working models. We each interpret existing information in our own way, selecting and processing it to arrive at our particular view of the world, our individual 'reality'. It is through these interpretations that information attains meaning. Our working models enable us to rearrange the world we know, to imagine new contributions and possibilities, to imagine how things would appear in different circumstances and to predict the possible consequences of action to be taken. If this model is to be successfully used in novel situations, it must be extended imaginatively to cover potential realities as well as experienced ones. Thus from which working models provide a platform to test and evaluate.

We cannot approach any situation or fact as totally unbiased observers, free from the learning of the past. If we are always biased observers, then the problem is to see whether it is possible to be biased only to an optimal degree and whether our biases can be modified by experience.

Internal working models show a strong propensity for stability and self-perpetuation. However, they are not fixed templates. They are not exact copies or 'photographs' of other people or interpersonal events.

Working models of attachment figures and of self

Bowlby (1973) said:

> Each individual builds working models of the world and of himself in it, with the aid of which he perceives events, forecasts the future, and constructs his plans. In the working model of the world that anyone builds, a key feature is his notion of who his attachment figures are, where they may be found, and how they may be expected to respond. Similarly, in the working model of the self that anyone builds, a key feature is his notion of how acceptable or unacceptable he himself is in the eyes of his attachment figures. (p.203)

On the basis of these complementary models, a person makes forecasts of how accessible and responsive his attachment figures are likely to be should he turn to them for support. As I have already mentioned, the events on which internal working models of the self in relation to significant others are formed are, by definition, attachment-relevant events.

Once formed, internal working models have an existence outside of consciousness. Bowlby (1973) said:

> It is not uncommon for an individual to operate simultaneously, with two (or more) working models of his attachment figure(s) and two (or more) working models of himself. When multiple models of a single figure are operative, they are likely to differ in regard to their origin, their dominance, and the extent to which the subject is aware of them. In a person suffering from emotional disturbance it is common to find that the model that has greatest influence on his perceptions and forecasts, and therefore on his feelings and behaviour, is one that developed during his early years and is construed on fairly primitive lines, but that the person himself may be relatively, or completely, unaware of; while simultaneously, there is operating in him a second, and perhaps radically incompatible model, that developed later, that is much more sophisticated, that the person is more nearly aware of and that he may mistakenly suppose to be dominant. (p.205)

A number of current research projects are assessing the social and intergenerational transmission of internal working models, as well as the processes that explain the existence of multiple and mutually incompatible models of the attachment figures.

Clinical applications

Attachment-oriented psychotherapy can be defined as a way of eliciting, exploring, integrating and modifying internal working models.

In order to illustrate these points I shall refer to the case of Mrs Y, a patient I treated once a week for a period of seven years. Mrs Y (who is now dead) came to see me at the age of 73 when she suddenly became depressed for no apparent reason. She had been a marital counsellor and was an intelligent and psychologically minded person. In the course of her therapy, she revealed the fact that as a child she often felt neglected and rejected. She was one of six children, living in a small village. Father was busy during the day and went to pubs with male friends in the evenings. Her mother was often tired, lonely and overwhelmed with the demands put on her by all her children.

In some sessions Mrs Y was able to remember very vividly, with tears in her eyes, episodes of her childhood when she felt ignored by father and rejected by mother. Mrs Y had a difficult adolescence, but at the age of 21 she married a young doctor who was very successful professionally but also very caring and devoted to her. When he died, many years later, Mrs Y lived on memories of this happy and secure relationship.

Some years after her husband died, a close female friend of Mrs Y's fell ill and went into hospital. The night before her friend went into an irreversible coma, Mrs Y went to visit her but her friend refused to admit her. Soon after this event, Mrs Y became depressed and remained so for some months until she decided to consult me.

What became clear in the course of the therapy was that Mrs Y was insecurely attached to both parents in the course of her childhood. Therefore she built internal working models of parents as unloving and of herself as undeserving of love. However, not all was bad in childhood. There was an unmarried aunt nearby, who used to engage her in conversations about the family and help her to reflect on everyday life issues.

When she was 19 she met the man whom she later married. They got married in the late 1930s and had two children. During the war her husband became a military surgeon and had to be positioned near the Front. She was left in a depressed state with the two small children. That was the only time she remembered having been depressed prior to the depressive spell which motivated her to seek help from me. When her husband returned, he obtained a senior hospital medical post and family life became very enjoyable and secure. Her marital relationship lasted 35 years and Mrs Y had realistically good memories of those times. It was during that long period that she construed a working model of herself and her husband (also partly based on her relationship with her aunt), where she saw herself as lovable and him as reliable and loving.

After her husband's death, Mrs Y's children got married and moved far away from London. They seemed to be competent but emotionally aloof and somehow uncaring. Mrs Y related this to the fact that she was depressed when they were young and that, as a reaction to their early deprivation, they developed avoidant traits. She missed their company, but she was consoled by the fact that they did contact her from time to time and were doing well in their lives.

Therefore, during a period of many years, Mrs Y's psychic life was under the dominance of a model of a secure attachment that essentially developed as a result of having had a satisfactory marriage. What she was not aware of was that she had an underlying and radically incompatible model which had formed much earlier in her life. This model was suddenly reactivated by an external and specific trigger: rejection by her female friend who was dying in hospital.

In working with this patient, I was following the principles formulated by Bowlby (1973) when he said:

> In terms of the present theory much of the work of treating an emotionally disturbed person can be regarded as consisting, first, of detecting the existence of influential models of which the patient may be partially or completely unaware and, second, of inviting the patient to examine the models disclosed and to consider whether they continue to be valid. (p.205)

In understanding these processes, I always use the computer as a model. The fact that a program is not seen on the screen does not mean that it is not installed in the hard disk. You only need to press the right key to activate it. Something similar happens when a dormant working model is reactivated. The switch of predominance from one model to another can happen quite suddenly and may be short-lived. To illustrate this model further, I shall use another clinical vignette. In order to preserve confidentiality I shall slightly distort some details but without modifying the essence of the case.

Mr A is a man in his mid 30s who has been in analysis with me for some time. This is a man who was neglected by his two parents as a child. When he was ten his parents separated and he was sent to boarding school. Professionally he is doing well and holds a high position in an industrial manufacturing firm. It is not surprising to see that he is very involved with this type of work as he has always had the tendency to make greater investments in inanimate objects than in human relationships. I should not omit the fact that from time to time he has to make business trips abroad. After a series of short-lived relationships with women, Mr A is now in a new relationship with Jessica.

I am going to refer to one of his Monday sessions, which take place in the afternoon. He had missed the previous Friday session because he went to Barcelona with his girlfriend for the weekend to celebrate his recent promotion at work. He came back and said: 'I do not know what is wrong with me. I had a very successful weekend in Barcelona with Jessica. It was a good way of celebrating my promotion. We really enjoyed each other's company. Yet, by the end of this morning, I felt depressed. I do not see any reason why I should feel depressed now!'.

So I said: 'It seems that you were feeling reasonably happy during the weekend and this morning you got depressed for reasons you cannot see'.

'Yes,' he agreed.

'Well,' I said, 'I wonder if anything happened this morning which you did not notice, yet it had a depressing effect on you'.

Mr A said: 'All that comes to my mind is that when this morning I went back to work, my secretary was not there. Apparently she had phoned the office on Friday, saying that she was ill. So she was replaced with a temp. When I walked into my office this morning I found this other woman and I felt a bit lost'.

In response, I said: 'So, there may be something in it. I wonder if you felt abandoned by your secretary…'.

Mr A confirmed this hypothesis by saying, 'Yes, I did!'.

Then I asked: 'What sort of ideas come to your mind when you think about her?'.

Mr A said: 'She looks after me'. Then, after a pause, he added: 'It seems silly, but what comes to my mind is the fact that when I go abroad she often takes me to the airport or fetches me from the airport'.

Then there was a pause and he continued: 'I tell you what comes to my mind… When I was at boarding school, my parents were separated and I did not see much of my father. I must have been 10 or 11. The school was about five miles away from Cheltenham, where my mother was living alone. Some weekends I used to go and visit her. I remember taking the bus. I normally carried a bag with my dirty laundry. It felt too heavy for me. My mother had a car but she never went to fetch me at the bus stop. So I had to walk 15 or 20 minutes from the bus stop to my mother's house. She must have been depressed. She was watching television all day. She hardly talked to me. On Sunday afternoon she would say 'Off you go. It's time for you to catch the bus!'. She never gave me a lift to the bus stop. I walked all the way there with my bag full of clean clothes. I had a dreadful feeling in my stomach but I could not put a name to this feeling…'. At this point my patient became tearful.

So, what became clear in the course of the session was that the absence of his secretary had reactivated in him an early working model of his relationship with his mother, when he was neglected by her.

This technique follows Bowlby's suggestion that an analyst guided by attachment theory is striving, jointly with the patient, to understand how the patient's emotional reactions, behaviour and forecasts are based on multiple working models. At the same time, both analyst and analysand try to examine how these models may have come into being. As Bowlby pointed out:

During those inquiries it is often found that a model, currently active but at best of doubtful current validity, becomes reasonably or even completely intelligible when the actual experiences that the patient has had in his day-to-day dealings with attachment figures during all his years of immaturity are known. This leads again to the controversial question of the extent to which actual experience is of influence in the development of working models of self and others. (Bowlby 1973, p.207)

One of the interesting aspects of eliciting underlying working models is that, when such a discovery occurs, often both the analyst and the analysand are taken by surprise, as happened with Mr A. Often the patient reacts with emotion and this seems genuine, it comes from his true self.

The emotional component

Working models are emotionally charged. In other words, there is an emotional component to the cognitive system. Working models of oneself and others form in the course of attachment-relevant events and contain the emotions inherent in these events. Because of the fact that these events always have an emotional component, their representation must necessarily be associated with these emotions. Therefore painful representations may be defensively excluded from the consciousness. In this way the person may be relieved of these painful emotions, but at a price. For the act of excluding working models or representations from consciousness forces a person to work at a conscious level with an inadequate model of reality, leading to inappropriate, perhaps even pathological, behaviour (Bretherton 1985).

Clinical experience shows that patients are more likely to be consciously and unconsciously predisposed to rediscovering those representational models which are associated with painful emotions when they feel safe with a kind and empathic therapist. When this occurs and painful affects emerge in the context of a mutually co-operative therapeutic relationship, this may in turn reinforce the therapeutic alliance.

On coherency

Internal working models of relationships provide rules for the direction and organization of attention and memory (Bretherton 1985). These rules facilitate or restrict the individual's access to certain forms of knowledge regarding the self, the attachment figure and the relationship between one and the other. One important discovery made by attachment researchers is that these rules also influence the organization of thought and language as it relates consciously and unconsciously to attachment issues. In other words, a person's degree of clarity in thinking and narrative about relationships and his attachment history reflects the organization of his representations.

Because of the fact that unconscious representational processes cannot be witnessed directly, they can only be elicited by inference. The Strange Situation provides an instrument to make such inferences about young children. This is done by observing the child's behaviour during the critical moments of separation and reunion with an attachment figure. In child analysis, such inferences are made through observing the child's play in interaction with the therapist. In adult analysis, this is achieved through verbal language: free associations and transference communications.

A major finding of research work around the Adult Attachment Interview (see Chapter 6), regarding representation and language, is that the degree of coherency with which a person describes early events (whether these events were regarded as adverse or not) is indicative of the way that person's representational models are organized.

CHAPTER 6

Semi-Structured Interviews to Assess Representations of Attachment Relationships and Related Issues

Introductory remarks

Several semi-structured interviews have been designed to assess representations of attachment relationships for research purposes. Of these, perhaps the best known is the Adult Attachment Interview (A.A.I.), which focuses on the subject's recollection of his attachment history and current thoughts about it (George, Kaplan and Main 1985; Main and Goldwyn 1985). This interview was designed in Berkeley in 1985. However irrelevant it may seem, I would like to say that I was extremely fortunate in obtaining an early manuscript discussing the interview and its coding and classification system from John Bowlby in 1986.

There is something mysterious and paradoxical about the A.A.I. It has been widely used for a good number of years in several countries. Recent research literature making reference to the A.A.I. is vast (see, for instance, Colin 1996). Yet the authors of the A.A.I. have not formally published a detailed description of the interview and its coding system, presumably acting on their belief that it is important to safeguard scientific reliability, which can only come with intensive face-to-face training. Conducting and processing the interview requires a specific and approved training; people who have not had easy access to it have been left without a sense of its full value.

During the AAI, questions are asked in a set order and specific probes are used when questions are not answered. The interviewer follows the subject's phrasing in order to understand the meaning of what he says and to assess the coherence of his narrative. The interview is conducted according to a natural conversational and empathic style.

The AAI is normally audio recorded and its analysis depends upon extended and careful study of the transcript as a whole. This interview offers a systematic way of applying John Bowlby's ideas to assessing patients' representations of their attachment relationships. The interview also tries to elicit the subject's overall evaluations of autobiographical recollections.

The questions

The first question, which is aimed at establishing the earliest family and environmental background, is followed by others aimed at eliciting information about grandparents, siblings and their roles in the child's life. Once the subject appears to be more relaxed and oriented towards the exercise, the interviewer begins to assess the subject's view of the quality of his early relationship with each parent.

Next the interviewer tries to find out to which parent the subject felt closest, and why. Gradually, the conversation moves on to explore an important aspect of internal working models of early relationships: the degree of confidence that, in times of adversity or crisis, a parental figure would be available to provide empathic support.

Subsequent questions try to deal with memories of early separation and their emotional significance. The interviewer then begins to explore whether the subject – during his years of immaturity – had ever felt rejected by his main attachment figures and, if so, to what extent. How the subject interprets such rejection is also an important topic of analysis.

Then, this question is asked: 'Did your parents use to threaten you, maybe for discipline, maybe just jokingly?'. This is a relevant topic, no doubt based on the fact that John Bowlby thought that repeated parental threats of abandonment or punishment (normally made to the child to impose discipline) can create insecurity of attachment (see Chapter 7). Furthermore, threats may acquire a distinct meaning when the child has already experienced some kind of abuse.

The subsequent questions are aimed at assessing how the subject makes links between early and current interpersonal experiences and conceptualizes these links. At some point, the interviewer tries to find out whether the subject experienced the loss of a parent or other close loved person (whether a sibling or any other significant person) while he was a child. The circumstances surrounding the loss and the age of the child at the time are taken into consideration. If an important attachment figure died, the interviewer tries to find out if the subject was allowed to attend the funeral and what this was like. The interviewer makes sure that responses to all these questions cover earlier and recent losses of any siblings (whether older or younger), loss of grandparents, loss of any person who seemed to be a substitute attachment figure and, of course, in adult life, loss of a sexual partner or spouse. The interviewer is not only interested in factual information but in the way the subject describes these feelings and events and the extent to which he may have resolved mourning. No doubt this section of the AAI springs out of Bowlby's (1960b, 1980) studies on childhood mourning.

At some point, the interviewer also tries to find out whether the subject went through a period of rebellion against his parents and whether he has forgiven them for their past inadequacies. The interviewer may then ask: 'What is your relationship with your parents like for you now as an adult?'.

If the subject is a parent, the following questions can be asked: 'How do you respond now, in terms of feelings, when you separate from your child? Do you ever feel worried about your child?'. One purpose of these questions is to elicit signs of role reversal between parent and child. We must bear in mind that the A.A.I. was originally formulated for the purpose of highlighting intergenerational links, and therefore some correlations between the way a subject describes his childhood and his attitude towards his own children are relevant.

Finally, there is a question aimed at eliciting anxieties and worries that the subject may have about his child's future, particularly in terms of the child's vulnerability to fears of political, social and/or environmental disaster.

Processing the interview

Mary Main has pointed out in her lectures that the main purpose of the A.A.I. is to elicit and classify the subject's state of mind with respect to attachment. On the basis of the study of each interview, two main aspects are taken into account: (1) probable childhood experiences in accordance with the subject's account; and (2) coherence of the subject's narrative.

In addition, the assessor tries to detect: (1) idealization of one or both parents; (2) unresolved or chronic anger towards one or both parents; (3) insistence upon inability to recall childhood experiences (which, if present, is seen as an indication of defensive organization); and (4) lack of resolution of mourning for each important person who the subject has lost.

Probable childhood experiences

Among the tasks of the A.A.I. is the assessment of:

1. *The extent to which the subject experienced mother or father as loving or unloving.* (Memories of being held or hugged for comfort and of being made to feel better in times of trouble, instead of being scolded, can provide indications of parental love.)

2. *The extent to which the child felt rejected or prematurely pushed to be independent.* (Memories of being frequently picked on, criticized, teased, given cold or contemptuous responses when upset, and so on indicate rejection.)

3. *The extent to which 'role reversal' may have occurred*; in other words, the
    extent to which the subject felt that a parent's psychological or physical
    well-being was a concern for, or responsibility of, the child. (Memories
    of having to look after an incompetent or ill parent, particularly in the
    absence of other adults in the household who could help; or – at the
    lower end of the scale – memories of some subtle interactions between
    parent and child, in the course of which the child felt he had to inhibit
    expressions of feelings in order not to upset an over-reactive parent,
    indicate role reversal.)

In addition, the A.A.I. tries to elicit memories of traumatic experiences. The
interview is organized according to Bowlby's notion of 'informed inquiry'.
Knowledge of normal and dysfunctional patterns of interaction in the family (see
Chapter 7) can provide a conceptual framework to guide the questions the
clinician or researcher may ask. Bowlby believed that in order to understand
another person, we need to know much more than pure generalizations about past
experiences.

For instance, discussing a clinical record on Julia, a patient whose mother was
described as 'extremely demanding, domineering, critical and often disparaging
and humiliating', Bowlby (1980, p.220) said: 'As occurs so often in the literature,
although we are told of the tyrannical ways of Julia's mother, no content is given
of what she actually said.... What, we wonder, were the words and phrases in
which mother expressed her demands and criticisms? In what terms and tones did
she disparage and humiliate Julia?'

In the A.A.I. the interviewer asks questions such as: 'When you were upset
emotionally when you were little, what would you do? Can you illustrate with
specific incidents?'; 'Can you remember what would happen when you were hurt
a bit physically? Again, do any specific incidents come to mind?'; and 'Were you
ever ill when you were little? Do you remember what would happen?'. In this way,
the interviewer is trying to elicit: (1) if the subject can remember particular
episodes of his early life; (2) the content of these memories; and (3) how these
memories relate to the subject's overall appreciation of the relational and
historical context in which these events occurred.

Coherence

One innovative aspect of the A.A.I. is its attempt to assess the way a person
organizes his thoughts and verbal language in relation to attachment; in other
words, the 'coherence' of the narrative. Here, the notion of 'coherence' refers to
the subject's ability to make his communications easily understood and accepted
as plausible, as well as his capacity to make clear and common-sense connections
between past events, outcomes, thoughts and feelings.

Coherence is lacking to a lesser or greater degree when the subject makes contradictions and/or irrational connections within or between sentences. The subject may tell long stories that are unrelated or irrelevant to the main point, make strange remarks or comments that seem out of place, or use unnecessary jargon or inappropriate metaphors, and so on.

One very important discovery made by Mary Main and colleagues is that the degree of coherence of speech is indicative of the subject's overall capacity to have access to information related to his attachment history and to keep it organized in a thoughtful way. This, in turn, is related to attachment security. This aspect of psychological functioning has been termed 'metacognitive knowledge' (Main 1991). This work is partly based on Bowlby's (1980) assumption that there is an interaction between internal working models and cognitive biases that influences the way a person encodes information about himself and others.

Classification of responses to the A.A.I.

The authors of the A.A.I. formulated four categories for classifying the adult's state of mind with respect to attachment: *secure, dismissing, preoccupied* and *unresolved*. The secure pattern, which is the one considered to be optimal, has also been labelled 'autonomous' or 'balanced'. The dismissing category has also been termed 'D', 'detached' or 'avoidant'. The preoccupied category has also been called 'E', 'enmeshed', 'ambivalent' or 'resistant'. The unresolved category is often referred to with a capital 'U'.

The secure adult

Adults classified as secure find it easy to remember and explore through dialogue and reflective thinking their attachment history. They particularly feel at ease in describing specific episodes of their distant past. In this context, they seem to be able to integrate autobiographical recollections into an overall view which has a relatively independent and objective quality. Either their memories are mainly positive or they appear to have good enough internal resources to cope with adversity in a relatively healthy way (that is to say, with little use of defence mechanisms such as derogation, idealization, splitting, and so on). They also explicitly recognize that attachment-related experiences influence psychological well-being.

Within this category there are two sub-groups: (1) individuals who grew up in a stable and supportive family group; and (2) individuals who had difficult experiences during childhood but show resilience and are presently exceptionally thoughtful and developed (these are often referred to as the 'earned secure' to distinguish them from the basically secure group).

The dismissing type

It seems that this category relates to Bowlby's formulation of a 'disposition to assert independence of affectional ties'. According to Bowlby (1980), individuals disposed strongly to assert their self-sufficiency fall on a continuum ranging from those whose proclaimed self-sufficiency rests on a precarious basis to those in whom it is firmly organized (p.224–228).

Using Bowlby's model of attachment behaviour, we can say that these individuals have their attachment systems activated at a low level for defensive purposes. This means that they are less prone to seek intimacy with, and comfort from, significant others than secure individuals. The underlying defence is self-protection against painful feelings, which in many cases stem from consistent neglect, emotional distance or rejection.

According to Bowlby (1980), two rather different types of childhood experience seem to be prevalent:

> One is the loss of a parent during childhood, with the child being left thereafter to fend for himself. The other is the unsympathetic and critical attitude that a parent may take towards the child's natural desires for love, attention and support. Not infrequently, it seems, a person who grows up to assert his independence of affectional ties has been exposed to a combination of experiences of these kinds. (p.224)

I have also found this disposition in patients who have had hospital admissions in childhood (without having had continuous access to parental figures and received continuous comfort from them), and also in patients who have had intrusive parents.

In the A.A.I., many individuals who may be included in this category report little in terms of personal history. They may idealize the parent. They may also provide details about difficult situations but be cut off from related feelings or dismiss their significance.

In terms of the present, these persons appear to minimize at a conscious level the significance of close and intimate relationships in thought, feeling or daily life. If they speak about the importance and later influence of early experiences, their understanding seems to be mostly intellectual.

The preoccupied type

These people, instead of having their attachment system activated at a low level (as occurs with the dismissive type), have it activated at a higher level. Thus they tend to seek relationships all too easily, but once in a relationship they tend to behave in an ambivalent and clinging way. This category relates to Bowlby's definition of individuals with a 'disposition to make anxious and ambivalent relationships' (1980, p.218–222).

Bowlby (1980), said:

> Nevertheless, although those who make anxious and ambivalent attachments are likely to have experienced discontinuities in parenting and/or often to have been rejected by their parents, the rejection is more likely to have been intermittent and partial than complete. As a result the children, still hoping for love and care yet deeply anxious lest they be neglected or deserted, increase their demands for attention and affection, refuse to be left alone and protest more or less angrily when they are. (p.219)

Some of these individuals report having had a weak parent, usually the mother, who failed in her supportive role and promoted role reversal. The mother may not have been overtly rejecting but she may have been unable to contain the child's anxieties. She may have panicked in emergencies. If there were overt child–parent difficulties, they most likely took the form of parental nagging, guilt-inducing communications and persistent criticisms.

In their responses to the A.A.I., these individuals appear to be confused, incoherent and unable to apply objective criteria to understanding relationships and their influences. Their interviews may be long and difficult to follow with unexplained oscillations of viewpoint. Their responses are often tangential or irrelevant. In some cases, they may show an unconvincing self-analytic style. They often appear to be intensely preoccupied with past relationships while unable to move beyond a sense of the self as enmeshed in early relationships. They may often appear still to be embroiled with their family of origin, still struggling to please the parents or caught in a conflict of rebellion and dependency. They seem not to have achieved an identity away from these struggles.

The unresolved type

The fourth category is termed 'unresolved'. Many adults so classified have experienced losses, abuse or other traumatic events. They appear to be confused about the loss or trauma, or disoriented and incoherent in describing it or its effects. They may oscillate repeatedly between positive and negative viewpoints, show lapses in the monitoring of their reasoning and discourse, and be unable or unwilling to stay with the topic of the interview or the most recent question.

A necessary clarification

It is important to make a distinction between a classification of responses to the A.A.I. and a classification of attachment styles or dispositions. Clinical experience indicates that there is a close correlation between one type of classification and the other. However, strictly speaking, for the researcher, what is being classified is the response to the A.A.I., nothing else. In other words, what is classified is the interview, not the subject. Further research is needed to establish if responses are stable. Currently, there is evidence that responses are stable, at least over a year (Howard Steele, personal communication).

However, this classification has predictive value for parenting styles and psychopathology. If we match this classification with clinical observations in psychoanalysis, it is possible to assume that the interview gives a good indication of what the overall disposition of an adult may be.

Reliability, discriminatory validity and usefulness of the A.A.I.

There is growing evidence that the AAI is a useful, reliable and valid research tool. Bakermans-Kranenburg and Van Ijzendoorn (1993) in a careful study found a very respectable level of validity. There is general agreement that the A.A.I. measures something specific: an adult's state of mind with respect to attachment. However, in the existing literature this concept is not clearly formulated.

In summary, the A.A.I. tries to assess:

1. An adult's internal working models of attachment relationships.

2. The metacognitive processes associated with these internal working models, together with the way in which these processes manifest themselves through language.

3. The state of correspondence between episodic and semantic memories.

4. The organization of defences against insecurity of attachment and associated anxieties.

5. Linked with the above, the use of strategies for maintaining self-organization and the notion of being connected with significant others in the face of insecurity.

6. The degree of resolution of anger and/or mourning.

However, as I have already mentioned, an important point is that the A.A.I. is intended to predict the quality of the interviewee's attachment relationship with his own child, as observed in the Ainsworth Strange Situation. The validity of the A.A.I. in this respect is well established (van Ijzendoorn 1995). Attachment research has been substantially advanced by the development and application of the A.A.I.. In fact, the most promising results have been achieved in the study of the intergenerational transmission of disturbed patterns of attachment. Parents classified as secure-autonomous with the A.A.I. are statistically more likely to impart security to their children than parents who do not fall into that category.

Studies carried out in London (Fonagy *et al.* 1991) demonstrated that the A.A.I. applied to pregnant women had a predictive correlation with the Strange Situation, carried out after the child was born, at 12 months of age. Seventy-five per cent of secure mothers had securely attached children; 73 per cent of mothers classified as 'dismissing' or 'preoccupied' had insecurely attached children.

The full interpretation of these findings is not easy and will be further and significantly advanced when and if we reach a better understanding of, and consensus over, the causal correlations between the quality of actual experience, attachment representation and the overall organization of mental functions (including memory, language, and so on).

On reflective function

Peter Fonagy et al. (1995) propose that the capacity to reflect over personal and interpersonal issues, and to see others as people with mental states of their own, is a developmental achievement. It seems that, by and large, this capacity only fully emerges in the context of a secure attachment relationship.

This capacity involves the subject's ability to think of himself and others as separate people, capable of thinking and feeling, whose behaviour is motivated by underlying mental states and knowledge which emerges from sources which can be clearly identified and defined (see Chapter 13).

The concept of reflective function partly evolves from Mary Main's (1991) work on metacognitive monitoring and partly from the work of a good number of psychoanalysts who discussed the characteristics and importance of being able to think about personal and interpersonal events, particularly in terms of the connection between one's own mental states and those of others. For instance, Bion (1962a, 1962b) described the transformation of raw or concrete mental states ('beta-elements') into tolerable thinkable experiences ('alpha-functions'), while Fairbairn (1952) and Kohut (1977) recognized that the self develops through perception and reflection of oneself in someone else's mind.

Initially, Peter Fonagy and colleagues talked of 'self-reflective function'. However, they have recently dropped this term and replaced it by 'reflective function' (Howard Steele, personal communication). The term 'self-reflective' may be interpreted as something taking place within the individual in relation to himself, whereas the reflective function is inherently interpersonal in its manifestations and the way it expresses itself.

Fonagy and other members of his team have studied transcripts of A.A.I.s for the purpose of assessing the quality of reflective functioning. They have also demonstrated that individual differences in reflective functioning are rooted in the presence or absence of attachment security (see Fonagy et al. 1991, 1996, 1997).

Perhaps reflective functioning is a more specific way of thinking about oneself and the world which is intertwined with ego functions (see, for instance, Bellak, Hurvich and Gediman 1973): the capacities for reality-testing, judgement, sense of reality of the world and of the self, regulation and control of affects and impulses, thought processes, synthetic-integrative functioning, and so on. Clinical experience shows that optimal functioning in all these areas depends upon the quality of early attachment relationships and, in turn, affects the way adults treat their children. Consistency of behaviour, predictability, emotional stability, good judgement, and non-distorted perception of the child's emotional states, motives and needs are all related to ego functioning.

Attachment styles among adults

Bartholomew and Horowitz (1991) devised a semi-structured interview asking subjects to describe their friendships, romantic relationships and feelings about the importance of close relationships. Participants were asked about loneliness, shyness, their degree of trust of others, their impressions of other people's evaluation of themselves and their hopes for any changes in their social lives. On the basis of the interview audio recordings, each transcript was rated on four nine-point scales describing the subject's degree of correspondence with each of four prototypes: secure, dismissive, preoccupied and fearful.

The *secure prototype* is characterized by a valuing of intimate relationships, the capacity to maintain close relationships without losing personal autonomy, and a coherence and thoughtfulness in discussing relationships and related issues.

The *dismissive prototype* is characterized by a downplaying of the importance of close relationships, restricted emotionality, an emphasis on independence and self-reliance, and a lack of credibility in discussing relationships. In the face of interpersonal problems, self-concept is maintained by putting the greater responsibility on others.

The *preoccupied prototype* is characterized by an overinvolvement in close relationships, a dependence on other people's acceptance for a sense of personal well-being, a tendency to idealize other people, and incoherence and exaggerated emotionality in discussing relationships. In the face of interpersonal conflicts, these people tend to blame themselves for perceived rejections by others and are thereby able to retain a positive view of others.

The *fearful prototype* is characterized by an avoidance of close relationships because of fear of rejection, a sense of personal insecurity and distrust of others.

This information was complemented by other assessments which included factual information about family, personal activities, friendships, sociability, interpersonal problems, a self-esteem inventory, and so on. The degree to which subjects presented a coherent, integrated and internally consistent portrayal of their experiences and feelings in close relationships (coherence); the degree to which specific memories were recounted to support generalizations (elaboration); the degree to which emotions were openly expressed or controlled whenever appropriate (emotional expressiveness); the capacity to use others when upset (reliance on others); and the tendency to look after others (caregiving behaviour) were assessed.

In this way, multi-dimensional scalings confirmed the hypothesized underlying structure. However, none of the subjects uniquely fitted any one prototype. Instead, many subjects reported a mix of tendencies across time and across relationships. However, the study suggested that: (1) patterns of relationships among adults reflect in some ways patterns of early parent–child relationships; (2) in processing social information, people seem to produce behaviours that evoke specific reactions from other people, and that this social feedback is interpreted in ways that confirm the person's internal working models of the self and others; and (3) people tend to induce social partners to engage in patterns of interactions which confirm existing internal working models. The author proposed further research on how internal working models of early attachment relationships manifest and promote confirmation in relationships with friends and sexual partners.

The Attachment Style Interview

Another interview measure of attachment style for adults, the Attachment Style Interview, is perhaps more accessible for use on the European side of the Atlantic, with training available in London (Bifulco, Lillie and Brown 1994). Developed alongside a battery of other semi-structured investigator-based instruments, including measures of life events and difficulties and of childhood experience of care and abuse, the interview seeks to contrast the external nature of support on offer from other people with the internal nature of the respondent's attitudes and behavioural tendencies within relationships, looking at friends, children and even pets, as well as family of origin and partners.

The interview, which takes about half an hour, contains a set of stem questions and additional probes which are used to encourage the subject to talk freely about how he feels about relating to the people mentioned above. The final categorization resembles other attachment measures in distinguishing standard (or secure) attachment from several sub-groups of non-standard styles of relating. It discriminates fearful and simple avoidant from dismissive, and also possesses a similar rating of preoccupied/enmeshed to the A.A.I. and Bartholomew's measure.

In building up the picture that underlies this final categorization, the investigator must rate tendencies to mistrust; attitudinal constraints over confiding and help-seeking; intolerance of separation; anger felt in relationships; fear of intimacy and sexual intimacy (contrasting fear of rejection with fear of engulfment); desire for engagement/enmeshment in relationships; self-reliance; and an overall ability to make and maintain relationships. Particularly important in scoring high on this last scale is the ability to form close bonds with people outside the family and to engage in communications where reciprocal confiding is possible. Lacking a standard or secure attachment style has been found to be a predictor subsequent onset of depression (Bifulco *et al.* 1997) and, in another sample, failure to recover from depression (Harris, Brown and Robinson 1997). Tirril Harris (personal communication) points out that it is not only as a predictor of symptomatology that this instrument has its use; by focusing systematically on particular aspects of relating, it can give a psychotherapist an all-round picture of a prospective patient and where any future therapeutic work might profitably be concentrated. Therefore, the interview may have a diagnostic value in clinical practice.

Dysfunctional Parenting

Introduction

The assumption that parental styles have an important influence on child development has a long history. Many books and articles have been written on this subject. Locke's (1693) and Rousseau's (1762) educational methods were early manifestations of this concern. From within the psychoanalytic field, explorations of the negative outcome of dysfunctional parental practices have been discussed. However, Bowlby's attachment theory has the merit of proposing a systematic framework for relating dysfunctional early parent–child interaction to the child's development along a sub-optimal pathway, with its sequalae of anxious attachment and psychopathology (Perris 1994).

It seems that the patterns of interaction between parents and children, once established, tend to persist in most cases. One reason for this is that the way a parent treats a child, whether for better or for worse, tends to continue unmodified. How a caregiver treats a child is to a large degree related to his personality and, unless this person undergoes in-depth psychotherapy, his pattern of interaction is not going to change. If this pattern is pathogenic, it is going to be so when the child is 2 years old, 5 years old, 10 years old and...even 50 years old!

Much attachment-oriented psychotherapeutic work is related to examining the influence that such patterns of interaction have had on personality development over a long period of time.

A securely attached child is a happier and more rewarding child to care for, and also less demanding than an anxious child. An anxious ambivalent child is likely to be clinging and emotionally taxing, while an avoidant child is likely to be distant and lacking in engagement. In both of these cases the child's behaviour is prone to provoke negative responses from the parents, so that a vicious circle develops.

Fathers and mothers

As I have already pointed out in Chapter 4, there is increasing evidence that the role of father is very important (Phares and Compas 1992). Clinical experience indicates that there is a substantial association between paternal characteristics and child and adolescent psychopathology. In most cases the degree of risk associated with paternal behaviour towards children is comparable with that associated with maternal behaviour.

Some pathogenic styles of parenting

A number of studies (e.g. Winefield, Tiggemann and Winefield 1994) show that correlations between recall of parental behaviour and current psychological functioning were as predicted by attachment theory. Subjects with supporting, non-rejecting and non-overinvolved parents were less depressed, less socially alienated and more satisfied with their lives. Maltreating, abusive or overprotective parents and those suffering from addictions, depression or other psychiatric illnesses tend to be major agents in deviating their children's developmental pathways to a sub-optimal course. On the other hand, parents who are warm, affectionate, playful, supportive and respectful of their children's sense of initiative and need for exploration tend to have children who grow up to be mentally healthy and psychosocially mature and creative (Franz *et al.* 1994).

A. Pathogenic communications

Here we are going to list and describe some communications that parents may use which can be regarded as unsupportive or lacking in sensitive responsiveness. It is assumed that the constant repetition of these communications, rather than occasional expression, is what may contribute in a substantial way to insecurity. The following list is not intended to be comprehensive and is the result of my own clinical experience as well as what I learned in my supervision sessions with John Bowlby. I have identified many of these patterns in the course of my work as a hospital psychiatrist, when I have interviewed and observed many families with young members. Some descriptions appear in the attachment literature and correlate with my own observations.

INVALIDATION OF THE CHILD'S REQUESTS FOR COMFORT

Differences in parents' responses to a child's request for comfort can have extensive impact on the content of semantic memory and internal working models of the self and other. For example, when frightened and seeking assistance from his attachment figure, a child might be told, in soothing tones as he is picked up, 'Oh, were you afraid to be alone? Don't worry, mommy won't leave you'. Another child in similar circumstances might be told, as his mother pushes him away, 'Don't be such a scaredy-cat! Nothing will hurt you!'. This child will not only form an internal representation of mother as unaccepting of his care-eliciting communications, but also will begin to form a semantic representation of himself as 'scaredy-cat' (Crittenden, 1992, p.583).

Crittenden (1992) says:

> The power of semantic labels on developing personalities is shown by Tim, a maltreating father. When asked if he had been a 'good kid', Tim answered that he had been 'a mean kid'. Upon further query, Tim stated that he knew this because his mother had repeatedly told him so and 'after a while, it just gets to be part of who you are'. (p.583)

A patient of mine once came to her session and said that she did not have much to say. She also felt 'ridiculous and silly'. In the course of the session, it emerged that she was in fact upset because of some incident at work. She then recognized that she was reluctant to tell me that she felt upset. She felt it would be irrelevant. It was part of an old pattern (which, in fact, developed early in childhood) of bottling up her feelings. She remembered that as a child, if she had a problem at school, she would keep it to herself. She also recalled some incidents when she tried to express to her mother feelings of disquiet in relation to incidents at school. On all those occasions her mother reacted in a dismissive way and called her 'ridiculous'.

A parent who resents the child's desire for comfort is likely to interpret the child's care-eliciting signals in terms that are unfavourable to the child's self-concept or self-esteem. This would be the case, for instance, with a mother who says to her crying child: 'You are so selfish! Do you think I should spend all my time with you?'.

DISCONFIRMATION OF THE CHILD'S PERCEPTIONS OF FAMILY EVENTS

The evidence that adverse experiences with parents or other significant others during the years of immaturity play a large part in causing psychological disturbance is now substantial. However, many parents who create adverse conditions do not wish to be seen as responsible for creating such conditions. They need to minimize the perception of their negative aspects and maximize the perception of their positive aspects. Therefore they may indoctrinate their children into believing that they – as parents – are much better than they seem. Such indoctrination may not only cause undue guilt but may account for cognitive disturbance. Communications such as, 'You should be grateful to have such a dedicated parent' may not only cause guilt and conflictual feelings, but may also interfere with the development of cognitive and perceptual abilities.

Bowlby (1988b) said:

> Children not infrequently observe scenes that parents would prefer they did not observe; they form impressions that parents would prefer they did not form; and

they have experiences that parents would like to believe that they have not had. Evidence shows that many of these children, aware of how their parents feel, proceed then to conform to their parents' wishes by excluding from further processing such information as they already have; and that, having done so, they cease consciously to be aware that they have ever observed such scenes, formed such impressions, or had such experiences. (p.101–102)

Most children prefer to see their parents in a favourable light and overlook many deficiencies. They also have too little experience of the world to be able to compare their parents' behaviour with what is going on in other families, perhaps less pathological. Yet they do not easily conform to seeing a parent only in the light the parent requires or to feeling towards him or her only in the way demanded. To ensure that, pressure must be exerted. This pressure is mainly exerted through what the parent says to the child.

A patient of mine recalled in a session an episode of his childhood. One night he heard his parents having a terrible row in their bedroom. The following day he gathered courage to question his mother, who responded: 'You got confused! They were the neighbours!'.

GUILT-INDUCING COMMUNICATIONS

Parents may use guilt-inducing communications in order to impose discipline, often with benign consequences. However, over-controlling and role-reversing parents may use this type of message in order to retain the child in their vicinity and inhibit exploratory behaviour. Repeated communications of this kind may contribute to the formation of a harsh and guilt-ridden super-ego.

INVALIDATION OF THE CHILD'S SUBJECTIVE EXPERIENCE

One way of adapting reality to parental wishes is to invalidate feelings that the child has, particularly when these feelings are unpleasant because they stem from a reality that the parent wishes to deny. As a result, the child is required always to appear happy and to be well disposed towards his parents. The child is also discouraged from expressing sorrow, loneliness or anger. Bowlby (1988b) quotes a patient of his who one day, after a good deal of therapy, said: 'I see now that I was terribly lonely as a child but I was never allowed to know it'.

When I was working in a hospital as a general psychiatrist, one day I interviewed a family with an adolescent daughter, Mary, who was slowly recovering from a breakdown. Mary had been admitted to the hospital three weeks earlier and had then gone home on leave for a week. When Mary and her parents returned for a re-assessment, I asked her how she had been. Her answer was: 'Terribly unwell!'. Her mother immediately reacted by saying to me: 'That's not true! She has been fine!'. Then she turned to her daughter and said: 'You have been happy, Mary! Haven't you?'.

This was an apparently normal middle-class family. Both parents were professional people in their late 40s. Mother was engaged in higher university studies. In the course of further family meetings, it transpired that mother lost both parents in puberty and spent her adolescence in a rigid institution. It became clear that for her any unhappy feelings in the family would reactivate painful feelings of her past, feelings that she felt she could not afford to have. It was interesting that after a few sessions, father – who basically remained aloof in family sessions – requested an individual interview with me. In the course of that session, he told me that besides his 'normal professional and family behaviour' he had another life: he was visiting prostitutes on a regular basis, sometimes as often as three or four times a week. His wife knew nothing about this. He requested a referral for individual therapy and subsequently I put him in contact with a psychoanalyst.

Mary's breakdown had a favourable outcome for all members of her family, and further damage was prevented. That was not the case with a patient of mine who, aged 50, after several years of analysis, exclaimed with tears: 'I want to feel I have the right to feel angry or unhappy! I wish I had had family therapy in my teens!'.

THREATS

Bowlby was particularly aware of the way in which parental threats undermine security of attachment. Parents, either in a naive or malignant manner, make threats to their children in order to impose discipline and control or discharge anger. These communications include threats not to love the child, to abandon the child, to commit suicide in response to bad behaviour, and so on. A parent may say things like this: 'If you do not do your homework dutifully I'll send you to boarding school!'. Bowlby (1988b) quoted one of my cases, where a father told his daughter repeatedly that if she did not behave in the way he expected (namely not to go to his bedroom on Sunday mornings) he would send her to a school on a remote rock surrounded by sharks (Marrone 1984).

In the course of a supervision session, I told Bowlby that a patient of mine remembered violent rows between her parents. In response, he suggested I ask her what her parents used to say when they had these rows. Once I had the opportunity to ask such a question to my patient, she said with tears in her eyes: 'My mother always said to my father: "If you go on like that I will go away, and take my daughter with me. You will never see her again!"'

UNPRODUCTIVE CRITICISMS

Some parents or caregivers constantly subject their children to criticisms in such a way that their main effect is one of undermining the child's sense of self-esteem. These criticisms seem to be accompanied by meta-communications which have a rejecting quality. This type of negative communication contrasts to that of a supportive and accepting parent who may convey the following message: 'I like you, I love you, but you must revise this aspect of your behaviour'.

People who, as children, have been subjected to unproductive criticisms, tend to become allergic to any type of criticism (including well-intentioned and friendly comments).

SHAME-INDUCING COMMUNICATIONS

Some children are subjected to shame-inducing communications, which are often cruel and humiliating. In some cases it seems that the purpose of the verbal degradation is to impose discipline. A patient of mine, who suffers from a social phobia, was deserted by his parents when he was a child and subsequently looked after by grandparents who seemed to take great pleasure in making him feel ashamed of himself in public.

INTRUSIVENESS AND MIND-READING

There are some parents who do not allow their child to have much mental space of their own. Such a child can be the object of intrusive questioning and interpretations to the point that the child feels he cannot keep inside any thought which will not be taken away and exposed.

DOUBLE-BINDING

Double-binding is a form of communication which contains a statement followed by a second one which contradicts the first. A mild example would be that of a parent who says to his child: 'Yes, of course you can go and play with your friend but you know what I think of him!'.

The main effect of double-binding is that it provokes in the recipient irreconcilable conflicting feelings. However, there are malignant forms of double-binding which result in the child feeling that whichever way he goes is unacceptable or impossible. Often double-binding takes place in the context of an intense relationship which has a high degree of physical and/or psychological value for the recipient of the message. The double-binding message is structured in such a way that there is no escape: it must be disobeyed to be obeyed. If it is a definition of the self, the person thereby defined is this kind of person only if he is not, and is not if he is. Moreover, the recipient of the message is prevented from stepping outside the frame set by this message: he is not allowed to challenge it through reflective communication; neither can he withdraw (Watzlawick, Helmick and Jackson 1967). In my clinical experience as a general psychiatrist, I have found that this type of communication often occurs in families where there is a young member suffering from psychosis.

Analytic work with parents who double-bind show that this type of communication stems from internal dissociation and ambivalence.

PARADOXICAL COMMENTS

These are comments that simultaneously mean their opposite, and such meaning can only be deciphered by the tone of voice. An example would be that of a mother who says to her child in an angry tone of voice: 'Yes, I'm so pleased with your behaviour!'.

Often these comments have a benign quality, but in certain cases they can create cognitive confusion.

UNFAVOURABLE COMPARISONS

These are comments which involve comparing the child with siblings or peers in an unfavourable way. An example is that of a parent who says: 'Look at your sister. She can do it!'. The effect of repeated comments of this kind is that of undermining self-esteem and self-confidence. The child may develop the conviction that his parents wish he was like somebody else, which has a very rejecting connotation.

COUNTER-STIMULATING COMMENTS

These are comments based on the parents' assumption that the child is incapable of achieving a higher goal. An example would be: 'You cannot go cycling! You will be exhausted before you leave!'.

Again, the effect of a comment like this is to reduce self-confidence.

CONSTANT BLAMING

This type of communication may have a guilt-inducing quality. However, its main characteristic is its intensely hostile quality. The child is accused of being the cause of all ills, particularly of a parent's suffering. Sometimes, blaming is a response to the child's care-eliciting attempts. A patient of mine recalled that on one occasion he was upset because he had a conflict with his teacher. His father, not knowing enough about the event, exclaimed: 'I wonder what you have done!'.

COMMUNICATIONS WHICH UNDERMINE THE CHILD'S BEST INTENTIONS

These are comments which are based on the assumption that the child does not do anything in a genuine sense, always acting in a tricky or manipulative way. One example would be that of a parent who responds to a child's achievement at school by saying: 'I wonder what you want to get out of me with this!'.

COMMENTS THAT DENY THE CHILD'S ENTITLEMENT TO HAVE OPINIONS

These are communications that indicate that either the child has no right to have opinions or that the child's opinions are unworthy of serious consideration. A patient of mine said that in her house, her parents used to state: 'Children have nothing to say!'.

PARENTS' SELF-REFERRING COMMENTS

In this case, when the child talks about a personal issue, the parent immediately appropriates the topic to talk about himself. A patient of mine gave me an example of his mother's usual reaction to him. He came back from school and said that he had fallen down and hurt his back. In response, his mother said: 'I often have back-aches', and went on talking about her ailments, ignoring the child's message.

DISMISSIVE OR HARD-HEARTED RESPONSES

These are verbal reactions to a child who is upset and seeking support, which in fact minimize the child's reason to be distressed (or make it illegitimate) and carry an implicit criticism of oversensitivity. An example would be that of a child who, having a conflict with a friend, seeks support from a parent. The parent responds: 'Oh! Come on! Don't bother me with silly issues!'.

OVER-REACTIVE RESPONSES

These are extreme responses to the child's anxieties or difficult emotions, so that the parent's emotional reactions are greater than those of the child. Often, the parent's response to the child's present situation is one of making pessimistic predictions. As a consequence of repeated experiences of this kind, the child may learn not to confide in the parent in order to protect himself and, perhaps, the parent as well.

THE POSSIBLE ROOTS OF SUCH COMMUNICATIONS

These parental communications often have a hostile, rejecting, punitive, sadistic, controlling, clinging or ambivalent quality. In some cases, these communications take place several times each day. As a result the child may experience lowered self-esteem and self-confidence, excessive guilt or shame, lack of trust in his own opinions or perceptions, cognitive confusion, and so on.

These forms of communication often occur in intact families where there is no history of child abuse, gross neglect, violence or severe losses or separations.

Possible reasons why a parent may communicate to the child in this way include:

1. The parent's projection of his/her own sense of guilt, shame or negative discrimination.

2. Identification with parents who treated him/her in that way, so that the parent treats their child as he/she had been treated in the past.

3. The child may have been unwanted by one or both parents.

4. The child may have been made a scapegoat as a result of an unfortunate family situation which has been attributed to him.

5. A parent may want to retain strict control of the child and discourage him from exploring the world because of their own insecure attachment and need to cling to the child.

6. In a reconstituted family, a child may be the result of a previous marriage or relationship and in such a context the step-parent rejects him.

7. A child may have some resemblance to another person (usually a grandparent) who the parent hates.

8. A child may be of the wrong sex in a family in which the parents hoped for a boy or a girl.

9. The child is treated as an extension of the parent, so that he has vicariously to satisfy the parent's narcissistic need for achievement, company, glamour or fame. If the child cannot meet this need, he must be attacked.

THE NAMELESS DREAD: WHAT IS NOT REFLECTED UPON

The term 'nameless dread' was first used by Karin Stephen (1941) to describe extreme states of anxiety in childhood, interpreted as a fear of impotence in the face of instinctual tension. Bion (1962b; 1967) used the term in order to describe a state of anxiety without meaning which results from the mother being unable to provide 'reverie' (that is to say, a state of calm responsiveness and containment of the child's anxieties). In my view, Bion's idea of a 'nameless dread' is essentially correct. However, it has to be updated and expanded upon.

A nameless dread is intense anxiety or anxiety-ridden feelings which a person experiences at a subjective level but to which they cannot give a name. In other words, this is anxiety or pain which has no meaning. In terms of attachment theory, the main source of anxiety is insecurity of attachment. Furthermore, the anxiety is less likely to be processed when it is not possible to make sense of it, to reflect upon its sources. In some families it is difficult or impossible for children and parents to discuss attachment-relevant events in a reflective way. When these explorations do not take place, the child is left alone with unprocessed anxieties. Therefore, the impact of the anxiety is greater than it would have been if shared reflective communications had taken place. A patient of mine once said: 'In my family, emotions had no name'.

It is not uncommon to see patients who come to therapy in a state of being unable to conceptualize their affective states, and then recognize in the course of the therapy that in their families it was not possible to talk about feelings, to discuss interpersonal events and to interpret them in a meaningful way.

B. Parents' attitudes and patterns of relating

In most cases the communications I have described are indicative of a parent's general attitude towards the child.

In clinical practice we often find that the parent seems to show stable behavioural patterns which can be broadly classified in the following way.

INABILITY TO RESPECT THE CHILD'S SENSE OF INITIATIVE

When a parent interacts with his child, he may be respectful of those processes that Winnicott (1965) called 'going-on-being'. This is the natural tendency that exists in the child to have a sense of self with a past, present, and future'. Any 'impingement' on the part of the parent causes a reaction in the child, and the reaction breaks up the going-on-being.

Although Winnicott talked about impingement as an act of interference with the infant's going-on-being, it is possible to extrapolate his notion to the continuous relationship that children of any age have with their parents. Some parents are able to find a good enough way of providing guidance and supervision while at the same time allowing space for the development of the child's sense of autonomy and initiative, particularly through play. Other parents need to exert too much control over the child, to the degree of restricting (some times severely) the child's initiative.

Hoffman (1994a, 1994b, 1995), an Argentinian psychoanalyst and researcher, has studied parent–infant dyads. He says that from the sixth month of life a baby is increasingly capable of personal initiative. The parental response may be favourable or adverse. An adverse parental response is likely to generate compliance and inhibition, or else rebelliousness.

As the child develops, his sense of initiative may conflict with the parent's proposals and projects. Parent and child may be able to negotiate this conflict or they may not. In favourable conditions, as the child grows older his initiatives continue to increase in frequency and become more complex. A good enough parent shows respect, empathy, timely responses and a capacity for negotiating conflicts.

REJECTION

Research evidence (Bowlby 1980) suggests that there are parents who, for reasons stemming from their own childhoods and/or from difficulties in the marriage, find their children's desire for love and care a burden. So they respond to them irritably, by ignoring, scolding or moralizing. Other children are brought up by foster parents who do not feel genuine love for them.

As Bowlby (1988b) explained, a child may never have been wanted or fully accepted by one or both parents for one or many reasons. In all these cases the child may be treated by one or both parents, step-parent or substitute parental figure in a rejecting way. Aspects of rejection seem to be lack of interest and hostility. However, hostility may be present in more accepting parents and may not in itself be an indicator of rejection. Perhaps the key aspect of rejection is the persistent turning away of the child's requests for affection and relatedness and the implicit or explicit message that the child is not liked.

Some parents may prematurely push the child towards independence; others may be reserved, distant, cool, unexpressive. A parent may reject his child continuously or intermittently and partially. In more severe cases, the parent may actively and continuously reject the child, and may even confirm his acts with verbal communications which explicitly state his wish that the child was not there.

NEGLECT

Sometimes it is difficult to make the distinction between rejection and neglect, because both attitudes have in common a lack of loving involvement with the child. However, in the case of neglect, the parent may not reject the child in a noticeable way. Instead, the parent does not make his child a priority. The parent may be depressed. He may be addicted to alcohol or drugs. He may prefer to work long hours away from home; spend weekends in leisure activities without the child; go on holiday leaving the child behind; or delegate his parental function for exceedingly long periods of time to nannies or other caregivers (with whom, perhaps, the child is not familiar).

The parent may not want to get involved with school activities or attend parent–teacher meetings; he may send the child alone to the doctor, and so on. Also, the parent may place the child in boarding school and fail to keep in close contact with him. The parent may not be emotionally supportive or show an active interest in the child as an individual. He may fail to supervise the child outside school hours and not be aware of his whereabouts. Nonetheless, the parent may make good material provision – good food, clean clothes, formal education – and not give the impression that he does not wish to have the child in his life.

A neglected child may not be able to put words to his feelings, yet he may consciously or unconsciously struggle with a sense of lacking love. The child may form the notion that the parent cannot be trusted in times of crisis. The child may also fear that lack of compliance with parental wishes may result in abandonment or unforgiving aloofness.

In more severe cases, the child may be neglected to the point of cruelty. For instance, he may be left alone inside the house or in the street for periods which are highly inappropriate for his age.

The key factors in neglect are: (1) a lack of emotional warmth and support; and (2) a lack of protection and appropriate supervision.

INABILITY TO PLAY TOGETHER

This is a more specific form of neglect that may exist in the absence of generalized neglect. In most cases, it occurs in the context of a parent's aloof stance. Some patients say that they do not remember having played with their parents. They have no memory of sitting on the floor with one or either parent and playing together with toys. They cannot recall going to the park or flying a kite. They have no past image of running around and laughing in the garden. What they have instead are memories of mother and/or father being busy with domestic chores or with their own social and professional occupations, with no time to spend with their children in mutually enjoyable activities.

Direct observation of families shows that, in fact, some parents do find it difficult to involve themselves in spontaneous and imaginative play with their children. Therefore, it seems, adults' accounts of such a style of relating to parents during their early years should be regarded as plausible.

PUSHING FOR ACHIEVEMENT

A parent may push his child to achieve to an excessive degree. The parent may make the child feel rejected because acceptance is not based on what the child actually is today, but posed as conditional upon future achievements.

Often these parents need their children vicariously to repair their own narcissistic wounds, their own sense of failure, often through academic achievements, sport and competition, and so on.

ROLE REVERSAL

Role reversal occurs when the child is made to feel that the parent's psychological or physical well-being is a concern or responsibility of the child. Role reversal can occur with varying degrees of persistence and intensity. Often the pattern of role reversal persists throughout the life of the parent–child relationship (even after the child becomes an adult).

The reasons why a parent may engage a child in role reversal vary with each case. The parent may have an anxious personality and need the child to contain his anxieties. The parent may be clinging for fear of abandonment. The parent may be incompetent or ill. He may be emotionally at the edge of a breakdown and the house may be in chaos. The child may feel concerned with the parent's psychological well-being in response to: (1) explicit, implicit or double-binding requests; or (2) witnessing parental illness, disability or incompetence.

According to my clinical observations, there are basically two types of role-reversing parents: (1) low level and (2) high level.

The *low level* role-reversing parent may have a striking childish, chaotic or incompetent quality. The parent may be psychiatrically or medically ill. He may be histrionic and dramatic, and may over-react to emotional events. Perhaps the child feels that he cannot confide his own problems to the parent, because – if he did – the parent would fall apart with anxiety or chaotic anger. The parent may induce guilt in the child by saying that the child is not doing enough for the parent. Therefore the child may try to please or placate the parent by keeping his problems to himself.

The *high level* role-reversing parent, instead of showing weakness or vulnerability, shows apparent strength. He can be over-controlling and inhibiting and indicate that his restrictions on the child's exploratory behaviour are based on the need to protect the child from danger or hazardous situations. However, underneath it all, there is the parent's need to retain and control the child for fear of losing him.

Individuals in analysis who have been subjected to role reversal often show a conscious or unconscious conflict between compliance with parental figures and profound resentment.

ROLE DELEGATION

This is the case of a child who may be the oldest of several siblings and to whom a parental role in relation to the younger siblings is delegated. Parents may be unavailable because of work commitments, mental illness or physical disability. In this context, the child may be denied the right to his childhood and be pushed prematurely to function in a more mature or precocious manner. Unconscious resentment together with a compulsive care-giving attitude in adult life may be one of the possible outcomes.

INCONSISTENCY

Inconsistent parents fluctuate in their availability and sensitive responsiveness. These parents may have no aversion to close bodily or emotional contact, so that moments of intimate interaction are possible. However, their oscillations make the child feel alarmed and hyperaroused.

THE PSYCHIATRICALLY ILL PARENT

Of course, we should not forget that some parents are clinically ill and that their illness is likely to affect the way they care for and treat their children. The parent may be housebound with agoraphobia, have frequent psychiatric admissions or oscillate between periods of depression and elation, and so on. Of course, alcoholism and violent behaviour have to be included in this list, even if it is not possible to offer a comprehensive account here.

THE TRAUMATOGENIC PARENT

Inconsistency, role reversal, neglect and rejection can occur in different degrees and, of course, in extreme degrees they can become severely traumatic. I am not sure where the dividing line between what is detrimental and what is traumatic lies. Nor do I know if there is consensus and clarity in relation to the meaning of the word 'trauma'.

We often refer to a traumatic event as something that has a dramatic quality and occurs at one moment, leaving a devastating effect which – at best – overtaxes the coping abilities of the individual or the social group. However, Masud Khan (1963) talked about 'cumulative trauma', that is to say, the repetition of unfavourable events that has a cumulative effect of a traumatic quality.

Although sudden disruptions do occur, it seems that repeated disruptions of a severe kind are to be found in the attachment history of many of our patients, particularly in those who have a serious personality disorder.

Perhaps we could talk about a 'traumatogenic parent', a parent who is likely to inflict a high degree of cumulative trauma: sexual or physical abuse, emotional cruelty, exposure to adults' promiscuous sexual behaviour or unnecessary separation and abandonment.

It is not my intention to explore in detail all these different modes of parental communication and behaviour. What I want to do, instead, is to draw attention to areas of patients' detailed attachment histories which are fundamentally important and yet seldom studied in psychoanalytic case histories. However, the reader will have no difficulty in recognizing some of these patterns.

Bowlby (1988b) said that there will be many occasions when a therapist can usefully ask for more detail or raise questions about situations of childhood and adolescence that the patient has not so far referred to directly, but which seem plausible possibilities in the light of what he has been describing and the particular problems from which he is suffering.

PART 2

In the Psychoanalytic Realm

Some aspects of the relationship
between attachment theory
and psychoanalytic thinking

CHAPTER 8

In the Psychoanalytic Field

Some Comparative Notes

On object relations

The purpose of this chapter is to locate attachment theory in the context of some influential schools of thought in contemporary psychoanalysis. Inevitably, this review cannot be comprehensive and is presented as a general, albeit partial, reference framework.

In broad terms, attachment theory can be considered an offspring of object relations theory. However, there are several versions and interpretations of object relations theory. The term 'object relations' is in itself troublesome, for it may refer to people's relations with others or it may refer more specifically to mental representations of a significant other.

The concept of 'object relations' is originally linked with Freud's drive theory. The 'object' in Freud's terms is the libidinal object. (In his later theory, it is also the object of the aggressive drive; see later.) In this context, the word 'object' has a dual meaning, and this is so in English and Spanish as well as in other languages. In other words, an 'object' can be a 'thing' or the 'target' of a drive or intent. Therefore, in its original usage, the concept of 'object' was inherent to drive theory. Yet today many psychoanalysts who speak in the name of 'object relations theory' have not only abandoned the classical Freudian drive theory but see one theory as opposed to the other. To make things more complicated, we should remember that Freud formulated two different drive theories in the course of his life. In his first theory, he identified two instincts: (1) the libidinal or sexual instinct; and (2) the self-preservation instinct. However, in *Beyond the Pleasure Principle* (1920), Freud established aggression as an independent motivational source, as an instinct in its own right, as a pervasive self-destructive tendency. Since then, while some object relations theorists, such as Winnicott, have discarded the death instinct as a valid concept, others, such as Melanie Klein, have made a shift of emphasis from libidinal to aggressive issues and built many of their propositions on the latter.

The word 'object' has been used in the psychoanalytic literature to connote a wide range of concepts. For example, 'object' may refer to an in-born conception of the other (which, in the view of certain authors, precedes interpersonal experience), as it may refer to mental representations of another person which originate in real life. Furthermore, the object may be regarded as a 'whole object' (the representation of the other person as a complete being) or as a 'part object' (this often being seen as the representation of a part of the other person's body).

The object may be conceptualized as the static image of something but also as an active factor, which by its very nature (benign or malignant, good or bad, alive or dead, persecutory, and so on) may constantly influence psychic functioning. Although the word 'object', in its common usage, refers to something tangible, in psychoanalysis it may refer to something intangible, symbolic, endowed with or emerging from phantasies; something that can be cut into two, destroyed, repaired, reshaped, manipulated, and so on.

Bowlby abandoned the use of the word 'object', because – in his view – it is an inaccurate concept which lends itself to divergent interpretations. Instead of referring to the primary caregiver as an 'external object', Bowlby preferred the term 'attachment figure' or, more simply, 'father', 'mother', 'parent' or 'caregiver'. And, instead of referring to the internal representation of the other as an 'internal object', he preferred to use the concept of 'internal working model of attachment figures'.

An important element in making distinctions between different versions of object relations theory is the importance given to real interpersonal experiences in psychic life and, particularly, in early development. In this context, it is almost an impossible task to define object relations theory. Even if we recognize that the object of study is a set of theories rather than a unitary theory, it is not easy to define what all these theories have in common. It could be said that what all these theories share is the view that relations with others are central, particularly in the clinical field. But this is such a basic common-sense statement that it can hardly be used to identify a school of thought.

Perhaps, it could be argued, what is characteristic of all object relations theorists is the fact that they have distanced themselves from an early position which understood the role of objects largely in relation to the notion of discharge. In Freud's early formulation, disturbance arose as a result of dammed-up libido and the purpose of the analytic treatment was to lift the inhibition and make it possible for the patient to use other people as 'objects' of discharge. However, this early theory was soon replaced by the notion that disturbance was a result of unresolved conflicts. But the formulation of the essence of the conflict changed over the years: the conflict being between the pleasure and the reality principles, the ego and the id, the death and life instincts or dependency and autonomy needs.

The Kleinian school saw psychopathology as a result of the individual's failure to negotiate the internal conflict between death and life instincts. It is in this context that projection, projective identification and splitting are given a special role, as these are seen as mechanisms aimed at obtaining a false solution – as it were – to the failed instinctual negotiation. However, in this scheme these defence mechanisms are seen as existing both in the course of normal development and in adult psychopathology. The individual's appreciation of significant others is seen as imbued from the first with projections of split-off internal parts. Therefore, there is little room left for non-distorted perceptions of the other.

As I indicated in Chapter 2, Bowlby modified and re-defined without ambiguity Freud's metapsychological assumptions, respecting some, discarding others. Bowlby shared Fairbairn's idea that the primary motivational force is relationship-seeking. Like Fairbairn, Bowlby saw classical Freudian theory as rooted in an anachronistic model taken from nineteenth-century physics and biology. But, unlike Fairbairn, Bowlby tried to update a biological model for psychoanalysis, in line with contemporary developments in biology and ethology.

Bowlby suggested that instinctive behavioural systems underlie much of the psychosocial life of man and serve specific biological functions, the most important being the attachment system. This was selected as such during the early evolution of the human species because it made survival more likely: children accompanied by their familiar and primary caregivers are less vulnerable to life-threatening situations.

Bowlby's point of view came close to what J. Sutherland (1980), in a seminal paper, identified as the 'British object relations theory'. Sutherland found sufficient common elements in the works of Balint, Winnicott, Guntrip and Fairbairn so as to be able to group them together as distinct from the line of thought represented by Melanie Klein and her disciples. Although these people did not literally constitute a group (in the same sense that they did not do any joint work), their contributions eventually embodied a common development. The key point they shared was that it is impossible to understand psychic functioning without reference to the developmental and social contexts. The infant's innate potential has to be activated by an input of loving and empathic care from his mother. Very simply, to be able to love and enjoy, the baby has to be loved and enjoyed.

Sutherland (1980) put Klein in a separate camp. He thought that she appeared at times to create a kind of biological solipsism rather than a conceptual framework for the evolution, from the earliest stages, of structures based on experiences with objects.

For Bowlby, as well as for Fairbairn, the human infant is seeking a relationship with its primary attachment figures from the start. Pleasure is an accompaniment of these relationships when they go well but not a fundamental motivation. The original anxiety is related to separation from attachment figures and can readily be experienced with terrifying intensity.

Both Balint and Bowlby rejected the psychoanalytic concept of 'primary narcissism', which implies that at the beginning of life the infant is without the external other. This is a view currently validated by most developmental psychologists. In this context, the infant's pursuit of 'primary love' (in Balint's words (1952)) is a strong motivational force which underlies most forms of behaviour. When the mother–infant tie has been disturbed or prematurely severed, the remainder of life can become a search for restitution (albeit in a dysfunctional and counter-productive form) of that primary tie. However, unlike Fairbairn, Balint preserved to a large extent Freud's original metapsychological assumptions and instinctual theory. Therefore, Balint's position is a juxtaposition of new relational concepts and classical theory. It is here that Bowlby and Balint parted company.

Bowlby and Winnicott

Of the four British object relations theorists quoted by Sutherland, Winnicott has remained the best known and most influential in contemporary psychoanalysis. Winnicott, like Bowlby, began his training within the Kleinian school and eventually distanced himself from it. Being both a paediatrician and a psychoanalyst, Winnicott was very familiar with mothers and babies: their relationships have been a central subject of his writings. Winnicott provided a powerful and poetic account of the child's development of his sense of self in an interpersonal matrix. In this account, the mother–baby relationship constitutes the inherent context in which the child's personality evolves. The mother's ability to resonate with the baby's wants and needs in an empathic, dedicated, timely and responsive way is an important factor in facilitating healthy development. However, the mother's capacity to experience herself as empathic with, yet separate from, the baby, creates the necessary distance which pushes the baby towards separateness. In this way, the infant begins to learn the reality of the world outside his control and to experience the limits of his power. Therefore, it seems, Winnicott's analysis emphasizes the delicate dialectic between contact and separateness, which will allow the development of the capacities both to relate and to be alone. This is certainly congenial with Bowlby's position.

Perhaps the key statement that Winnicott has made is his well known, 'There is no such thing as a baby. What there is is the caregiver–child relationship'. As Nicola Diamond (1996) points out, the fundamental meaning of this idea is that the primary unit of existence is not the individual but the relationship. This point of view challenges the notion that from the first there is an internal world without context.

The most radical conception of the 'internal world' is that it is the primary unit of psychic experience. In this ideological context, the external world is reduced to a mere epiphenomenon of internal processes. A less drastic notion is that first there is an internal world, and then society comes along and aspects of it are internalized. According to this model, the internal world is a self-enclosed system within which purely autogenerated processes take place.

An alternative model, which is implicit in Winnicott's work, is that the internal and the external are contained in each other. This mutual containment is only possible by virtue of the fact that the relationship between one and the other is fundamental. In Winnicott's framework, the self emerges and acquires coherence through experiences with an empathic mother, who provides a 'holding' function. In this sense, Winnicott's position is close to Kohut's self-psychology and basically compatible with attachment theory.

In Winnicott's view, the development of a sense of self-confidence and self-esteem; the capacity to form and sustain intimate relationships; the capacity for a sense of concern and guilt; the capacity to feel grief, to react to loss in an organized way; the capacity for playfulness and happiness at appropriate times, are related to the care the person has received during his years of immaturity. In other words, the health of the adult is laid down at all stages of infancy and childhood.

It follows that in psychoanalytic therapy, the material has to be explored in its social and developmental context. Winnicott (1965b) said:

> When an analyst takes us deeper in the understanding of the material presented by the analytic patient, it is not enough for the analyst to state that the external factor is recognized as having its importance. If a formulation of a complete child psychology is being made, one that can be tested by direct observation, the analyst must imaginatively clothe the earliest material presented by the patient with the environment, the environment that is implied but which the patient cannot give in analysis because of never having been aware of it. (p.113)

Winnicott thought that an analyst can only reach the patient's true self if his general attitude towards the analysand is benign and responsive. The aim of the therapy is to break through the false self-organization. But this is only possible when the analyst is open to the experience of his patient without making new impingements. (In Winnicott's framework a parent is 'impinging' when he is imposing on the child his own agenda or preoccupations instead of responding with empathy to the child's true self.) Bowlby fully endorsed these ideas.

Attachment theory and self-psychology

Kohut (1913–1981) has been one of the most influential authors in American psychoanalysis in the past two or three decades. One of his key ideas was that normal healthy development is highly contingent upon the consistent and empathic availability of parental figures. The vision of psychological functioning, psychopathology and therapy which Kohut called 'self-psychology' has some similarities with some important points in Winnicott's and Bowlby's thinking.

The basic element of Kohut's theoretical framework is the self, 'a center of initiative and a recipient of impressions'. Here the self is endowed with active attributes, which in Freud's model were given to the 'ego'. So, it seems, Kohut regarded the self as both a representational structure and an active agent or set of functions. Bowlby, instead, basically linked the idea of self with a representation of oneself as a person (separate from the set of functions that the individual exerts in order to organize his behaviour and psychological homeostasis).

In any case, Kohut thought that the self emerges in an interactional matrix. The infant's self is immature and rudimentary and cannot become cohesive and resilient unless the parents provide through their empathic responsiveness a 'self-object function'. Kohut used the term 'self-object' to name the parent or attachment figure, particularly in his role of provider of an empathic function. Although I find the term confusing, I assume that it is a short version of the following concept: 'an object that is essential for the self'. This notion is not fundamentally different from the concept of 'sensitive responsiveness' formulated by attachment theorists.

According to Kohut, the infant has two important emotional needs which emerge sequentially: (1) the need to be admired by his parents so that he can feel, 'I am perfect, you admire me'; and (2) the need to idealize or overvalue at least one of his parents and to experience a sense of merger with such an idealized figure, so as to be able to feel, 'You are perfect and I am part of you'. Kohut used the term 'selfobject transference' to refer to these archaic needs. He called the first 'mirror transference' and the second 'idealizing transference'.

However, I think that the needs to be admired and to merge with an idealized figure are compensatory wishful phantasies that a person deeply wounded in his self-esteem has. In other words, the person was made to feel so imperfect and unlovable (perhaps by constant criticisms or through neglect) that he now desperately needs to counteract these unbearable feelings by seeking extremely reassuring responses from people.

Bowlby suggested that the child needs to experience his parents as wiser, stronger and better able to cope with the world than himself, but this idea is very different from Kohut's notion that children want perfection. Although Kohut's ideas about self-object transference are based on clinical experience, he was wrong in assuming that such a phenomenon occurs in normal infants. Kohut's weakness was the same as many other analysts: to make inferences about early development from observations made in the treatment of adults with manifest psychopathology. Bowlby tried to avoid such a fundamental error by proposing to use direct observations of cross-sections of the infant population. Although Kohut was on the right track, he seemed to lack acquaintance with modern developmental research. This may have limited the value of his ideas and perhaps explains why at times he expressed them in such a convoluted way.

In Kohut's view, under normal circumstances, everyday transactions between a child and his empathic parents provide the framework in which a cohesive and healthy self develops. Minor or sporadic failures of empathy are not deleterious, but chronic failure of empathy provokes psychopathology. Since Kohut attributed lack of empathy to parental psychopathology, he was formulating an adequate model of intergenerational transmission of psychic disturbance. In the face of the parents' failure to serve a self-object function, the child's original search for empathic responses is directed through dysfunctional channels: aggression, neurotic symptoms, deviant sexuality, grandiosity, and so on.

Kohut's view of the analytic process is consistent with his developmental ideas. The analytic situation is not one in which a distant observer (the analyst) constantly makes interpretations to the patient. Instead, the analytic situation provides an interpersonal field within which the analyst acts as an 'introspective observer'.

In terms of metapsychology, Kohut did not openly challenge Freud's early instinctual model in any fundamental way. He created a separate system of ideas without seemingly worrying whether it could easily co-exist with the old model. Bowlby, instead, was very keen to reformulate the core aspects of psychoanalytic theory.

With each book, Kohut (1971, 1977, 1984) added to, amended and revised his theoretical proposal. Other self-psychologists have since continued to revise and expand this paradigm, sometimes taking divergent pathways. Lichtenberg and Wolf (1997) have recently reviewed the basic principles of self-psychology. It does seem that self-psychology and attachment-based clinical psychoanalysis have much in common: the importance given to empathy and reflective thinking; the interest in exploring episodic memory; their understanding of motivational systems, and so on.

Bowlby and Mahler

Margaret Mahler stimulated new thinking on the early mother–child relationship. In the same way as Bowlby, she thought that psychoanalysis would benefit from empirical research. Mahler began her career in Vienna as a paediatrician and, like Winnicott, was very familiar with mothers and babies. After her arrival in the United States in the late 1930s, she began to make laboratory observations in the field of early development. She was a pioneer in this area, even if she attracted criticism because she did not employ a rigorous methodology or generate testable hypotheses. Perhaps she did what she could in those early years.

Mahler emphasized the crucial importance of parental behaviour in early development. The pathway that a child is going to follow will be the result of the interaction between his own needs and the personality of his parents. The mother's holding behaviour, her feeding, smiling, talking, supporting, cradling and many other responses provide the infant with the first organizers of psychic life. As the child grows, optimal regulations and fluctuations of the child–mother distance promote a sense of separateness and individuation that the growing individual needs in order to feel securely attached, yet able to venture alone into the world in order to explore it and joyfully learn from these explorations. The child goes away into the world and comes back for 'refuelling'. For Mahler, the child becomes a person through this pendular process of submersion within, and emergence from, the personality of his mother.

Mahler (Mahler *et al.* 1975) proposed that normal development occurs in four phases: (1) the normal autistic phase, (2) the normal symbiotic phase, (3) the separation-individuation phase, and (4) the phase of libidinal object constancy. This formulation implies a theory of the individual's achievement of a sense of being separate, yet in meaningful contact with others. To a large degree, this is a theory of representations of oneself and significant others. It shows how the individual's emotions and organization of behaviour depend on such representations. However, these processes take place in connection with motor and cognitive maturation.

In Mahler's scheme, the separation-individuation phase is crucial because it opens the way for the establishment of a stable concept of self and a stable concept of the significant other. However, in her view, the child needs to negotiate successfully a conflict between: (1) his fear that separation from mother in times of distance may result in losing her love; and (2) his fear that reunion with mother in times of refuelling will result in being captured, trapped or 'fused' in a symbiotic relationship. The successful negotiation of this conflict at least partially depends on the mother's sensitive responsiveness and her capacity to adjust to the child's changing needs.

A main point of interest in Mahler's studies is the development of: (1) the individual's sense of being separate; (2) the individual's recognition of others as separate people with their own minds; and (3) the ability to relate to the other.

Bowlby (personal communication) appreciated Mahler's contribution, which in some respects is congenial to attachment theory and concerned with key issues in contemporary attachment research. However, Bowlby criticized three aspects of Mahler's theory:

1. Mahler postulated an early stage of self–other undifferentiation. This is a hypothesis which has not been confirmed by attachment research.

2. Mahler 'collapsed' the life-long negotiation between the need for security and closeness on the one hand, and the striving for exploration on the other, into a specific phase of development (the separation-individuation phase). The search for emotional and physical proximity with the attachment figure and the drive towards autonomy and individuation are poles of an open-ended process.

3. Mahler remained loyal to Freud's metapsychological formulations. By virtue of this she felt constrained to explain her observations with language that did not do justice to them. This resulted in unnecessary ambiguity and contradictions.

However, Mahler was one of the many authors of her generation who paved the way for others to make fundamental shifts in psychoanalytic theory.

On undifferentiation

While discussing Mahler's work, in the early 1980s Bowlby drew my attention to a seminal paper by Peterfreund (1978) in which he questioned the assumption that there is an early stage of 'undifferentiation' or 'autistic phase', in which the child is unaware of the existence of the other as a separate individual. Peterfreund also strongly criticized the use of terms borrowed from psychopathology (and particularly adult psychopathology) to describe early stages of normal development. The idea of a period of undifferentiation that is subjectively experienced by the infant as a form of merger with mother is very problematic and is not confirmed by contemporary developmental research.

For instance, Stern (1985) points out:

> Infants begin to experience a sense of an emergent self from birth. They are pre-designed to be aware of self-organizing processes. They never experience a period of total self/other undifferentiation. There is no confusion between self and other in the beginning or at any point during infancy. They are also pre-designed to be selectively responsive to external social events and never experience an autistic-like phase. (p.10)

More recently, Peter Hobson (1993) has reviewed an impressive list of papers which give observational and experimental evidence that very young infants engage in forms of interpersonal relatedness and attachment. He points out:

> In each of the studies described, therefore, we can see how young infants showed organized expressions of affect and attention when the form and timing of their mothers' natural style of engagement were disrupted. The person-with-person configuration of mutual gaze and facial, vocal and gestural interchange seem to

involve not merely the co-ordination of behaviour between infant and mother, but also some kind of psychological linkage which when established – or when broken – has emotional consequences for both participants. (pp.36–37)

Bowlby and Anna Freud

Anna Freud, like Bowlby, was deeply concerned with the way families treat their children and aware of the need to inform wide audiences. In 1975, towards the end of her life, she emphatically stated that people in the helping professions should be made aware that the child's or adolescent's behaviour does not exist in isolation but needs to be seen and assessed in the light of his emotional relationship within the family.

Anna Freud was, as Arthur Couch (1995) explains, a wide-ranging contributor to psychoanalysis for nearly 60 years. She believed that the psychoanalysis of young children and direct observation of them in natural settings would support and make valuable additions to psychoanalytic developmental theory, which originally derived mainly from analytic reconstructions from the analysis of adults.

Bowlby (1969), in Volume I of his trilogy *Attachment and Loss* dedicated a good number of paragraphs to assessing the relationship between Anna Freud's ideas and attachment theory. He said that the accounts given by Anna Freud and Dorothy Burlingham of the children in the Hampstead Nurseries during wartime included one of the few descriptions of the development of the child's tie that had been written by analysts on the basis of direct observation. Anna Freud observed, for instance, that children cling even to mothers who are continually hostile and sometimes cruel to them. In other words, the attachment of a young child to his mother is based on familiarity and not on discrimination of her personal qualities. Bowlby noted that Anna Freud was aware that the child's early need to establish specific attachments is an instinctual need. He expressed his indebtedness to Anna Freud in several of his works. One important idea that Bowlby took from her is that a child organizes his attachments according to a hierarchical order.

Anna Freud (1972) thought – as Bowlby did – that, regarding the origins of intensified separation anxiety in later years, an explanation that carries weight is that a person who as a young child had experienced mother as unreliable, or had periods of separation from her, is likely to become vulnerable to any subsequent sign of insecurity in the relationship.

CHAPTER 9

On Transference

Background Aspects

Mario Marrone and Nicola Diamond

Introduction

Transference is a very specific concept in attachment theory. However, it does not essentially differ from some early psychoanalytic formulations. In classical psychoanalytic theory, 'transference' was viewed as a form of displacement since it referred to a process whereby feelings, wishes or expectations were deflected from one person to another. The term was originally used by Freud in his *Studies on Hysteria* (1893–1895) and conceived of as a 'false connection', because feelings originally associated with parental figures were disconnected from their early context and object and revived elsewhere with somebody else. The idea of a 'false connection' emerged out of the observation that an affect can be misplaced. In the individual's early history, the affect was linked to a primary parental figure; but now it appears again, this time inappropriately placed in another relationship and with a different person. In this context, the subject believes that the affect is evoked by this new person but, in fact, it belongs to an earlier relationship.

Freud observed that in psychoanalytic therapy affects are displaced from an early parental figure to the person of the therapist. However, this point gives rise to several issues. First, does transference only occur in the analytic situation or is it in fact inherent to all types of interpersonal interactions? Second, is transference, within the analytic situation, a very specific phenomenon or is it – as some authors seem to suggest – a bucket concept that broadly contains every interaction and communication between analyst and analysand?

The phenomenon of transference was observed initially not by Freud but by the Viennese physician, Joseph Breuer in the treatment of Anna O, which evolved between 1880 and 1882 (Freud 1893–1895). Anna O, who had been intensely involved with her father (especially during his terminal illness), in her treatment with Breuer developed passionate feelings towards the physician. These feelings manifested themselves through the unconscious fantasy of having been made pregnant by the analyst, with the concomitant development of a phantom pregnancy. Therefore the passionate feelings she had with her father, together with the conflicts she had in relation to him, were revived in her relationship with the physician. Here we can see that conflict accompanied the displacement of affect.

Greenson (1994, p.151) said: 'The main characteristic [of transference] is the experience of feelings to a person which do not befit that person and which actually apply to another. Essentially, a person of the present is reacted to as though he were a person in the past'. He added (p.152): 'Transference may consist of any of the components of an object relationship, i.e., it may be experienced as feelings, drives, wishes, fears, fantasies, attitudes, and ideas or defenses against them. The people who are the original sources of transference reactions are the meaningful and significant people of early childhood'.

Initially, Freud saw transference as an obstacle to therapy, as a resistance which obstructs the recall of repressed memories (Freud 1905, p.116). Yet, later on, he recognized the importance of transference as a way of understanding and analysing the patient.

Freud thought that, in the course of treatment, the revival of early issues created a phenomenon which he called 'transference neurosis'. This process was capable of replacing the patient's original neurosis because it was lived out in the transference to the analyst. In this context, the therapeutic process basically consisted in the resolution of the transference neurosis. In saying this, Freud was making the assumption that transference reactions were both economically and structurally equivalent to ordinary symptoms.

However, the idea that there can be a final resolution was questioned by Freud himself in *Analysis Terminable and Interminable* (1937a). One way we can read this paper is to argue that it puts into question that there is a final end to the analytic process. Likewise, one can suggest that there may be no end or finale to transference. The subject never escapes from finding himself in transference relationships, the difference being that the analytic relationship enables the analysand to become more aware of what differentiates present from past relationships.

Some authors seem to believe that transference is a by-product of analysis, that is to say that it is exclusively elicited by, and occurs in, the therapeutic situation. For example, Waelder (1956) pointed out:

> Transference may be said to be an attempt of the patient to revive and re-enact, in the analytic situation and in relation to the analyst, situations and fantasies of his childhood. Hence, transference is a regressive process. Transference develops in

consequence of the analytic experiment, viz-a-viz, of the analytic situation and the analytic technique.

Such a formulation implies that transference occurs only in the therapeutic situation, leading to a great deal of confusion. However, Freud (1905, p.117) was explicit when he wrote: 'Psycho-analytic treatment does not create transferences, it merely brings them to light, like so many other hidden psychical factors'.

As Szasz (1963) rightly pointed out, to define transference in terms of the analytic situation is like defining microbes as little objects appearing under the microscope. As the occurrence of bacteria is not confined to laboratories, so the occurrence of transference is not confined to the analytic situation.

However, transference in the analytic situation can become a central theme to be explored. In this context, transference has been seen both as an obstacle to, and a facilitator of, the therapeutic process. Freud (1905, p.117) said: 'Transference, which seems ordained to be the greatest obstacle to psychoanalysis, becomes its most powerful ally'.

Preliminary discussion

Since Freud, the concept of transference has undergone substantial modifications (this according to each school of psychoanalytic thought). For instance, a particular view of transference is that it consists of the 'internalization' of an early relationship and its 'externalization' in the present. In the context of these debates, Fairbairn (1952) talked about transference as a process of repetition. He pointed out that it is not an object or its representation that is internalized and later manifested in the transference, but a representation of the self in relation to the object (the other). As we shall see later, this idea comes close to Bowlby's notion of transference.

Some authors have suggested that transference cannot be purely concep-tualized as 'an externalization of an object representation'. Instead, it should be seen as an interpersonal enactment of 'self and object representations' in the form of pressure unconsciously exerted by the subject on the other, so that the subject–other relationship conforms in some essential way to the self and object constellation depicted in the internalized relationship. This process has often been described in terms of 'projective identification'.

What transference may not be

One incorrect, yet widely held view, is that all communications in the analytic session should be interpreted as transference manifestations. For instance, Ezriel (1963) said that it seems possible to treat all material as transference material and hence use it for 'here-and-now' interpretations. He added:

In this event, everything the patient says or does during a session – e.g. his movements, gestures, correct or distorted memories, reports of dreams or phantasies, and even deliberate lies – would have to be considered as the idiom used by him to give expression to his need in that session for a particular relationship with the analyst. Thus even the patient's reports to the analyst about his relations with other people, past or present-day, would be taken as attempts to involve the analyst as an active participant in relations which the patient entertains with his unconscious objects as they seem to exist here and now, and with their representatives in external reality. (pp.117–18)

In our view, this is a reductionistic view of transference. It excludes any possibility that the patient's communications may have validity in themselves. It takes away the specificity of the transference phenomenon as it may occur both inside and outside the clinical situation. It implicitly assumes that transference only occurs in the therapeutic situation. It may lead to a type of psychoanalytic technique that can be disconcerting to the patient.

Pearl King (personal communication) said that the idea of the 'here-and-now' was originally formulated by Rickman to denote the fact that representations of previous relations can re-emerge in the here-and-now of the analytic situation. However, there is now a trend in some quarters to reduce to the 'here-and-now' the interpretation of the material. This concept is literally equated to the present moment as such in the analytic situation, in a way that misunderstands the temporal and historical nature of the analysand's experience and of the analysand–analyst relationship. In a sense, there is no here-and-now as such. The temporal experience involves an incessant movement of past in relation to the present which in turn anticipates the future, and this is a dynamic rather than a linear process. There is no pure present. What we are trying to say here is (a) that transference is a specific phenomena which cannot be forcibly collapsed into the here-and-now (decontextualized from the social and historical situation) and (b) that the notion of 'here-and-now' cannot be formulated without recourse to a deeper understanding of temporality.

We believe that only certain communications, in their specific meaning (as well as in the context of their historical significance), can be seen as indicative of specific transference phenomena.

Furthermore, when the emphasis is placed on what goes on internally for each subject, then the reference to the external reality is left relatively unexplored. Often there is the assumption that the internal world experiences a highly complex symbolic construction and elaboration, whereas there is little attempt to explain the individual's sense of being in the world (in a highly complex symbolic network of communications).

If we interpret everything the analysand says as a manifestation of internal reality (as Ezriel did), where do we leave room for the expression of perceived interpersonal reality? If internal reality is seen as where symbolization takes place, then there is the assumption that the construction of the symbolic world is entirely generated out of the subject's individual experience. Such a view ignores the fact that symbolic reality finds its raw material in a shared language that is communicated between persons, in specific relationships and in given socio-cultural contexts.

Another incorrect, and again widely used, meaning of the term 'transference' refers to the overall quality of feelings that a patient has towards his analyst: whether there is a 'positive' or 'negative' transference. It is often assumed that a positive or negative transference comes from the 'internal world' of the patient. In this way, a whole array of potential responses within a relationship is reduced to one or two overall attitudes that the patient may have towards the analyst. In this framework, the way the analyst's behaviour may influence these attitudes is overlooked. In other words, these so-called 'transferences' may have much to do with the overall quality of the analyst–analysand relationship. There is no relationship, not even the analytic relationship, whose quality is independent from what each part puts into it.

The Kleinian view of transference

The Kleinian contribution to the concept of transference is to emphasize the centrality of the role of phantasy, innate destructiveness and the earliest anxieties and defences. Here, Freud's late theory of life and death instincts is fundamental. The death instinct is the source of all aggression and destructiveness. Phantasies are the mental representations of the instincts and, by implication, internally generated. Transference is an enactment of phantasies.

In Klein's view (1952), there is a relation between past and present interpersonal experiences in the origins of transference. However, this relation is subsumed under the impact of early anxieties and defences. Her conception of transference is based on the earliest stages of development (p.433–437), in the presence of fear of annihilation. By means of projection the source of anxiety is located outside the individual.

In the transference, early persecutory anxiety is revived and manifests through 'negative transference'. Although Klein indicated that negative as well as positive transference need to be explored (p.436), some analysts influenced by the Kleinian framework are noted for their tendency to highlight the patient's 'negative transference' as central to the analytic process.

When too much emphasis is placed on these ideas, it seems as if the less is known about the reality of the subject's interpersonal history the better it is for the analytic task. However, this may not be strictly related to Klein's position. She said '...every phantasy contains elements of actual experience, and it is only by analysing the transference situation to its depth that we are able to discover the past both in its realistic and phantastic aspects' (p.437).

However, Susan Isaacs contribution (1948) has added additional weight to the idea that what matters in analysis is the exploration of unconscious phantasies, which underlie every mental process, accompany all mental activity and, hence, constitute the substance matter of transference. In this context, the interpretation of phantasy in the immediacy of the analytic situation is the master key to achieve psychic change.

Kohut and transference

As has already been indicated (see Chapter 8), one of the central points of Kohut's paradigm is the notion that the empathic responsiveness of the primary attachment figure is essential for the optimal functioning of the self. Both attachment theory and self-psychology put emphasis on the necessity for 'responsive attachment figures' (in Bowlby's terms) or 'selfobjects' (in Kohut's terms) throughout the life cycle.

In the Kohutian frame of reference, transference processes are understood as the revival in a present relationship of the search for, and frustration of, the need for self-objects. In this context, Kohut would say, all existing defences in the self become spontaneously mobilized as 'selfobject transferences'. In other words, the structural damage caused by early failures in the self-object function calls for specific defences which show in the present relationship.

Kohut's studies on transference were basically circumscribed to phenomena observed in the analytic situation, especially in the treatment of narcissistically damaged patients. He reduced the concept of transference to some specific processes, to the exclusion of transference in its wider, general everyday occurrence.

According to Kohut, some early, archaic or 'transitional' self–selfobject configurations do not resolve through maturation in narcissistically damaged patients and, consequently, re-emerge in the analysand–analyst relationship.

In normal circumstances, the child seeks from the parent a type of confirmation of inner subjective experience that Kohut called 'mirroring'. This term refers to the way in which the parent gives back the image to the child. However, the term 'mirroring' is also used to describe a form of transference: 'mirroring transference'. This is when the analysand seeks to be admired by the analyst. This is unconsciously aimed at promoting a grandiose experience of the self.

Moreover, in normal development, the child idealizes the parental figure. The idealizing stage does not last for ever because the realistic and inevitable frustrations and disappointments due to the imperfections in the parent no longer allow for the idealization. In the analytic relationship, the patient seeks out the experience of idealization in the person of the analyst in an attempt to create the possibility of a narcissistic self-object. This is what Kohut called 'mirroring transference'.

But also, for Kohut, transference is about working through the breakdown of the empathic relationship between caretaker and infant. The idealizing and mirroring transferences are not interpreted but allowed to emerge as an archaic situation which will allow the subject to go through an intersubjective experience which has never before been a possibility.

The case study of Mr Z (Kohut 1979) demonstrates the shift in approach that Kohut offered. Kohut analysed Mr Z in two different periods. After Mr Z terminated his first analysis, he came back for further therapy. Kohut resumed work with this patient, but at this point he had changed some of his ideas and technique. Therefore, during Mr Z's second analysis, Kohut interpreted the patient's problems under a new light.

Mr Z presented initially as a man who narcissistically required an idealizing relationship with the analyst. This was interpreted initially by Kohut as the patient's omnipotence, as his refusal to encounter the oedipal reality that he could not have mother all to himself because father existed as part of the triangle. Kohut saw the analysand's need to be adored by the analyst as an expression of the patient's refusal to share the maternal figure. This is where Kohut offered a classical psychoanalytic account of the transference, which in this case was linked with the oedipal situation and also with the internalized relation to the parental figure.

In the second analysis, the interpretation of what, at this new stage, Kohut referred to as the 'idealizing' and 'mirroring' transference, had a totally different emphasis and meaning. Kohut related the need for an idealizing transference not to a purely internal mental state but, instead, to the early and actual experience with a narcissistically intrusive and all-possessive mother (a mother who imposed her own needs on to the child instead of providing an empathic understanding of him). The second analysis related to the discovery that mother acted as a noxious self-object which was not counteracted by a male parental figure because father, in fact, was absent during a significant part of the child's formative years.

Self-psychology offers a bipolar conception of transference: at one pole of the transference is the patient's need for the analyst to serve as a source of self-object function that had been missing or insufficient in early interpersonal experience. In this dimension of transference, the patient hopes and searches for a new self-object experience that will enable him to resume and complete an arrested developmental process. At the other pole are the patient's expectations and fears that the original experiences of self-object failure will be repeated once again in the analytic relationship.

Perhaps it would be useful to clarify at this point that, in terms of attachment theory, the first pole is seen as reactivation of attachment behaviour in the context of the analytic relationship. The second pole is transference proper.

Lacan's concept of transference

Psychoanalysis in the Latin world has been very influenced by Lacan's ideas. Lacan presents a way of thinking that is fundamentally different from the school which emerged in the Anglo-American context. An inclusion of Lacan's view in this book may be seen as irrelevant and forced. Certainly, Lacan's thinking is as far away from British psychoanalysis and attachment theory and its empirical elements as you can get. However, Lacan's views cannot be ignored as if they do not exist. Furthermore, one can find in Lacan not only a contrasting model (which stimulates critical discussion) but also some points which can be taken up (albeit in a different form) by attachment-oriented psychotherapists. Here we are not trying to represent Lacan's views in their complexity; we simply wish to select some of his ideas about transference.

Lacan, from his early thinking onwards, rejected the idea of transference as an affect that occurs inside the individual and then becomes externalized. On the contrary, he viewed transference as a structural relation, whereby an exchange takes place, 'which changes the nature of the two beings present' (Evans 1997, p.212; Lacan 1953–1954, p.109). In other words, transference cannot be understood as an individual phenomenon. It is not reducible to either party and has to be conceived of as the outcome of an intersubjective relation.

What becomes a key feature of conceptualizing transference is through the analysand's assumption that the analyst is 'the subject who is supposed to know'. As Evans (1997, p.197) explains, this can be seen in the analysand's attribution to the analyst, that the analyst knows the secret meaning of his or her own words. Of course, in actual clinical practice, this comes about in a number of ways. It can be the case that even before the patient begins treatment, he presumes that the analyst has power and knowledge. This may also happen at the moment of entry into treatment. Alternatively, it can take some time for the transference to be established. In contrast, the analysand may view the analyst as not intelligent enough to understand.

However – even in these circumstances – a gesture or some sign that the analyst makes at some point will be read by the analysand as an indication of some hidden knowledge or secret intention. This process has to be understood as a function that the analyst comes to embody in the treatment. When this function is on its way, the transference is then in operation (Evans 1997, p.197).

It is most important how the analyst deals with this transference, that is, to 'refuse the power' given to the analyst. In this context, the analyst should not contribute to create or collude with the analysand's attempt to make him the centre of the world and the repository of all meaning (in other words, to put him/her in a God-like position which no human being can occupy).

Here it is perhaps necessary to say something about Lacan's terminology. Lacan referred to both the 'other' (with a small 'o') and the 'Other' (with a big 'O') and also to the *objet petit-a*. Early on in his thinking, the 'other' connoted both other human beings and otherness. However, as his ideas developed, Lacan (1955) began to make a distinction between 'other' and 'Other'. From then on, the 'other' referred to other human beings whereas the 'Other' implied an otherness which is irreducible to a 'narcissistic identification' (to use British language), and also inferred that there is a lack in being, that there is no Other who can make us feel complete and whole.

The *objet petit-a* is the object of desire which we seek in the other. It may be perceived as the most precious object that is hidden from view which we can seek in the other (as is the case in the transference). However, the *objet petit-a* is an unobtainable object which can never be had or found and is certainly not in the analyst's possession.

Lacan talked about an object that is unrepresentable. This is the object that has always been missing, the lost object which was never present but which the subject reconstructs as a nostalgic longing, as if it was once there. But in fact, dissatisfaction is basic to the human experience.

It appears in the transference that the other (or the analyst) can be the one who causes the subject's dissatisfaction (desire) or the one who can offer fulfilment and completion; the one who is the true object of desire. For Lacan, no one can in fact occupy this position, for the other can never be the 'Other' as such, or take the place of the *objet petit-a* (the cause of desire and all-satisfying object).

The analyst who takes up the stance of occupying a position as if he could be the object that can fill the subject's 'lack' in as well as his own 'lack', buys into an illusional state that does not acknowledge his own 'lack' and the patient's 'lack'. He cannot know everything about the patient nor can he be the patient's source of total psychic nourishment. By 'lack', in this context, we refer to an aspect of Lacan's thought, most marked in his earlier writings, when he referred to the subject's lack of being. This implies an inherent incompleteness in the human condition. There is no object that can fill this insufficiency (see Chapter 15).

For Lacan, the function of the analyst is not to occupy a place that can be filled up by imaginary imagos (in an imaginary plenitude of something that can be seen as all-powerfully destructive or all-powerfully satisfying). Instead, the analyst is there to open up the subject to an empty space in the subject and in the other. In this way, the analyst confronts the subject with what he tries to avoid: his incapacity to face loss.

Lacan was critical of the view that the analyst can simply step outside of the transference altogether and define reality as one-dimensional. He also said that interpretations should not all be about transference.

Bowlby's view of transference

Bowlby thought that transference is the direct manifestation in current interpersonal situations of the individual's internal working models. In this context, the main aim of interpreting transference is to elicit, examine and – if possible – modify underlying working models. Bowlby (1973) wrote:

> In terms of the present theory much of the work of treating an emotionally disturbed person can be regarded as consisting, first, of detecting the existence of influential models of which the patient may be partially or completely unaware, and second, of inviting the patient to examine the models disclosed and to consider whether they continue to be valid. In pursuing this strategy an analyst finds that how the patient perceives him (the analyst), and what forecasts the patient makes about his likely behaviour, are particularly valuable in revealing the nature of the working models that exert a dominant influence in the patient's life. Because certain of these perceptions and forecasts appear to the analyst so clearly to be based on a patient's pre-conceptions about him and to be derived from working models that stem from experiences with other people during earlier years, rather than from current experience, how the patient perceives and conceives the analyst is often known as 'transference'. When an analyst interprets the transference situation he is, among other things, calling the patient's attention to the nature and influence of those models and, by implication, inviting him to scrutinize their current validity and, perhaps, also, to revive them. (pp.205–206)

Bowlby added:

> Seen in the perspective of Piaget's theorizing, the concept of transference implies, first, that the analyst in his caretaking relationship to the patient is being assimilated to some pre-existing (and perhaps unconscious) model that the patient has of how any caretaker might be expected to relate to him, and, second, that the patient's pre-existing model of caretakers has not yet been accommodated – namely, is not yet modified – to take account of how the analyst has actually behaved and still is behaving in relation to him. (p.206)

Bowlby pointed out that a strong feature of a patient's forecasts is his strong expectation of being treated by the analyst as he (the patient) was treated by significant others in childhood. Often, this expectation is based on negative experiences of childhood and adolescence (namely, experiences of being abandoned, ridiculed, attacked, abused, and so on). These expectations may not manifest in the form of direct communications but in a symbolic or derivative form. Once elicited, they tend to persist, often in spite of repeated falsification in real life, or in spite of reassurances that they are unfounded. Many of these expectations can be modified, but only through a long analytic process.

Some illustrations

One summer afternoon, the following incident was witnessed: a boy, probably aged around three, was running in freedom near his mother along a pebbled path. Suddenly and accidentally, he fell over and hurt his knees, which began to bleed. He obviously felt hurt and tears began to roll down his cheeks. When mother realized what had happened, she reacted by smacking the child very hard on his face while saying: 'You are always so stupid!'.

If his mother did that on that occasion, she would probably do something similar on other occasions. The mother used the word 'always': 'You are always so stupid!'. In this context, it is conceivable that this child could form an internal working model of himself as stupid and incompetent, and a working model of mother as punitive and lacking in compassion. As a consequence, in the future he could also have difficulties in showing vulnerability.

A 24-year-old woman in therapy described the following incident. She went to visit her father. In the course of the visit her father upset her with criticisms. Then he accompanied her to the bus stop. Distracted with negative thoughts, she missed the bus. Her father then exclaimed: 'What's a grown up woman of 24 doing, crying in the street because she missed the bus!'.

Sometimes the transference situation can remain undiscovered for a long period of time. This was the case in the following example. A patient in five-session-a-week analysis was very punctual and assiduous in terms of her attendance. However, in her sessions she often felt bored an unmotivated. After a relatively long period of therapy, one day she asked her analyst if he would object to her missing the Friday session as she wanted to have an extended weekend in the countryside with a friend. Given the analyst's neutral response she felt allowed to take time off and enjoy herself. But suddenly and surprisingly, she burst into tears. When the meaning of her emotional reaction was explored, she recalled the fact that during her school years her father constantly pushed her for achievement. He forced her to do a great deal of homework and, in addition, constantly to attend evening and weekend courses on a variety of extra-curricular subjects. At the same time, he discouraged playful activities with her peers. In this session, it became clear that, in spite of the fact that she started therapy under her own initiative, at an unconscious level she was seeing her five-session-a-week analysis as another parental imposition which prolonged her working day and inhibited leisure with her friends.

Transference and projection

In the psychoanalytic literature and clinical seminars, transference is often seen as projection. According to this view, the patient projects on to the analyst internal objects or feelings and this is conceptualized as transference. However, Bowlby (1975) was very apprehensive about this way of understanding what is going on in the analyst–analysand relationship. He was particularly concerned with the fact that many therapists seem to interpret as projection too much of what is going on in the session.

For instance, the concept of projection has been used very extensively to attempt to explain any fear that a patient may have. In this context, the fear could then be attributed to the projection of a 'persecutory internal object'. This is often attributed to an internal process when in fact there may be many other factors intervening, which are not readily intelligible at first glance.

Another use of the term 'projection' is to denote the process whereby a person attributes to another some feature of his own self, especially some aspect of himself that he dislikes or of which he is afraid.

Bowlby (1973) pointed out:

> This trend in theorizing has been carried furthest by Melanie Klein who has postulated that the process of attributing to others undesired and frightening features of the self occurs on a major scale during the earliest phases of normal development, with far-reaching effects on later personality. During his first year of life, in the Kleinian view, an infant regularly attributes to parent figures impulses that are in fact his own and then introjects (namely creates working models of) parent figures already distorted by these misattributions. In this view, then, the reason a child develops working models of hostile, rejecting, or unresponsive parents ('bad introjected objects') is not so much because of any actual experience he may have had of being unsympathetically or adversely treated by them as principally because, almost from the first, his perception of his parents is gravely distorted by his own prior projections. (pp.172–173)

Bowlby added:

> Not infrequently a person is afraid that someone else intends him harm, but to another's eye this expectation seems misplaced. In such circumstances, as we have seen, psychoanalysts are very apt to postulate that the person who is afraid is projecting onto the other hostile intentions that are in himself but that he denies exist. Though there can be no doubt that this can happen it probably happens much less often than is supposed. (1973, p.173)

He continued:

> In fact a situation of the kind described is explicable in at least four ways; and it is necessary to examine the evidence in each case before deciding which explanation, or which two or more together, is most likely to apply:

1. The subject has rightly detected harmful intent in the other person and in so doing has been more sensitive to the situation than the onlooker.

2. The subject during childhood has learnt that significant people are often hostile when they claim to be friendly and is therefore apt, through a process of assimilation, to suppose that figures met with in later life are hostile also when they are not.

3. The subject, aware that he is no friend of the other person and even that he is disposed to do him harm, not unnaturally expects his ill intent to be reciprocated.

4. The subject, unaware of his own ill intent, maintains that, whereas he is friendly to the other, the other is hostile to him. (p.173–174)

Of these four possible explanations only the process postulated in the fourth can properly be called projection when the term is used in the restricted sense of attributing to others unwelcome features of the self.

THE DANGER OF OVERINTERPRETING PROJECTION

There is no doubt that some analysts tend to interpret much of the patient's material as projection, whether the projection is made on to the person of the analyst or on to somebody else. A psychoanalytic technique that overemphasizes projection has various problems. First, it is reductionistic. The excitement and richness of exploring the patient's complex interactions with his world is reduced to one particular defence mechanism. Furthermore, because of the fact that projections are often seen as a way of getting rid of internal nasty bits of the self, persistent interpretations of this kind can undermine the patient's self-esteem by making him believe that these bits are all he has.

Another point is that if we, as analysts, overemphasize projection, we are likely to mistake the patient's true perceptions of reality for projection. When a patient says 'my boss is an angry person' and the analyst interprets such communication as a projection, he may conclude that the boss was not angry. This can turn out to be a plain and unfair disconfirmation of the patient's perceptions.

Bowlby (1988b) has discussed how, in some dysfunctional families, the children's perceptions of what is going on are continuously disconfirmed. The long-term effect of these experiences is that the individual develops a basic mistrust of his own perceptions, together with an impaired sense of competence in interpersonal situations.

On projective identification

The concept of projective identification (Bion 1957, 1959a, 1959b; Goldstein 1991; Grinberg 1956, 1979; Klein 1975; Ogden 1982) is useful. It is essentially a clinical concept. Although Bowlby himself did not highlight the validity of this concept, it has an important role to play in understanding attachment relationships (see, for instance, Lieberman 1992a). Although Klein saw projective identification as an essentially intrapsychic process, the contribution of Bion and other authors has been that of showing how this mechanism takes place in the area of interplay between the intrapsychic and the interpersonal. Generally speaking, it is assumed that projective identification takes place in three steps. Step 1 is the subject's projection of a part of himself on to another person. Step 2 is an interpersonal interaction whereby the projector actively pressures the recipient to think, feel and act in accordance with the projection. In step 3 the recipient complies with the pressure exerted on him to fulfil the projector's expectations and behaves accordingly. A further step, often described, is that the subject reinternalizes the projection after it has been processed by the recipient. These processes can also be observed in small groups, between the subject and part of the group or the whole group (Marrone 1982).

There is scant literature explaining what people do, what strategies, techniques or modes of communication they use, in order to make the recipient comply with the projection. In other words, what actually happens between the subject and the other in order to make projective identification possible at an interpersonal level is rarely explained.

Early psychoanalytic writings refer to the way the child projects on to his mother. However, more recent studies are also looking at the way the parent makes projections on to the child and the child enacts the parent's projections (Lieberman 1992b, p.560).

Likewise, in the analytic situation, some degree of projective identification from the analyst to the patient may be used when the former has a way of working that continuously makes the analysand feel vulnerable. In cases like this, the analyst may unconsciously be getting rid of his own sense of vulnerability by putting it on to the patient.

Strategies enacted in the treatment situation

Children learn to use strategies or patterns of behaviour, either as a defence against anxiety or as a way of maintaining access to, or eliciting care from, the attachment figure during periods of perceived danger. These strategies may continue to be used in relation to other people in adult life and can indeed be used in the analytic situation.

A young professional woman (in analysis with Dr Marrone) often behaved as a clown in her work situation, with the effect of losing respect among her colleagues. She also behaved as a clown in relation to her analyst. As analysis proceeded, it was revealed that, during her childhood and adolescence, behaving like a clown was for her the only way of attracting attention from her peers.

Attention from peers in these circumstances seemed to compensate for the experience of being ignored by her parents.

The identification and understanding of dysfunctional strategies in adult life, as well as in relation to the analyst, are often an important part of the analysis.

The centrality of the analyst in question

From the discussions in this chapter, it seems that the idea that the analyst is the central figure of the patient's life is problematic. If an analysis is to succeed, the analysand must be deeply engaged with it: he must be in a mental state of 'being-in-analysis'. When this mental state is not achieved, the patient may be inclined to terminate therapy prematurely, opt for lower frequency of sessions in the absence of practical limitations, or simply not treat the analytic process with enough depth and consistency.

On the other hand, if the analysand does develop this sense of being-in-analysis, he will give the analyst a prominent role in his life. This important role will be ascribed by the analysand but it cannot be claimed by the analyst. In this context, the analyst will be able to study in detail the vicissitudes of the analyst–analysand relationship, the way the patient reacts to weekends and longer breaks, and so on. However, there is a school of thought that puts the analyst in an absolute central position (and here we would like to stress the word 'absolute'). According to this view, all interpretations must be confined to the analyst–analysand relationship. This notion of centrality also implies that the analyst always knows best.

Dr N, a London analyst, believed that any analysand should – by definition – transform his analyst into the primordial figure of his psychic life and the sole source of understanding. Should the patient not accept this demand, Dr N would conclude, it was because the patient's psychic life was dominated by splitting.

When his patient, Mr Y, was having difficulties in his marriage and wanted to have marital therapy with his wife, Dr N exclaimed: 'What are you doing to me? You want to bring to another arena what belongs to our relationship!'.

However, whenever Mr Y brought to analysis some of his marital problems, Dr N would reduce them to the analytic relationship. One of Dr N's typical phrases would start as follows: 'The reason why you are now talking about your conflicts with your wife is that you indirectly want to refer to conflicts between you and me'. Moreover, Dr N was never interested in the way Mr Y's marital conflicts affected the children, he was only interested in Mr Y's 'internal world'.

At some point, Mr Y, eager to understand the dynamics of his marital relationship, discussed it with some of his close friends. As a result of these conversations, he gained some insights which he then wanted to share with his analyst. In response, Dr N said again: 'What are you doing to me! You go to talk to your friends! You bring to another arena what belongs here!'.

Mr Y insisted that he wanted to comment on his friends' insights, for they linked the patterns of his marital relationship with the patterns of his relationship with his mother. In order to illustrate his point, Mr Y described a past scene, a piece of interaction between his mother and himself. Dr N responded: 'I cannot comment! I wasn't there! I can only comment on what is going on between you and I here and now!'.

In this way, instead of allowing the patient to have a life outside the analysis, Dr N transformed the analysis into a sacred cage. An attachment-oriented psychoanalyst would have worked in a very different way. First, he would have helped the patient to explore the nature of his marital difficulties in the overlapping area of his past experiences and current marital interactions as well as in the transference. He would be open to the possibility of marital therapy, also considering that Mr Y's wife could benefit herself from an independent source of support and understanding. This analyst would also have tried to incorporate into the analysis the insights gained by the patient through conversations with friends.

Final comments

Bowlby's position in relation to transference can be seen as a development of Freud's original thinking (see the first part of this chapter). As we have already pointed out, Bowlby's addition was his understanding of the transference as an expression of internal working models.

Bowlby would agree with the self-psychologists that the patient enters analysis in order to have a better quality of relationship than he had with his early caregivers, yet the patient will be constantly apprehensive that the analytic engagement will be predominantly a repetition of past negative experiences.

Bowlby, like many other analysts (some of whom we have discussed), would be opposed to the idea that the analyst should claim a central position in a patient's life. The analyst is there in a specific role with his assets and limitations. The quality of the analyst–analysand relationship depends on various factors, one of which is the analyst's capacity to respond sensitively.

Bowlby's understanding of transference also included the notion that a person has a wide repertoire of possible responses to others. Some of these responses can be regarded as transference phenomena, but they appear when there is an external trigger. In other words, a working model can be re-activated (and expressed in the transference) when there is an interpersonal situation in the present capable of producing such a reaction. For example, an analyst's long silence re-created in a patient (who had parents whom he experienced as indifferent) the feeling of being ignored.

CHAPTER 10

Ghosts on the Couch

Ghosts in the nursery

The above is the title of an article which appeared in the *Journal of the American Academy of Child Psychiatry* in 1975. A later version was published as a chapter of the book, *Clinical Studies in Infant Mental Health: The First Year of Life,* edited by Selma Fraiberg in 1980. The authors were Selma Fraiberg, Edna Adelson and Vivian Shapiro. Of them, the best known was Fraiberg, now deceased. She was Professor of Child Psychoanalysis in the Department of Psychiatry and Paediatrics at the University of California, San Francisco, and Director of the Infant–Parent Programme at San Francisco General Hospital. However, the clinical studies to which the paper referred evolved as part of the Child Development Project of the Michigan Department of Mental Health in the early 1970s.

The paper, which was warmly recommended by Bowlby in his lectures, seminars and supervision sessions, contains several elements which give it a pioneering character. First, it is a paper that gives an interesting account of the intergenerational transmission of disturbed patterns of attachment. Second, it proposes a form of infant–parent psychotherapy. Third, it highlights the importance of eliciting representational models in their historical context as part of a good therapeutic technique.

The ghosts referred to are the pain and suffering that an adult (who may now be a parent) experienced in his own childhood as the result of disturbed, insecure or broken attachments. The pain and suffering may be excluded from conscious recall in the present. However, the defence mechanisms against these feelings may influence in a negative way his behaviour towards his children. This, in turn, is likely to affect his children's personality development.

Fraiberg *et al.* (1975) say that these ghosts, 'are the visitors from the unremembered past of the parents, the uninvited guests at the christening'.

They continue:

> In our infant mental health program we have seen many of these families and their babies. The baby is already in peril by the time we meet him, showing the early signs of emotional starvation, or grave symptoms, or developmental impairment. In each of these cases the baby has become a silent actor in a family tragedy. The baby in these families is burdened by the oppressive past of his parents from the moment he enters the world. The parent, it seems, is condemned to repeat the tragedy of his own childhood with his own baby in terrible and exacting detail.(1980 edition, p.165)

However, there are 'families in which a parental history of tragedy, cruelty and sorrow has not been inflicted upon the children'. We have often heard from parents a conscious desire not to repeat their history: 'I want something better for my child than I have had', they say (p.166).

Therefore, the intergenerational transmission of disturbance is a complex matter which cannot be reduced to simple formulae. Yet the clinical studies undertaken by Fraiberg's team showed that a history of anxious attachment was present in the parents of disturbed infants with significant frequency.

Clinical illustrations

A baby aged five and a half months showed little interest in her surroundings; she was listless, too quiet, she rarely smiled. She did not spontaneously approach her mother through eye contact or gestures of reach. There were few spontaneous vocalizations.

A video-tape which recorded one moment of interaction between the baby and her mother gave important clues. In her mother's arms the baby is screaming hopelessly and does not turn to mother for comfort. The mother looks distant, self-absorbed. She makes an absent gesture to comfort the baby, then gives up. She looks away. The screaming continues for five dreadful minutes on tape.

The baby's mother was herself a neglected child. Her own mother (the baby's grandmother) was psychiatrically ill. The family history was dominated by more than one symptom of serious disturbance. As Fraiberg and colleagues put it: 'the mother's story of abandonment and neglect was now being psychologically reenacted with her own baby' (1980, pp.167–178).

This seems to be a pattern observed in many clinical settings: parents who have been neglected tend to neglect their children; parents who have been abused tend to abuse; parents who have had inconsistent parenting tend to be inconsistent with their own children. In supervision sessions Bowlby often said: 'people tend to treat others as they have been treated'.

So when we see cases like these, what can we do in order to break the 'intergenerational circle'? It seems that the most important element is to help the individual revise his own internal working models of attachment relationships. Another very important aspect of the treatment programme is to work with the family as a whole as well as with the child. The first task is to provide a secure base, so that trust can emerge in a parent who perhaps has not known trust. The second task is to help the parent to remember and relieve his own attachment history, in particular painful or distressing episodes of his childhood. A very interesting observation was made by Fraiberg's team: to produce psychic change, eliciting memories is necessary but not enough.

The child's parent may talk about having experienced losses and emotional shocks, about having being hurt and not being able to talk – as a child – about his feelings to anyone. But no significant psychic and behavioural change is seen until the parent feels now what he felt in the past, when he was bereaved, shocked, anxious or hurt; that is to say, until such a time when the warded off feelings can be trusted to the therapist. These mothers remembered factually the experiences of childhood abuse. What they did not remember was their suffering. 'It was finally a relief to be able to cry, a comfort to feel the understanding of the therapist' (Fraiberg et al. 1980, p.173).

A condition of these therapeutic interventions was to move quickly to protect the baby. A conventional analysis may take years to reach the point of conclusion. The baby cannot wait. Such a timescale may be too slow for a developing infant who is being damaged in everyday interaction. Fraiberg clung to the belief that it will be the parent who cannot remember his childhood suffering who will inflict his pain upon the child. Therefore, it was an essential part of the therapeutic technique to assist the parent in recalling painful events of his own childhood, together with the associated emotions.

A parent in therapy said: 'But what's the use of talking? I always kept things to myself. I want to forget. I don't want to think'. The therapist responded with sympathy but also explained how trying to forget does not resolve the underlying feelings. The therapist's message was: 'It will be safe with me to speak of the frightening memories and thoughts, and when you speak of them you will no longer need to be afraid of them, you will have another kind of control over them'.

Normally, as the treatment progresses, the therapist helps the individual adult to see how fear of the parental figures of his childhood had led to an identification with their fearsome qualities. Yet, as happens in some cases, it may be possible to identify an adult figure in the parent's past who stood for protection, tolerance and understanding. In the chaos and terror of his childhood, there may have been someone who saved the person from total collapse: an aunt, a neighbour, a teacher, a father or mother who died young.

The clinical studies presented in 'Ghosts in the Nursery' referred to parents who had experienced gross neglect or abuse in their early years. One can easily conclude that the therapeutic technique proposed by Fraiberg's team is mainly applicable to working with the victims of such dramas. However, when Bowlby first drew my attention to this paper, he wanted to highlight that any patient with a history of insecure attachments (whatever their degree) may benefit from this type of technical approach. By this I mean an approach based on detailed exploration of the patient's past. This may seem a basic notion in psychoanalytic psychotherapy, but it is a notion that needs to be underlined. This technique does not exclude making transference interpretations, but it does not force everything into the transference.

Identification with the aggressor

Fraiberg's team saw a pattern that they defined as 'strikingly uniform': that of the individual forming a pathological identification with the negative aspects of his parents. They said:

> Yet, if we name this condition in the familiar term 'identification with the aggressor', we have not added to the sum of our knowledge of this defense. Our literature in this area of defense is sparse. Beyond the early writings of Anna Freud which named and illuminated this defense in the formative period of childhood, we do not yet know from large-scale clinical study the conditions which govern the choices of this defense against other alternatives, or the dynamics which perpetuate an identification with the enemy, so to speak. (1980, p.194)

It is true that the whole issue of identification with negative aspects of others is a neglected subject in the psychoanalytic literature. Some interesting discussions of this theme are to be found in Joseph Sandler's book *The Analysis of Defense* (1985), which is a transcript of discussions held by Anna Freud, Joseph Sandler and others at the Hampstead Clinic. An interesting point made in this book is that the identification occurs with an 'anxiety-provoking other'. Identification combines with the impersonation of the other so that the child transforms himself from the person threatened into the person who makes the threat.

Of course, this identification can occur as transient behaviour soon after experiencing anxiety. This would be so in the case, for instance, of a six-year-old boy in analysis who attacked various objects in the consulting room not long after feeling attacked by his dentist. However, what seems more difficult to explain in simple terms is how this type of identification becomes a character trait and, consequently, a pattern of behaviour which may manifest years later in countless interactions. We may, however, assume that in these cases the anxiety-ridden situation occurred many times in the course of the individual's early development.

This type of identification may also involve projective identification: if I treat you as I was treated, I will make you feel vulnerable. In this way I will get rid of my own sense of vulnerability.

Perhaps, rather than talking about 'identification with the aggressor' we should talk about 'assimilating oneself with the other', a concept which Anna Freud herself mentioned by using the German word *angleichung* (Sandler 1985).

Fraiberg *et al.* said:

> We are on sound grounds clinically and theoretically if we posit that a form of repression is present in this defense, which provides motive and energy for repetition. But, what is it that is repressed? From a number of cases known to us in which 'identification with the aggressor' was explored clinically as a central mechanism in pathological parenting, we can report that memory of the events of childhood abuse, tyranny and desertion was available in explicit and chilling detail. *What was not remembered was the associated affective experience.* (1980, p.194–195; italic in original)

In other words, in many cases memories of painful events are not repressed. What is repressed is the pain itself. Fraiberg *et al.* said:

> The key to our ghost story appears to lie in the fate of affects in childhood. Our hypothesis is that access to childhood pain becomes a powerful deterrent against repetition in parenting, while repression and isolation of painful affect provide the psychological requirements for identification with the betrayers and the aggressors. (1980, p.195)

Three types of memory

Fraiberg's experience showed that the revival of painful scenes of the patient's early life, together with their associated emotions, had therapeutic value. My own experience of working both in individual therapy and with groups confirms that assumption. It seems that with the right therapeutic technique, it is possible to retrieve memories of such episodes and that these memories are normally linked to unresolved issues from the past. Normally the therapist (and the group in group therapy) respond to these emotional accounts with belief and empathy.

The key to conscious recall of memories of particular events is the affective resonance between unresolved current and past feelings. In other words, the patient may start talking about a difficult situation of the present and suddenly feel surprised by the spontaneous retrieval of a past event. The nature of such an event seems to relate to the current difficulty. These clinical observations may require some theoretical explanation, however imperfect or incomplete this may be.

In Volume III of *Attachment and Loss*, Bowlby (1980) drew attention to the distinction, introduced by Tulving (1972), between two ways of storing information about one's own history. One way is that of storing information in relation to specific events or scenes of the past, autobiographically. Another way is that of storing history according to a more general appreciation, according to its meaning, its contribution to personal knowledge.

D.N. Stern (1985, p.94) also refers to Tulving's work in a way that is congenial to Bowlby's point of view. He says that the study of memory systems is crucial for understanding how the different self-invariants embedded in lived experience are integrated.

In the *episodic* type of storage, information is stored sequentially in terms of temporally dated episodes or events and temporo-spatial relations between events. When someone says: 'I remember one day, I must've been ten years old or so, I was on holiday with my parents in the south of France. I was playing with my father and my mother approached us smiling and told us that she really enjoyed being with the family. I can remember her smile!', this person is reviving information stored in an episodic mode.

In summary, episodic memory consists of remembered scenes, sequentially ordered, located in a specific moment. Particularly important is recall of the feelings experienced in the course of the event (Bowlby 1980). Bowlby believed that episodic memories, when recalled, by and large are relatively non-distorted versions of what actually happened. However, it has recently been held (i.e. Crittenden 1992) that episodic memories can be re-created, particularly in young children.

In clinical practice, the recall of episodic memory seems never to be free of interpretive components. However, the recalled episodes seem to be plausible; they have a convincing quality, they express some direct perception that the subject had of his immediate reality. They represent a small but coherent chunk of lived experience (see Stern 1995, p.196–199).

In the semantic type of storage, by contrast, information exists as generalized propositions about the world, derived either from a person's own experience or from what he has learned from others, or from some combination of the two. Inflows into the semantic memory system are always referred to an existing cognitive structure. An example of semantic memory would be given by the person saying: 'In my childhood we often went on holiday to France and had a lovely time'. This type of memory is presumed to be first constructed from the generalizations offered by others (Bowlby 1980). It mainly represents reality from the caregiver's perspective.

Bowlby (1980) said:

A corollary for the distinction between episodic and semantic storage, and one likely to be of much clinical relevance, is that the storage of images of parents and of self is almost certain to be of at least two distinct types. Whereas memories of behaviour engaged in and of words spoken on each particular occasion will be stored episodically, the generalizations about mother, father, and self enshrined in what I am terming working models will be stored semantically (in either analogical, propositional or some combined format). Given these distinct types of storages a fertile ground exists for the genesis of conflict. For information stored semantically need not always be consistent with what is stored episodically; and it might be that in some individuals information in one store is greatly at variance with that in the other. (p.62)

In the case of the person who remembers his holidays in France, there is correspondence between semantic and episodic memories. But suppose there is another person who enters therapy and says to his analyst at the beginning of his treatment: 'As a child I had wonderful summer holidays in Devon and Wales'. Yet, as treatment progresses, he remembers a good number of specific episodes of his holidays when he felt frightened while witnessing terrible rows between his parents. In this patient there are contradictions between his semantic and episodic memories of his family holidays.

In clinical practice one often finds patients who describe their childhood as happy or satisfactory but, at some point in their therapy, there emerge many memories of abuse or neglect. So there seem to be discrepancies between episodic and semantic memories.

Bowlby (1980) said:

One reason for discrepancies arising between the information in one type of storage and that in another lies in all likelihood in there being a difference in the source from which each derives the dominant portion of its information. Whereas for information going into episodic storage the dominant part seems likely to derive from what the person himself perceives and a subordinate part only from what he may be told about the episode, for what goes into semantic storage the emphasis may well be reversed, with what he is told being dominant over what he himself might think. (p.63)

Bowlby often referred in supervision sessions to the fact that parents like to be seen by their children under a favourable light. Even when parental behaviour leaves a lot to be desired, they still want their children to maximize positive appreciations and minimize their negative perceptions. Therefore they tell their children that their behaviour is better than it seems, or at least they ascribe to it a more acceptable significance. In circumstances like these, the individual may have difficulty in integrating memories of specific events, as he perceived them, with a semantic storage which is highly influenced by the caregivers' version of what happened and their evaluation of the quality of the relationship.

However, there are cases in which episodic memories of adverse events are integrated with realistic semantic storage. I have observed in my clinical practice, that patients who are able to present a coherent account of adverse episodic and semantic memories, have had someone in their early lives with whom it was possible to discuss and reflect upon these adverse situations.

When Bowlby (1980) drew attention to these systems, Tulving had not yet advanced his studies. Some years later (when Tulving (1985) included the notion of a third system, *'procedural* memory'), the understanding of attachment behaviour in relation to memory advanced a step further.

Crittenden (1992) says:

> Procedural memory is thought to encode information regarding recurrent patterns of sensori stimuli and behavioural responses. These sensorimotor schemata (Piaget, 1952) operate preconsciously and consist of learned modifications of the species-specific repertoire of attention and response biases with which human infants are born. Procedural models (or representations of interactions that have been generalized [Stern 1985] of the self and of attachment figures reflect infants' learned expectations of their own behaviour and that of caregivers. These models function throughout the life span to regulate everyday behaviour. They represent an efficient means by which individuals use affect and prior experience to inform current behaviour without the lengthy process of actively evaluating current conditions and past experience to organize responses. (p.577)

Storing information of differents types (behaviour sequences, episodes, generalizations) explains the co-existence of multiple perspectives on reality which can have varying degrees of mutual correspondence or discrepancy. In early development, integration of procedural, semantic and episodic memories acts as a major organizer of internal working models or representations of self and others.

It seems that in the case of psychopathology, the individual has failed to integrate these multiple perspectives because he has not been able to accommodate his own perspective with that which he has 'borrowed' from his significant others. Another possible reason for the inability to integrate one type of memory and another may be the need to repress painful feelings associated with some episodic memories. One of the aims of the psychotherapeutic process must be, then, to elicit, explore, reflect upon and integrate these different memory systems.

Unlike semantic memory, episodic memory operates largely at an unconscious level. Neither of these memories is easily amenable for conscious review or modification. However, of the two, episodic memory seems to be more buried. This appears to be particularly the case with anxiously attached individuals. Without conscious processing of episodic memory, the internal working models rooted in these episodes will remain influential, yet unchanged.

I became aware of the clinical usefulness of recalling and reviving early scenes or episodes of the patient's past well before I became acquainted with attachment theory. I was living in Argentina and training in psychodrama. In psychodrama sessions, the therapist often assists a patient (the 'protagonist') to move gradually, through a free associative path, from describing scenes of the present to reviving and re-enacting scenes of the past. At the time there were a number of psychoanalytically trained psychodramatists, such as Fidel Moccio, Eduardo Pavlovsky, Hernan Kesselman and Carlos Martinez Bouquet (see Chapter 13), who were saying that the unconscious is organized in scenes and that it was therapeutically important to get through the scenes of the present ('manifest scenes') into the scenes of the past ('latent scenes'). Only in this way can we more fully understand the real meaning and historical roots of the current episodes with which a patient often begins a session. The outcome of reviving and re-enacting episodic memories in a psychodrama session can often be as intense as it is illuminating.

So when in the course of our supervision sessions, John Bowlby directed my attention to episodes of the patient's past, the idea of reviving past scenes was not unfamiliar to me. This is a technique that can be used in individual, group, marital or family therapy.

It has been suggested that past experience retrieved in therapy and representations of particular events are influenced and, to a certain degree, transformed by, the encoding of the original experience (Lindsay and Read 1994). The encoding of the original experience is determined – at least in part – by subsequent experiences. Therefore, it seems, memories of an event that took place at a certain point in the person's development may be affected by subsequent experiences and subsequent interpretations of those experiences. It is possible that this view is correct. In any case, one can explore such processes in the course of an analysis. A patient's responses to such inquiries are often plausible, informative and therapeutically effective.

PART 3

How the Attachment Paradigm May Influence the Psychotherapeutic Style

CHAPTER 11

Application of Attachment Theory to Psychoanalytic Psychotherapy

Introduction

In terms of attachment theory, psychoanalytic psychotherapy can be defined as a method of treatment which mainly consists of: (1) eliciting, modifying and integrating internal working models of oneself and significant others; and (2) promoting reflective thinking. Implicit in this formulation is the idea that symptoms, anxieties and defences are explored in the wider framework of an interpersonal context.

The way the analyst or psychotherapist behaves in the session is not fundamentally different from the way many professionals in the field – who have been properly trained – will conduct a treatment. However, this analyst or psychotherapist will incorporate attachment theory into his reference framework as a very important paradigm. This, in turn, is likely to influence the therapeutic technique and style.

The way transference phenomena are understood and interpreted is a fundamental part of this method. We have already discussed this issue in detail in the preceding chapters. Bowlby said that analytic therapy provides a 'secure base' from which to explore the patient's world. The therapist provides this secure base by being consistently available and responsive.

On sensitive responsiveness

In terms of attachment theory, a therapist's sensitive responsiveness to a patient must be an essential condition to make the therapy viable. John Bowlby pointed out that without sensitive responsiveness, a therapist cannot enlist the patient's co-operation. Bowlby suggested in supervision that the therapist moves backward and forward in the session from a position of observer to that of seeing the patient's situation from the point of view of the patient's own subjective experience. However, the analyst not only tries to see the patient's point of view through empathic understanding, but he also remains separate, as an independent thinker.

A patient who has not had enough sensitive responsiveness himself is highly unlikely to show sensitive responsiveness to other people. Therefore, the analyst should work towards identifying in the session the patient's empathic failures, in relation to the analyst and to other people as well. This involves the frequent and consistent interpretation of the mental state of both analyst and patient.

As Peter Fonagy suggests (unpublished paper, internally circulated within the British Psycho-Analytical Society):

> over a prolonged time period, diverse interpretations concerning the patient's perception of the analytic relationship would enable him to attempt to create a mental representation both of himself and of his analyst, as thinking and feeling. This could then form the core of a sense of himself with a capacity to represent ideas and meanings, and create the basis for the bond and that ultimately permits independent existence.

To function successfully as an attachment figure (and as a therapist), the adult person should be able to communicate effectively using reciprocal patterns of timely signals, take the perspective of others, accept responsibility for his part in regulating relationships and empathize with the person who is in distress.

The attachment-oriented therapist or analyst will take into consideration the character organization of a patient. He will pay attention to defensive traits and dysfunctional care-eliciting strategies that the patient may have developed early in life and assimilated into his character structure. The character organization of the patient will become evident through the patient's behaviour in the session as well as from his account of his behaviour elsewhere. The therapist will have to confront the patient with his character pathology. In this context, the knack of his work will be to strike the right balance between confrontation and empathy.

General principles

An attachment-oriented therapist is actively interested in establishing links between the present and the past in a historical, developmental and social context. He tries to help the patient recall and integrate semantic and episodic memories. He allows and encourages the patient to participate actively in the process of retrieval as well as in the working-through process. He is able to accept error-correcting feedback.

This therapist is able to recognize the suffering of the patient and his family as well as the intergenerational tragedy. He tends to formulate his interpretations in the form of questions and hypotheses, seeking the patient's confirmations or corrections.

This therapist is able explicitly to recognize the patient as a whole person with both pathological and healthy attributes. He works closely with experience as it occurs in the session, following the patient's emotional line. He allows the patient to explore the world freely, to develop his sense of autonomy and his own values. Although total neutrality is not possible, the analyst makes a constant scrutiny of his own personal values and biases, so that they do not excessively contaminate interpretations. He is open to discovering unique and personal meanings in each patient. If a patient has grown up in a different culture, the analyst should learn as much as he can about it from the patient. He sees himself and his patient as partners in a process of investigation that can lead to discovery. Whenever appropriate he will talk about 'we' rather than 'I' or 'you'.

The analyst's attitude of openness to his encounter with the patient should not be mistaken for breaking boundaries or his indulging in self-disclosure as a habit. In ten years of weekly supervision with Bowlby, I learned nothing about his private life. Much of what I learned about him was communicated to me by his wife Ursula and his son Richard after his death. In supervision sessions he never encouraged me to talk to my patients about myself. The risk of doing so would be to make the patient a container for the analyst's anxieties, and this might be a form of role reversal in the analytic relationship. However, I believe there may be occasions on which a moderate degree of self-disclosure may be useful to confirm a patient's perception of the analyst or highlight his empathic response.

On exploring the past

Bowlby believed that, as part of the process of analysing resistance and defence, the analyst should try to open for exploration scenes of the past that have become shut off but which continue to be extremely influential in affecting thought, feeling and behaviour. These scenes usually fall into at least three distinct categories: (1) those that parents wish their children not to know about; (2) those in which parents have treated children in ways that children find too unbearable to think about; and (3) those in which children have done, or perhaps thought, things about which they feel unbearably guilty or ashamed.

Of particular relevance is the revival of scenes that parents are inclined to disclaim so that they press their children to exclude from consciousness what they have seen or felt. This would be the case, for example, of parents prone to violence who try to obliterate the child's knowledge of a violent incident which they have witnessed.

Disconfirmation of the child's perception and knowledge often leads to permanent cognitive disturbance and other problems, such as chronic distrust of other people, inhibition of their curiosity, distrust of their senses and a tendency to find everything unreal.

A note on free association

It is well known that the procedure of free association is fundamental to psychoanalytic technique. Freud developed it gradually in the 1890s. According to this procedure, voice is given to all thoughts and feelings which enter the patient's mind during a session. The first goal of this procedure is to eliminate the voluntary selection of thoughts and feelings so that unconscious material is more easily revealed.

However, when we take a closer look at free association, we can identify all sorts of characteristics and complexities. We may begin the discussion by noting all the different precipitants of a stream of free associations: recent events, memories from the remote past, interpretations or remarks by the analyst, bodily sensations, fantasies, and so on.

Free associations are not easy. Some patients find it difficult to free associate, while other patients' free associations take the form of very long, incoherent and confusing communications. The analyst should be able to facilitate free associations but should not force them.

An analyst's request that his patient present all his thoughts in a session without censorship or selection may be intrusive. Moreover, a patient who strives to free associate may feel guilty or at fault if he believes that he is failing to meet the analyst's expectations. Some patients, particularly those who have a psychotic element in their personality, may experience excessive anxiety if they feel that free association breaks down a socially established logic which keeps them tied to reality.

But of course, the patient is not the only one who is free associating. The analyst is free associating as well through the process of free floating attention. Therefore, the analytic encounter takes place in the space 'in between' two people's free associative processes. But this encounter is not madmen's dialogue. It has its thread, its own coherence, its own aim.

A patient who has symptoms of social phobia and gets panicky when he eats in restaurants or public settings, comes to the session and says: 'I have a vague feeling that the first time I got anxious was soon after I arrived at boarding school at the age of nine. But I am terrified of recalling something I guess happened there'.

I invite him to imagine that he is now nine and eating for the first time in the school refectory. In response, he describes very vividly the physical aspects of the environment, his being seated at the corner of a large room with a large window at his back. Then he says: 'Certainly I feel exposed in this corner of the room, with splitting feelings that must come to an end if ever I am to be resurrected in one piece. I don't know what causes this terrible sense of shame, but the pain is too heavy to be acknowledged and too disturbing to keep pretending that it is not there...'.

At this point, neither the patient nor I know where we are going. I do have a number of images in anticipation of what he might tell me. Although I have never been to boarding school, I imagine being there for the first time, aged nine, missing my mother, not sure why I am there, feeling anxious in a strange environment, perhaps being subjected to cruel comments by unsympathetic teachers or pupils, not having anyone to turn to for comfort. But I do not yet know what my patient is struggling to deal with, so all I can do is to invite further exploration with relaxed curiosity and care.

In fact, as the session unfolds the patient recalls being frightened in this new and big place, missing his home and his mother's food, feeling intimidated at meal times while sitting in a very large refectory... Then he says: 'I am also frightened that you are going to tell me that this is a trivial matter, you are not going to take me seriously, you are going to laugh at me'.

I respond: 'Perhaps you see in me someone who at the time poured scorn on your distress'. The patient says: 'It rings a bell'. But it is the end of the session and I say: 'We are into something. It is now the end of the session but I hope that we will be able to continue exploring this issue'.

To a certain degree we have made some initial discoveries, which are the result of the interaction between our internal working models which are gradually elicited. But there is also uncertainty, which I need to tolerate.

My internal working models include my knowledge of some developmental and attachment issues. However, I need much more than this knowledge in order to be productively involved in a free associative interaction with the patient. Complex inferential processes are taking place. I sense that in my dialogue with the patient I am not following a particular recipe, I am not using a prescribed technique. What I am doing is spontaneously 'lending', so to speak, through my own free associations, my internal working models – which have earned a relative sense of security and integration through many years of personal analysis, supervision, theoretical learning, group work and life experiences. These, as Peterfreund (1983) says, are 'broad based models of human experience'.

Meanwhile, I am trying – as far as I can – to stay with my patient's subjective experience and avoid a rapid ordering and organization of the data which may be external to the patient. I certainly use theory to build a hypothesis about the patient's anxieties, conflict and defences, but I try to build up understanding from within the data and in co-operation with the patient. I identify with the patient momentarily but I also allow myself to react freely as an observer.

Peterfreund (1983) suggests:

> The fundamental reason for entering the patient's world is to obtain the relevant information to think about, organize, and generalize from – information based

both on what the patient conveys and what the analyst fills in. The analyst uses himself as a basic model, which is necessary because no other model can conceivably encompass the complexity of the patient's experience. The resulting cast amount of information may make for a temporary confused and disordered situation, but eventually, as the information is grouped and patterned and as hypotheses are formed and tested, uncertainty can be reduced. We then have a reasonable chance of being able to interpret something that is relatively on target, relatively accurate, and close to the patient's experience. (p.160–161)

A note on the true and false self

Winnicott (1975) used the term 'false self' to account for a defensive type of character organization or character trait. The false self is to be located, in Winnicott's own words, in the infant–parent relationship. He said:

> The mother who is not good enough is not able to implement the infant's omnipotence, and so she repeatedly fails to meet the infant gesture; instead she substitutes her own gesture which is to be given sense by the compliance of the infant. This compliance on the part of the infant is the earliest stage of the False Self, and belongs to the mother's inability to sense her infant's needs. (1975, p.145)

Winnicott suggested that the false self hides the true self, the latter being what feels real, what is creative, what comes from the aliveness of the body. Winnicott (1975) said: 'The true self appears as soon as there is any mental organization of the individual at all, and it means little more than the summation of sensori-motor aliveness'.

It seems, from Winnicott's account, that the false self is either a character structure (what he calls a 'False Self Personality') or a defensive organization that may colour some aspects of a subject's interpersonal behaviour. The difference only depends on the degree and consistency with which the defence is used.

A person develops a false self because his caregivers not only had failures of sensitive responsiveness but also required compliance on the part of the child with their own mental states. In order for the child to adapt to such requirements, he has to hide his own needs, his own 'aliveness'.

Nicola Diamond (personal communication) suggests that one of the issues in severe forms of false self is that if a subject has not had another to recognize, identify and metabolize his feelings, these feelings not only remain encapsulated but also unprocessed and non-symbolized.

Bowlby (1980) adopted the terms 'true and false self' from Winnicott. In Bowlby's view, a contributing factor to the false self organization is that the child's spontaneous expressions of his needs for relatedness and comfort were invalidated in the course of family interactions. Therefore, the individual has created an image of himself in accordance with parental expectations. Compliance becomes dominant.

A person acting under the dominance of a false self type of defensive organization is likely to show competence at work, be emotionally composed and self-reliant, and go through life without overt sign of breakdown. Yet he may be difficult to live with and may have little understanding of either others or himself. This person may go to therapy because of various ill-defined difficulties, including feelings of emptiness.

Should he develop enough trust in a therapist, as Bowlby put it, he may reveal feelings of being isolated and unloved. Here, one of the main purposes of the therapeutic endeavour is to break the defensive barrier.

A note on the interpretation of defence

In terms of attachment theory, anxiety is mainly related to attachment insecurity. The origins of anxiety cannot be reduced to internal sources. Anxiety has to be located in an interpersonal context. Because of the fact that anxieties are difficult to bear, they are likely to originate defences.

An individual may use some defence mechanisms against anxiety in a transient way. But some defences can become part of the person's character organization. They may influence in a predominant and continuous way the individual's pattern of responses or behaviour. Avoidant behaviour, omnipotent attitudes and many other features of a person may be the result of defensive organization.

A certain analytic style emphasizes the need to interpret defences as they manifest in the analytic relationship. This is all well and good. The problem is that when defences are identified without understanding the painful situation that created the underlying anxieties, the analytic work may become risky. I shall explain what I mean. There are many accounts of analysts telling their patients: 'You feel omnipotent' or 'You avoid intimacy with me'. Such remarks – made in this way – give a description, not an explanation. Furthermore, they may be perceived by the patient as attacks on his self-esteem. However, if the analyst proceeds to investigate the possible sources of these defences and show empathy for the patient's early plight, the interpretation of defence will be more adequate and the analysand may feel more accompanied. In other words, if we interpret the defence together with the underlying anxiety, and then invite the patient to explore ways of making sense of these anxieties in the context of early interpersonal experiences, we may be helping the patient to achieve greater insight over his psychic functioning while at the same time offering an empathic response.

CHAPTER 12

On Iatrogenia

Introduction: the persecutory therapist

Meares and Hobson (1977), in a very important article on iatrogenia in psychotherapy, stated that it would be foolish to imagine that psychotherapy, when it is not beneficial, is merely ineffective. In fact, it may do harm. I would like to use this chapter as an introduction to this topic.

Meares and Hobson drew attention to the fact that research in the field of psychotherapy was, in 1977, at its beginnings. It perhaps still is. There is a great deal of work to be done in relating reliable measures of the many variables in the therapeutic process to valid assessment of outcome. However, clinical observations made over many years can perhaps provide more than mere anecdotal accounts.

I believe that some psychotherapeutic treatments can be iatrogenic and that attachment theory can inform the detection and analysis of iatrogenic techniques. The evidence comes from several clinical sources, which I prefer not to name for the sake of discretion.

Meares and Hobson focused their study on certain kinds of therapeutic technique which evoke in the patient feelings of persecution. These techniques contain strong elements of the following:

1. *Frequent use of intrusive interpretations, probing or questioning.* This may involve forcing confessions. However, the most common form of intrusiveness in analysis occurs when the analyst is interpreting every 'corner' of the patient's mind in a persistent way. Such technique is often justified by sophisticated theoretical claims.

2. *Frequent use of derogation.* The therapist may derogate his patient while considering his interpretations to be 'confrontations' or 'insight-giving'. Meares and Hobson showed that telling a patient that he is angry or

that he wishes to dominate may be a covert way of calling him names. This derogatory attitude towards patients is often seen in clinical seminars where emphasis is put on the patients' destructiveness and envy to the neglect of positive or well-functioning aspects of these analysands.

By subtle or even brutal means the patient is made to feel that he is 'bad', 'ill' and abnormal; and hence completely different from the therapist.

By definition, a patient who seeks therapy is trying to deal with a greater or lesser degree of insecurity of attachment, which always carries a burden of low self-esteem. Therefore, derogation in psychotherapy, because of its detrimental effect on the patient's self-esteem, is anti-therapeutic.

3. *Invalidation of experience.* This might occur when the therapist considers that what his patient says does not mean what the latter thinks it means. There is an implicit suggestion that the 'real' meaning lies elsewhere. This is not an unusual situation, since psychotherapy is characterized as a search for 'deeper' explanations. However, analysis consists of amplifying and extending awareness and this cannot be done at the cost of invalidating the patient's subjective experience.

4. *False neutrality.* This is the stance of an 'opaque' therapist, who pretends that clean withdrawal from the intersubjective experience of two people in an analytic relationship is possible.

5. Meares and Hobson also describe the 'untenable situation'. This is reached when the therapist's communication to the patient renders him helpless, confused and unable to explore and learn. It is promoted by lack of clarity about the structure of therapy, imposing impossible requirements, giving conflicting messages and making conflicting demands.

6. Finally, there can be a *'persecutory spiral'*, which is an escalation of destructive interaction in which both therapist and patient are, or feel, persecuted. Ambivalence or hatred may dominate the relationship and neither can leave. This is made worse when the therapist is self-righteous.

A review of dysfunctional therapeutic styles

It might be possible to draw parallels between dysfunctional parental styles and dysfunctional therapeutic styles. In this context, it might also be possible to formulate a hypothesis. If, as Anna Freud, Selma Fraiberg, John Bowlby and others propose, we tend to treat others as we have been treated by important people in our past, then we can assume that an analyst may treat his patients as he has been treated, particularly if his own analysis failed to investigate in detail the patterns of interaction that characterized his early relationship with his parents or caregivers.

For instance, an analyst who – as a child or adolescent – was often subjected to derogatory comments (normally disguised as well-intentioned and helpful communications), may do the same to his patients. Many examples of this sort could be given to illustrate the process to which I refer. This process resembles the intergenerational transmission of disturbed patterns of attachment. However, in this case, the person who is exposed to the intergenerational tragedy is the patient and not the child.

The iatrogenic analyst may have had years of analysis and gone through a thorough training. He may have years of clinical experience and be able to explain his technique in a substantial and convincing manner. However, in the intimacy of his consulting room he may treat his patients (all of them or some of them) in a way that is consistently or intermittently lacking in empathy or sensitive responsiveness.

Many analysts who work in an iatrogenic way do so by means of verbal communications which involve one or more of the following characteristics:

1. They disconfirm the patient's real perception of other people (including the analyst) by emphasizing the influence that projection and unconscious phantasy have in causing perceptual distortions.

2. They invalidate the patient's subjective experience by making interpretations which imply: 'What you feel or experience is not what you actually say but what I think you actually feel or experience'.

3. They use double-binding, for instance by making the patient feel guilty and then saying that the patient's internal world is dominated by guilt; by indoctrinating the patient in subtle ways and then claiming neutrality; by demanding that the analytic relationship be central and then interpreting excessive dependency; or by increasing the patient's sense of vulnerability and then treating it as pathology.

4. They inhibit exploratory behaviour and autonomy. This is often achieved by constantly interpreting the patient's search for autonomy as a narcissistic defence against dependency and most actions that the patient takes as 'acting out'.

5. They always make the patient feel at fault. This is achieved by making 'fault-finding' interpretations, normally aimed at demonstrating that any failure or conflict in the patient's interpersonal life is the sole result of

his psychopathology or unconscious determinism. In this way adversity is invariably reduced to the patient's internal fault.

6. They treat the patient with rigidity. In this case the therapist makes interpretations with an axiomatic sense of validity, that is to say, his views cannot be questioned.

7. They create in the patient a sense of disempowerment. This can be done by combined use of some of the techniques described above. As a result of their use, the patient feels increasingly unsure about his capacity to make good enough decisions, to assess reality, to perceive others, to make realistic choices, to establish realistically ambitious aims, to be in control of his life. The patient feels emotionally weak, his self-esteem is declining and he may entirely delegate any sense of wisdom to his analyst.

Patients can be trapped in analysis that has some of these characteristics as dominant features. In many cases, the patient remains in analysis for extremely long periods of time because he feels very debilitated and unable to walk through life without the crutch that his analyst is supposedly providing.

There seem to be some interesting and common characteristics in the behaviour of many iatrogenic analysts. First, they are dismissive of their patients' attachment histories. Second, they tend to make the patient feel vulnerable and weak, while they do not recognize any vulnerability or weakness in themselves.

Both characteristics – a dismissive attitude towards the significance of attachment histories and a tendency to see vulnerability and weakness in others rather than in themselves – can be seen as character defences against insecurity of attachment (as is often the case with people who have been broadly classified as 'avoidant' or 'dismissive'). Of course, a chief defence mechanism here is projective identification: making the other person feel what one is resistant to feeling. This type of behaviour reminds me of the behaviour of avoidant schoolchildren described by Alan Sroufe in Minnesota (see Chapter 4). These are children who show a false sense of security and superiority, who are normally tense, who find it difficult to admit personal failure or to say 'sorry', who in situations of interpersonal conflict are more likely to play the role of victimizer than that of victim. They also have the capacity to make their ambivalent mates weaker and act towards them as if signs of weakness deserve nothing but aggression and contempt.

In the following pages I shall try to describe in greater detail some dysfunctional communications made by therapists as well as attitudes lacking in sensitive responsiveness. I shall also try to pinpoint similarities with parental communications of the same sort.

Lack of warmth

Lack of warmth is shown non-verbally as well as verbally. It appears in the form of a cold attitude when greeting the patient at the beginning of the session or when saying goodbye. It also appears in the form of long silences on the part of the analyst or in his tone of voice when making an interpretation. However, the most striking form of coldness occurs when the patient is going through a crisis or needs comfort and what he gets is a 'clean' interpretive response devoid of genuine empathy.

In clinical seminars, lack of warmth is often justified. It is seen as a protective shield which the analyst must use against the patient's 'seduction' or manipulation. It is often held that the patient is always trying to play tricks in the analytic relationship, to seduce the analyst, to make him be friendly, so that the analysand's destructive or nasty elements remain hidden and are ignored.

John Bowlby firmly believed that the starting and ending point of any analysis should be the analyst's stance of being on the patient's side. This requires from the analyst a basic trust in therapeutic relationships, compassion for the patient's plight, a deep sense of respect for the patient and, as a result, a certain warmth. Then, of course, it should be possible to explore the patient's hostility and dysfunctional strategies.

There are people who show more or less warmth in their everyday life. This is to do with personality and cultural influences. In terms of psychopathology, in some cases lack of warmth may be a manifestation of character defences. However, the type of warmth (or lack of it) to which I am referring here relates more specifically to the attitude the analyst has in relation to his patient and to the theoretical justification found for such an attitude.

Lack of warmth on the part of the analyst may reactivate in certain patients early memories of lack of parental warmth. This is an important point because a number of studies in the field of attachment (e.g. Franz *et al.* 1994) relate parental warmth to acceptance and affirmation of the child's worth. Overall rating of affection displayed in parent–child interactions was inversely proportional to hostility or rejection in these relationships. Having had a difficult childhood correlated with lack of maternal warmth. Meanwhile, having at least a warm parent was associated with better social accomplishment in later life, which in turn was correlated with a variety of indicators of general psychological, interpersonal and psychosocial functioning.

On support and assurance

There are analysts who consider that support and assurance have no role to play in analysis. A patient was going through a very difficult period in his life and expected support in his therapy. In response, the analyst said with a disapproving tone of voice: 'Mr X, you want reassurance! This is all you want!'.

Research in the field of attachment highlights the value of support in relationships and shows how unsupportive communications may have a detrimental effect on psychic functioning. Furthermore, there is no clear evidence to substantiate the hypothesis that support is incompatible with analysis.

Support is a way of showing the patient that one understands his plight, that one is essentially on his side and is prepared to listen and see the world from his point of view. The therapeutic alliance is essentially built on the analyst's capacity to offer sensitive responsiveness and support. It is on the basis of such alliance that the therapist can help the patient to explore his denial of reality, splitting, perceptual distortions, manipulations, dysfunctional strategies to get attention, hostility, and so on.

Attachment research has shown that there is a difference between 'lack of support' and 'unsupportive behaviour'. Lack of support implies a poor response to a person's care-eliciting communications. Unsupportive behaviour, instead, involves a derogatory or accusatory response to a person's distress. An example of the latter would be a patient of mine who reported that, throughout her life, every time she failed as a consequence of unwise decisions she had made, her mother would exclaim in a harsh and punitive tone of voice: 'You made your bed, you lie in it!' or 'It serves you right!'. The key aspect of unsupportive behaviour is that the person in distress, instead of getting a reflective response, gets an attack on his or her self-esteem.

Unfortunately, unsupportive behaviour can occur in analysis. A young patient who failed his exams was told by his analyst: 'You mess it up!'. Even if there was an element of truth in the analyst's remark, as the patient did not seem to perform as well as he could because of his own anxieties and inhibitions, this explanation may only refer to an aspect of a more complex interpersonal situation. Therefore, such a remark, said without reference to other factors at play, becomes reductionistic. We shall briefly discuss reductionism in the next section.

Overt or covert derogatory and accusatory elements in the analyst's communications are often disguised as 'interpretations'. Not infrequently, in clinical seminars or supervision groups, an analyst's behaviour is justified in fashionably couched technical terms. However, these terms can be roughly translated as, 'It is all the patient's fault'.

Reductionism and de-contextualization

I had my first training in psychoanalytic therapy in Argentina, in the tradition of Jose Bleger and Enrique Pichon Riviere. Bleger insisted that behaviour is always motivated by more than one factor, all these factors converging to produce an end result. This is what he called 'policausality'. Pichon Riviere conceptualized human behaviour in a given situation as an 'emergent', something that emerges out of the intersection between a person's history and personality (he called it the 'vertical line') and the context of current social interactions (the 'horizontal line'). This type of thinking is compatible with Foulkes' group analytic propositions and with attachment theory. It is also congenial with Freud's concept of complementary series (1916–1917), whereby 'exogenous' and 'endogenous' factors were seen as complementary in the aetiology of neurosis.

From this point of view, an analyst should help the patient realize that his behaviour and mental states may be the result of a number of factors coming together. Among these factors, the effect of social interactions must be considered. Not to do this may limit and inhibit the broader reflective processes that are required to achieve metacognitive knowledge. However, there are analysts who start their interpretations by saying, 'The reason why you do that is…'.

Often, the analyst does not give enough consideration to the possibility that disturbed functioning on the part of the patient could be a reaction to unfavourable interpersonal situations – past or present. It can happen, for instance, that while a patient's use of projective identification is frequently analysed, this same patient is not assisted in recognizing situations in which he is the actual recipient of somebody else's projective identifications.

Mr Y, a man in his late 30s living in England, missed his native country, where people are more expansive and the sun shines more often. Dr N, his analyst, was convinced that this patient (when referring to his nostalgia of a better place to live) was trying to convey in a symbolic and defensive way the notion that if he was with expansive people under a sunny sky his hidden depression would disappear. A subsequent analysis revealed that this patient had genuine reasons to miss his country of origin and that the 'depression' to which Dr N referred was actively induced by Dr N himself, who was constantly undermining the patient's self-esteem and self-confidence.

Invalidation of the patient's subjective experience

In the case of Mr Y, the man whom I mentioned in the previous section, it could have been possible that he was in fact longing for a better mental state, symbolically represented by good weather and nice people. However, Dr N's denial of the possibility that the patient had good reasons to miss his country was an invalidation of the patient's subjective experience.

The same patient, Mr Y, whose parents lived in his country of origin, once said to his analyst: 'I think that my ageing parents need me. Maybe I should go back'. Dr N responded: 'No, Mr Y! Your parents do not need you. You need them!'. In this way, the analyst interpreted Mr Y's statement as a projection of his own dependency needs.

Mr Y's subsequent analysis, with a different therapist, showed that: (1) Mr Y had a genuine concern for his parents' well-being and his appreciation of their needs was accurate; and (2) nevertheless, in his early years Mr Y was subjected to a mild form of role reversal in relation to both parents, who in a subtle way made him feel somehow responsible for their emotional well-being. If there was some pathology in Mr Y, this was specifically related to a moderate degree of role reversal in his attachment history and not only (as his previous analyst claimed) to a projection of disowned dependency needs.

As Meares and Hobson (1977) point out, in cases like this:

> the therapist behaves as if the patient is communicating in a curious kind of code, which it is the duty of the therapist to break. Under these circumstances, the patient finds his words a cage. However much he strives to find his freedom through them, he is imprisoned behind the iron bars of an explanatory stereotype. (p.352)

The patient may perceive this style of interpretation as worse than over-simplification and reductionism, particularly when interpretations are directed unremittingly to his 'unconscious':

> When he protests that he is unaware of the feelings attributed to him and his plea is dismissed as a resistance, he may sense a growing failure and unreality – an alienation from his own thoughts. That which he felt he knew is uncertain, and what seemed substantial, a mere figment. He enters a state of increasing bewilderment, despair, and helplessness associated with a sense of unreality. (p.352)

The stereotyped approach

Peterfreund (1983, Part I) defines a 'stereotyped psychoanalytic approach' whereby the analyst constantly tries unilaterally to fit the patient's material into his own theoretical framework. Typically, those who work in a stereotyped manner believe that they understand the case well and that they have important clues about it from the outset. Therefore they tend to fit the case into theory. In this context, meanings are assumed rather than discovered.

The psychoanalytic process is not viewed as a mutually co-operative project to search for the truth but as the analyst's attempt to get his patient to accept as correct and hence understand his hypothetical formulations. Although the patient is asked to 'free associate', data presented by the patient are all too often selectively filtered to fit the formulation, or else are merely forced or collapsed into the formulation. Alternative possible interpretations of the data presented are neglected and may not even be recognized. The 'analysis' is then reduced to a process of subtle indoctrination.

Next, the patient's difficulty to accept at face value and understand the analyst's interventions is regarded as resistance. In turn, the resistance may be interpreted according to yet another stereotyped model. But what could be worse is that the analyst, in order to make the patient be more receptive to his interpretations, may insist that the patient's inability to see the analyst's point of view stems out of his own psychopathology. Therefore, a way to proceed is to make the patient feel ill.

Dr N persistently said to Mr Y in the course of his analysis: 'You have fundamental problems!' and 'You don't have any sense of illness!'.

At some point, Mr Y began to feel increasingly bewildered, confused, despairing and lacking in self-confidence. Therefore he began to talk to his friends about his analysis and, of course, to Dr N about these conversations with friends. His friends gave him support and advised him to change analyst. In response, Dr N concluded that Mr. Y was fixed in the schizo-paranoid position and began to interpret that the patient had transformed his friends in 'all-good' and his analyst in 'all-bad'. The degree of splitting, Dr N suggested, was such that he would recommend that Mr Y abandon ambitious professional plans because he was not psychologically fit to carry them out. At this point, Mr Y decided abruptly to terminate his long-standing analysis with Dr N and to seek another therapist.

On the importance of being wrong

Peterfreund (1983) said that there is a striking tendency for the stereotyped therapist to believe that he possesses an understanding of the 'truth'; that he has a privileged awareness of the nature of the patient's deep unconscious. Tolerance of uncertainty and ambiguity is not a hallmark of his work. He tends to present formulations dogmatically. He attributes cliché-ridden meanings to highly complex phenomena, which may actually have multiple meanings that may even change over time. In this context, of course, the patient can only play a minimal role in establishing the truth of what may be going on or of what has happened to him. The therapist does not view the patient as an equal working partner, capable of confirming, revising or refuting suggested interpretations, capable of evaluating what he hears and capable of arriving at insights independently.

The analyst persists in making circular, self-confirming formulations in which refutation has no place or is taken as a sign of pathology. This type of analyst is unable to engage in a dialogue with the patient and negotiate with him any difference of opinion. In this way, the therapist presents a model of identification that is unrealistic, for the patient may begin to feel that in order to become healthier and more mature he has to become as dogmatic as the therapist.

Some years ago, I gave a lecture at the London Centre for Psychotherapy under the title: 'The Importance of Being Wrong', in which I suggested that a therapist who can admit that at times he may be wrong has enormous advantages over the dogmatic therapist who believes he is always right. Hans Cohn, who acted as my discussant, said:

Psychoanalytic interpretations tend to conclude some unconscious A from an apparent B. When someone is late for a session, the analyst may interpret this as a resistance to analysis. Is the analyst right or wrong? Is there a necessary connection between lateness and resistance? I do not think there is. There are a number of reasons why somebody may be late for a session, among them no doubt also resistance. A context has to be established within which one reason is seen to be more likely than another. An interpretation, in my view, is essentially not a statement but a question.

I often say to my patients: 'Look, listening to what you say, I realize that a part of myself responds in this way and another part of myself in this other way. Perhaps we need to have a "group discussion" with all these voices, including yours, to negotiate a solution'.

I believe that it is important to show humility and honesty in engaging a patient in a shared project. Without these conditions we could easily lose our way and even treat the patient as he may have been treated by his parental figures, whose dysfunctional style may ultimately explain why the patient has come to therapy.

A patient who has experienced in his childhood a dysfunctional form of parental treatment is likely to be further damaged by an analyst who, even in subtle or disguised ways, repeats the abuse. The result may be that the patient becomes more fragmented and depressed or that he reinforces his false-self structure and gains some stability through it without any fundamental change at a deeper level.

Iatrogenic influences in supervision

I have heard of many instances in which a therapist in training was treating a patient with sensitive responsiveness and common-sense, while being instructed by the supervisor to frame the interventions within a different model, resulting in difficulties in the therapeutic relationship if not its total breakdown. The model advocated by the supervisor contained several of the following elements: (1) a tendency not to believe the patient's account; (2) a tendency to disregard the analysand's attempt to explore his attachment history; (3) a tendency to collapse the understanding of the interaction into a very narrow view of the transference–countertransference interplay (whereby the 'here-and-now' is all that matters); and (4) a tendency constantly to interpret the 'badness' of the patient (that is, to say his defensive traits and dysfunctional strategies without examining the context in which they were formed).

In one case, the patient wanted to talk about his early pattern of interaction with his parents and the trainee went along with this. In response, the supervisor said: 'You must not accept the patient's account of his history. You should only try to see the history as it appears in the transference and countertransference'. It is a curious fact that some supervisors actively discourage their supervisees from accepting patients' detailed accounts of their experiences outside therapy (particularly past experiences) while at the same time demanding a very detailed account of each analytic session. The underlying assumption seems to be that a supervisee's account of events that occur outside the supervision (namely the session conducted by the supervisee) is undistorted by definition while the patient's account of interactions with others is inherently untrustworthy. As a consequence of this the trainee is indoctrinated into believing that (a) the meticulous retrieval and analysis of the patient's life events is clinically insignificant and (b) that the patient deserves to be treated – by virtue of being a patient – as someone whose communications can never be taken for what they mean.

In another case, the trainee explained to her supervisor that she accepted the reason her patient gave for missing the previous session. The patient (being a mother) said that she had to miss the session because her child had a temperature. In such circumstances, she decided not to send the child to school and to stay at home to look after him. This, inevitably, resulted in her having to miss her analytic session. After hearing this report, the supervisor exclaimed: 'You seem totally unable to interpret resistance!'

In a third example, the patient was trying to cope with the consequences of a very adverse social situation: she was a female journalist who had recently taken refuge in the UK after being seriously threatened by Islamic fundamentalists in her native country (particularly because she was a woman who dared to publish her own independent ideas). The supervisor commented: 'How are we going to help this patient to deal with the psychotic part of her personality (which is our priority) if it is matched with a mad political situation?'. The supervisor made these comments well before he knew much about this patient.

It is not uncommon for trainees to find themselves in serious difficulties when they try to deal with a conflict between their human responses and the technique and style that the supervisor demands. These difficulties often result in the trainees being constantly upset, feeling persecuted by the training institution, losing confidence in their abilities, obtaining negative responses from their patients and not being able to integrate – as they should – common-sense with a more sophisticated and clear analytic understanding of the patient and events in the therapeutic relationship.

Attachment Theory
and Group Analysis

Introduction

In this chapter I would like to suggest that:

- the theoretical bases of group analysis and attachment theory are mutually compatible

- group analysis, as a therapeutic tool, offers the possibility of eliciting, modifying and integrating internal working models of relationships

- group analysis is a very powerful instrument in helping people to develop reflective thinking

- group work with parents may prove to be effective as a form of intervention aimed at promoting mental health in the next generation

- the use of psychodramatic techniques may aid the process of recovering episodic memories and enhancing communication in the group

- attachment-based experiential group work with psychotherapists may increase their understanding of attachment theory and its clinical applications at a cognitive-emotional level.

Theoretical aspects

Group analysis and attachment theory share some essential principles (Marrone 1994). Foulkes, founder of group analysis in Britain, saw this discipline not only as a method of treatment but also as an ever-evolving theoretical body based on the confluence of psychoanalysis with sociology and other disciplines. Throughout its development, group analysis has defined and maintained its own theoretical and methodological identity. Yet, at the same time, group analysis has created for itself a territory which is capable of accommodating and integrating an interplay of different perspectives (Marrone and Pines 1990).

Group analysis is based on the notion that the essence of man is social, not individual. Each one of us occupies a nodal point in a family network and society. The great forces of conscious and unconscious psychological dynamics are transmitted through groups and social networks and we are deeply imprinted by these great forces, through to our very core. In other words, the main concern of group analysis, as a theoretical body, is the location of psychic functioning in a developmental and social context. As Nicola Diamond (1996) points out, group analysis not only represents a movement away from one-person psychology to a multi-person psychology, but also contains, fundamentally, an interpersonal conception of the human being as always situated in relations with others.

Foulkes (1990) said that psychological processes

> are not created by the individual in isolation, purely in accordance with his own make up; they originate in a context, i.e. in a multipersonal network of interaction, represented in the first place by the primary family. How such processes are strengthened in any one individual is influenced by the configuration, by the members' relationships to each other, their colouring depends on the patterns of interaction of the total family. (p.283)

In the same paper, Foulkes criticized the way of doing analysis which reduces complex phenomena to pure intrapsychic processes. He said: 'It is quite easy in the psychoanalytic situation to make an analysand feel such processes inside himself, by way of suggestion, and to convince him that he is on the track of a deep, true mental reality'. (p.282)

Foulkes' point of view seems to coincide with that of Bowlby (1988), who said:

> it is just as necessary for analysts to study the way a child is really treated by his parents as it is to study the internal representations he has of them, indeed that the principal focus of our studies should be the interaction of the one with the other, of the internal with the external. Believing that that would be possible only if we had far more systematic knowledge about the effects on a child of the experiences he has during his early years within his family, I concentrated my attention on this area. (p.44)

Transference in the context of group analytic therapy

Foulkes (1964, 1968, 1975) recognizes the fact that members can take one another as well as the conductor as transference figures. Whereas in individual psychoanalysis the analyst is the focus of the patient's transference phenomena (mother, father, siblings, and so on), in group analysis there are more people present and members are free, as it were, to make all sorts of misattributions among themselves. Even so, members tend to make strong and durable transference reactions to the group analyst, who is seen as a parental figure and a normative authority, and who is expected to provide care and comfort and to give rewards and punishment. The group members are often seen as siblings. Durkin (1964) as well as Agazarian and Peters (1981) agree that in the group the various infantile figures and the many ideas and affects attached to them need not be forced on to the therapist: there are several people to choose among. In many cases, another member's personality or physical appearance is more conducive to the development of a particular aspect of transference than is the therapist's.

On eliciting, exploring, modifying and integrating internal working models

Once a small group of people gather together and begin to communicate and meet on a regular and continuous basis, one of the dominant phenomena that occurs is that a new micro-social system is established. An important motivational factor contributing to maintaining a sense of being together is the activation of affiliative behaviour (which is one of the main behavioural systems described by attachment theory).

This new micro-social system is a place in which, inevitably, individuals' existing working models are reactivated and brought into play. In this way, each group member presents different notions and ideas, different perceptions and ways of understanding the world. These are manifested implicitly or explicitly. These notions, ideas, and so on, can refer to a wide range of themes, subjects, ideologies and areas of knowledge.

These working models are brought into the group analytic arena as a by-product or epiphenomenon of 'being-in-the-group'. Each individual reacts according to his own working models, but these may differ from those of other group members. These differences are what may highlight their non-shared quality and demand updating and modification through confrontation, dialogue and negotiation.

One of the main tasks of the group is to elicit and explore working models of oneself and significant others. Since transference is a direct manifestation of internal working models, a good part of the group analytic process consists of exploring transference as it occurs in the group context (Marrone 1984). Each group member has transference reactions to the therapist, another member, part of the group or the group as a whole.

A group analyst oriented by attachment theory has at least seven main tasks to accomplish:

- *Task 1.* To increase (through analytic means) cohesiveness and a sense of affiliation to the group, so that the group can become a secure base from which it is possible to explore the members' inner worlds and relationships.

The sense of cohesiveness and togetherness that makes the group feel like a secure base is most effectively achieved when each group member can relinquish his false self and get in contact with one another through his true self.

- *Task 2.* To assist the group members in exploring their present circumstances: what situations they find themselves in, what role they play in creating these situations, how they choose people they form relationships with, how they respond to them, and what the consequences of their behaviour are.

These explorations usually involve making connections between the patient's possible behaviour outside the group, his behaviour as it can be seen in the group and his attachment history. As a result, patterns of attachment in the family may be recognized.

I shall briefly illustrate this point with the following vignette. A professional woman in her early 30s (who works for a large company) was unhappy with the way she was treated by her female boss. She (the boss) was frequently using guilt-inducing communications to force her (my patient) to comply with demands for assistance that she rightly felt to be inappropriate. In order to escape from this situation, my patient successfully requested to be transferred to another department. The day she had to tell her boss that she was moving to another section of the company, she could not bring herself to do so for fear of upsetting her. She felt sorry for her boss and almost entirely responsible for her emotional well-being. The group members helped my patient to see that she was treating her boss as a representative of her mother, with whom she has had a moderate degree of role reversal since early childhood. Furthermore, the group showed her how easily she would ignore her own needs in the group for the sake of serving the needs of the others.

- *Task 3.* To assist the group members in finding out how they interpret one another's behaviour (including the group analyst's behaviour) and explore their expectations about the quality of responses they expect to get.

- *Task 4.* To assist the group members in making links between past and present and to consider how the internal working models they have built in the past influence the way they behave, react, interpret responses and forecast outcomes in the present, both in the group and outside it. Linked to this, to promote an exploration of semantic and episodic memories.

In order to do this, the group analyst uses the technical device that Bowlby called 'informed inquiry'. Being acquainted with the possible repertoire of pathogenic situations in childhood and adolescence, in the family or at school, the group analyst tentatively construes in his mind a set of hypotheses from which to develop the inquiries. Following the patient's own associative past, he may take certain opportunities given by the group and by each individual patient to ask certain questions about past events. In this way, the analyst offers a model of exploration that all group members can use to facilitate mutual reliving and reviving experiences of the recent and remote past, focusing on a process leading to discovery and insight. However, I would like to emphasize that abruptly proposing a particular traumatic event (such as incest) is out of order, even more so if the group is highly conflicted or tense.

- *Task 5*. To be ready to identify and highlight any breakdown of empathy between group members and minimize the possibility that insensitive behaviour on the part of some members may confirm the fears of getting unempathic responses on the part of others.

It is not unusual, particularly in the early stages of group membership, that a member responds to others without sufficient empathy. This is often to be expected since we know how difficult it is for a person who has not been treated with sensitive responsiveness in his early years to be genuinely sensitive to others. Of course, the group analyst is not perfect, and sometimes it is he himself who responds in an unempathic way. But group members may recognize the analyst's failure and then it is the analyst's duty to show that he too can learn from the group.

- *Task 6*. To assist the group in identifying a member's dysfunctional strategies to disown vulnerability, regulate access to, and proximity with, others and regulate self-esteem.

- *Task 7*. To promote a culture of reflection and use the group's intrinsic resources to increase interpersonal knowledge.

The group's intrinsic resources

The technique and style of leadership of the group analyst are important factors in conducting the therapy. However, it would be wrong to think that these are the only factors that matter. For there is something inherent to small-group processes that in optimal conditions contributes in a fundamental way.

Foulkes (1964) pointed out that the aim of group analysis is to achieve a genuine and lasting change in the patient's mental organization and that our clinical observations give us every reason to think that this aim can be achieved. He said: These results were in his opinion predominantly due to forces which are peculiar to the social setting and which cannot take effect outside it.

Therefore, group analytic therapy is not merely an economical alternative to individual therapy, and is neither a substitute nor a short-cut: it demands to be appreciated as an essentially new orientation in clinical practice. I do not wish to enter here into a debate about the comparative effectiveness of group analysis and individual psychoanalysis; nor do I want to assume that all patients in group analysis do well or that all groups function optimally. In fact, I think that many patients do much better in individual analysis than in groups. The selection criteria for one form of therapy or another are fundamentally important as a clinical matter. However, this is a very complex issue which falls outside the scope of this chapter.

What I want to stress here is the fact that the group has some inherent therapeutic ingredients that the individual situation lacks. One of them is, of course, what Foulkes (1957; 1977) termed 'resonance': a specific response and affinity by group members with the 'wavelength' of someone's subjective experience. Foulkes thought that in the group-analytic group individuals not only resonate on a large scale to each other, simultaneously and reciprocally, but also to the group as a whole and particularly to the group conductor, who in turn is influenced by resonance. Perhaps Foulkes referred to some form of pre-conscious empathy which is shared collectively.

In individual therapy, the differentiation of roles between analyst and analysand is such that there is an inherent tendency to put the patient in the position of the 'observed one'. In group analysis, instead, the equality of roles is of such a nature that each member inevitably gives himself up to the experience of being with the others. In this context of dialogue and mutual openness, there is a particular opportunity for each member to explore his mental states as well as those of the others.

On reflective processes

What I am going to say next owes much to the work of Mary Main (1991) and Peter Fonagy, Howard Steele, Miriam Steele and members of their team (Fonagy *et al.* 1995). As I have already indicated in previous chapters, a compelling model for the transmission of secure attachment is that of 'metacognitive monitoring'. This is the capacity to understand the representational nature of one's own and others' thinking. This involves the capacity to step beyond the immediate reality of experience and grasp the distinction between appearance and reality, between the psychic life of one person and another.

In terms of attachment theory, the parent's reflective capacity, his or her coherent understanding of mental states in the child, is a powerful predictor of the quality of the child–parent relationship. It is then assumed that the adult's capacity to understand other people's mental states is contingent upon the experience of being understood in childhood. A child who has the capacity to perceive that other people (including his parents) have mental states of their own may be more able to regulate his emotional responses and moderate the impact on his self-esteem of negative experiences with the parent.

It is quite possible that group analysis may be an optimal context for the development of reflective capacities. These could be summarized as follows: (1) the capacity to represent oneself and others as having mental states of one's/their own which involve thinking and feeling; (2) the capacity to understand that mental states can be determined by attachment-relevant events, past or present; (3) the capacity to locate the way one has acquired knowledge about an interpersonal event: whether it was through direct observation, inference or information given by others; (4) the capacity to anticipate other people's reactions to one's mental states; and (5) the capacity to acknowledge the complexity of causation in the social world and to recognize that people in relationships mutually influence each other, so that outcomes can be the result of interactions. Linked to this is, the capacity to see that a person's mental states, behaviour and attitudes can change and be influenced by the group situation.

This list should also include the capacity to recognize that

1. observed behaviour may be determined by underlying intrapsychic and interpersonal causes and that these can serve as satisfactory accounts of the former;

2. that people may express different emotions from those they feel;

3. that people may consciously or unconsciously wish to deceive; and

4. that people may not always be fully aware of their motivations and strategies.

As Fonagy *et al.* (1995) suggest: 'only through getting to know the mind of the other can the child develop full appreciation of the nature of mental states. The process is intersubjective: the child gets to know the caregiver's mind as the caregiver endeavours to understand and contain the mental state of the child'.

I believe that a similar dialectical process takes place in group analysis. As a result, the patient is likely to acquire a self-structure capable of containing conflict and distress: that of himself and that of others.

Groups in preventive work

If parental capacity for sensitive responsiveness and reflection is the main predictor of child security – as it seems – and if group analysis can facilitate the development of these capacities, then, we must conclude, group work with parents may be an adequate preventive instrument.

Preventive interventions can be classified in two types: supportive and therapeutic. The supportive approach aims at enhancing parental sensitivity through support, information, feedback and modelling. In parents' groups, peer interaction may enhance these objectives. However, it is possible that with parents who present some form of psychopathology, group work focused on eliciting internal working models of attachment relationships and tracing their origins in the parents' early attachment history may be helpful.

Although not strictly group analytic in orientation, Mel Parr and the organization of which she is Director (PIPPIN: Parents in Partnership – Parent Infant Network) have designed a new form of intervention for men and women becoming parents (Parr 1997). This consists of weekly group meetings for eight weeks in pregnancy, followed by home visits after birth and ten weekly postnatal meetings, until babies are three to five months old. The intervention was initially designed to influence: (1) the capacity of each parent to observe their newborn; (2) the meaning that each parent ascribes to their observations; and (3) each parent's perception of their competence or self-esteem, as an individual and as a parent.

In the group setting, parents value the fact that – instead of being told how to deal with their babies – they are helped to learn from each other (Madeleine Guppy, personal communication). This experience suggests that group work with parents in the period surrounding the birth of a child may facilitate optimal parenting and hence promote mental health in the next generation.

On psychodrama

Psychodrama is a method of group psychotherapy created by Jacob Levy Moreno (1889–1974) which uses theatre as a model. Group members not only talk about their life experiences, they enact them. Since life is about thinking, feeling, acting (and interacting) at the same time, psychodrama re-creates life with thoughts, emotions and actions in an 'as if' space. This is a dimension that Moreno (1972) called 'surplus reality': a reality that represents 'the intangible dimensions of intrapsychic and extrapsychic life'.

Moreno was born in Bucharest, Romania, and studied medicine in Vienna. In 1925 he emigrated to the United States where he developed psychodrama (which is both a theory of the therapeutic process and a method of treating people in group settings). As a theory, psychodrama incorporates some key concepts from psychoanalysis, such as transference. However, it also contains its own set of notions, which are distinct from psychoanalysis. Moreno, like Foulkes, thought that the essence of human beings is social and that one cannot understand a person without taking into account his history and the culture in which he has lived. Moreno believed that the unconscious tracts of several individuals are interlocked: this is what he called 'co-unconscious'. His thinking was also inspired by philosophy, the central point being that at the beginning there was interpersonal action: this is the fundamental matrix. The self emerges from this matrix. His position has been described as existentialist (Marineau 1989).

Moreno, like Kohut, saw empathy as a psychic organizer. He called it 'tele'. This can be defined as 'insight into', 'appreciation of' or 'feeling for' the other person. He believed that a person cannot find himself if not through reciprocal empathy and reflective interaction with others. He expressed this in a poem in which he said: 'I will look at you with your eyes and you will look at me with mine' (Moreno 1972). On this notion Moreno based his technique of 'role reversal', whereby in the course of a dramatization a protagonist exchanges his role with someone else so that a father can become son, a husband wife, an employer employee, and so on.

The psychodrama session evolves in three stages: (1) warm-up, (2) enactment and (3) sharing. During the warm-up group members are encouraged to move from the state of not being ready for acting and playing in the group to that of being ready. In the course of an enactment a scene is represented by a group member, called 'the protagonist'. Other group members may be needed to play complementary roles in the scene: they are called 'auxiliary egos'. Through free associative processes, this scene may gradually unfold to elicit or retrieve other scenes which were underlying the initial scene and that may belong to the protagonist's past or his world of dreams and fantasies. Finally, once the enactment is over, group members share their feelings and thoughts.

The scene has an 'as if' quality: it occurs in a way that symbolically represents reality. Yet it is not reality itself. When a patient selects a group member to be his father, he acts as if this person were his father but simultaneously knows that he is not. When the 'as if' fails, when the auxiliary ego is treated concretely, there is no psychodrama.

Gradually, Moreno instituted formal training in psychodrama in the 1940s. Some French psychoanalysts attended training events at the institute that Moreno set up in Beacon, near New York. As a result of these experiences, these analysts adopted psychodrama as a useful therapeutic tool but placed it more firmly in a psychoanalytic theoretical framework. In this way the 'French school of psychoanalytic psychodrama' was born, having as pioneers prestigious names in the psychoanalytic world, including Mireille Monod, Didier Anzieu and Serge Lebobici. In various hospitals and clinics, psychoanalytic psychodrama began to be used with children, adolescents and adults (Pavlovsky 1988). Clinical experience showed that psychodrama could be useful in working with populations that did not have access to psychoanalysis for socio-economic or clinical reasons, including schizophrenics.

In 1962 psychoanalytic psychodrama began to emerge in Argentina and, by extension, in other South American countries, through the pioneering work of Carlos Martinez Bouquet, Fidel Moccio and Eduardo Pavlovsky. They first published their ideas in 1970, in a book entitled (in Spanish) *Psychoanalytic Psychodrama in Groups*. A number of interesting points were explored in this book, establishing for instance the conceptual distinction between 'acting out' and 'dramatization' (an acting out involves an action that replaces and avoids reflective thinking, which needs to be analysed, whereas a dramatization is a form of analysis that integrates action, bodily movement and emotions with reflective thinking).

I have found psychodramatic work very interesting for several reasons. Analytic inquiry through 'pretend play' seems to be more helpful for people who have poor reflective function and have difficulty in making meaningful connections through verbal means. Playing seems to fill a missing gap between mental states and reflective thinking. Episodic memories can be retrieved and enacted. Often, memories are revived together with intense emotion. Moreno talked about 'catharsis of integration': the act of simultaneously expressing emotions and thinking about their origin and significance.

Often the group creates and re-creates the scene in a way that transforms the raw experience into a playful representation which facilitates a much deeper understanding. For instance, in a session that I conducted, a patient remembered how – during her childhood and adolescence – her father, her siblings and herself desperately tried to dry out her alcoholic mother by taking away and hiding the bottles she bought. The group created a choreographic representation of this person's memories: members of the family were moving around mother, snatching the bottle from her hands again and again, only to see her regaining possession of it. In this way, the protagonist, with lots of tears in her eyes, brought to an area of higher symbolization her episodic memories.

Group experiences with psychotherapists

I have devised a way of offering psychotherapists a group experience to explore their reactions to a modified version of the Adult Attachment Interview. I have experimented with this technique with groups of trained therapists and students in various South American and European cities, with similar results. The group can be formed by anything between 8 and 20 members. It meets for half a day or a whole day, usually on a Saturday. The room used has to be ample, comfortable and allow for privacy and confidentiality.

I initially invite the participants to pair off in such a way that one interviews the other. Questions are asked according to the model established by the Adult Attachment Theory, which I have adapted to: (1) make it more congenial to a clinical interview; and (2) make it applicable to experiential learning rather than research. Once this part of the procedure is completed, we all come together as a group and have an unstructured group discussion (conducted along group analytic lines) to share, evaluate and integrate the material that emerged in the first part of the session.

Perhaps because of the fact that all participants have been, or still are, in therapy, I have never had a casualty or uncontained reaction. Normally, people become very involved with the experience and describe it as surprisingly moving. Of a recent workshop, a group member said: 'I have been in analysis for many years! Yet today I have retrieved a number of very meaningful memories that I have never brought to analysis!'.

In these workshops, participants seem to be able to understand on both a cognitive and emotional level the following points:

1. One's whole attachment history, from birth to the present time (not just earliest events) is relevant to understanding internal working models.

2. Some pathogenic patterns of interaction with important others (particularly with one's parents) seem to extend from earlier times throughout the whole duration of the relationship.

3. One's appraisal of one's attachment history is often organized according to a clear split between a semantic view of important relationships and episodic recollection of past events.

4. The episodic recollection of past events tends to evoke associated emotions in a way that semantic recollection does not.

5. Internal working models are formed in the course of episodes or scenes of one's life and can only be modified if these episodes and their related emotions are revived and relieved.

Of course, what can be gained in the course of a single workshop is not a substitute for years of on-going therapy. However, what in these workshops is revealed to therapists from the innermost areas of their own subjective experience is exactly what this book aims at: highlighting the therapeutic value of empathic responsiveness and historical retrieval within a developmental, social and inter-subjective conception of psychic functioning.

CHAPTER 14

Psychotherapeutic Resources
in General Psychiatry

Introduction

Clinical experience in general psychiatry shows that many patients with severe
pathology report early experiences of trauma, abuse, maltreatment, disturbed
family relations and/or loss. These profound difficulties are often poorly
understood by psychiatrists, nurses and other members of the mental health team.
Therefore, there is no shared framework to design strategies aimed at providing a
secure base from which some reparation – however limited – may take place.

Often, psychiatric services leave a lot to be desired in terms of their capacity to
provide a continuous, reliable and sensitive network for their patients. The reasons
for such failures are partly related to the biological tradition in psychiatry and are
partly political. Within the biological tradition, patients' inner experiences and
life histories tend to be considered as mostly secondary to neurochemical brain
events. On the other hand, the organization and administration of psychiatric
services are often guided by a politics of exclusion rather than by concern with the
needs of the less advantaged section of the population. As Thomas *et al.* (1996)
point out, 'psychiatry cannot be separated from politics. A careful analysis of the
relationship between psychiatry and socio-cultural context makes it difficult to
support the view that we should keep political and psychiatric discourse apart'.
The organization of psychiatric services in many countries is often guided by
economic rather than humanitarian considerations. Public psychiatric provisions
are often basic and mainly aimed at containing the most serious forms of
behavioural disturbance.

I do not intend to explore in detail all these issues in this book. However, I
would like to point out that attachment theory can inform the following areas of
general psychiatry.

1. The study of aetiological factors

There are many theories to explain the aetiology and course of major psychiatric illnesses. In Britain and many other countries, psychiatry is enormously influenced by a biological and neurochemical approach. This approach may have some substance, but it is limited and leaves aside the fundamental importance of developmental, social and attachment aspects of mental illnesses. For instance, there is growing evidence that lack of social support from specific attachment figures in adult life constitutes a significant risk factor in the aetiology of chronic depression (Brown and Moran 1994; Brown et al. 1994).

Many general psychiatrists have been reluctant to accept the validity of the psychoanalytic contribution to understanding many forms of severe mental illness (such as psychosis, depression and personality disorders) on the grounds that the assumptions which substantiate such a contribution cannot be tested by scientific methods. However, developmental research (which is by and large congenial to psychoanalytic thinking) can now provide convincing evidence of the relationship between early attachment disorder and risk factors for psychopathology in later life (e.g. Cicchetti et al. 1990; Kahn and Wright 1980; Patrick et al. 1994; Toth, Manly and Cicchetti 1992).

2. The study of psychotherapeutic interventions aimed at helping patients with major psychiatric disorders

There is a vast literature on the psychoanalytic and group analytic treatment of severe psychiatric disorders, such as psychosis. However, the role of defences against fear of disintegration or annihilation is often emphasized, rather than the early experiences that may have created or increased these anxieties in the first place. Attachment theory can make a contribution to understanding these anxieties and applying such understanding to psychotherapeutic work.

Many general psychiatrists may say that, for the majority of seriously disturbed patients, psychotherapy is ineffectual if not contra-indicated. It is true that a significant number of these patients are unable to engage in conventional forms of psychotherapy, because they lack the capacity to establish a therapeutic alliance and engage with another person in reflective thinking. However, the provision of a secure and caring environment (within which patients can develop enough trust in key members of staff so as to be able to express their innermost feelings and ideas) is essential.

3. The study of mental health care policies

The provision of health care services is not independent of policies determined by governments, health authorities and hospital administrators. Knowledge of attachment theory can be useful for those who hold decision-making power in this field.

Psychotherapy in general psychiatry

Perhaps in many hospital services it may be recognized that psychotherapy can be beneficial to some patients, but the criteria to make psychotherapy referrals are restricted to patients at the less severe end of the psychopathology spectrum. In this section I shall try to demonstrate, on the basis of my own clinical experience, that an attachment-based creative approach to psychotherapeutic intervention in general psychiatry, with patients at the more severe end of the spectrum (such as those suffering from psychosis), may be highly productive.

Psychotic disorders are heterogeneous, and events in the immediate social milieu (particularly the family) in which the patient lives partially predict outcome. In some cases a family-therapeutic approach is essential. Psychological interventions aimed at restoring self-esteem and developing social skills are always necessary.

During a period of 11 years (1980–1991), I was fortunate to hold a post in adult general psychiatry, with in-patient and out-patient duties, in a hospital where there was room for creative work. Although many of my medical colleagues did not fully understand and support my work, I formed a team which included nurses, clinical psychologists and social workers. I was the only psychiatrist in this team. Two attachment-oriented social workers, Tim Root and Wanda Irwin, worked in close association with me. We planned the treatment of psychotic patients as 'case-specific', taking into account the presentation of the illness as well as the therapeutic needs of both the patients and the people closest to them.

We found that a good number of psychotic patients benefited from a psychotherapeutic approach, particularly those whose clinical picture was not dominated by rage and violence, manic excitement or extreme withdrawal.

In the following sections I am going briefly to describe some interventions we made. During those years, I had weekly supervision with John Bowlby and much of my work was inspired by his teaching. In order to preserve confidentiality, I shall change names and alter some other details which are irrelevant to the clinical picture.

LINDA, A WOMAN WITH DE CLERAMBAULT'S SYNDROME

'De Clerambault's Syndrome', also known as 'psychose passionalle' (de Clerambault 1942; Enoch and Trethowan 1979), is generally shown by a woman who has a delusional belief that a man (with whom she may have had little or virtually no contact) is in love with her. The person selected is unattainable. This belief dominates the woman's psychic life. This syndrome is not part of another form of psychosis. The DSM-IV defines it as a 'delusional disorder'. Treatment is extremely difficult as the syndrome tends to become chronic and show poor response to anti-psychotic medication.

Linda was a slim, 28-year-old, blonde, pretty, English woman, married to a very rigid and punitive man. She held a secretarial job, which she could surprisingly maintain, and had a young child who was basically cared for by the paternal grandparents.

I first saw Linda in the waiting area of the hospital where I had my out-patient clinic. She was shaking like a leaf, bending her head forward and holding it with both hands. As soon as she entered the consulting room, she told me that Roger, a local greengrocer was in love with her. She could not meet his demands for affection because she was married. Therefore, Roger had decided to organize a plot – involving hundreds of people – to remind her of his love. One of the things Roger had done was to send her coded messages through car number plates. For instance, a plate with the letters 'RLY' meant 'Roger loves you' and a plate with the letters 'LLM' meant 'Linda loves me', and so on. Linda felt harassed and persecuted. She thought she was suffering from an anxiety state due to real-life events.

Linda also told me that she had previously and unsuccessfully seen two other psychiatrists. First, she had seen Dr X, who gave her neuroleptics, which she took reluctantly. The medication produced extrapyramidal symptoms and did not relieve her persecutory anxiety. Dr X told her that all that nonsense about Roger was purely in her imagination. Having felt misunderstood by Dr X, Linda requested a consultation with another psychiatrist, Dr B.

Dr B insisted that she should take medication and increased the dose of Disipal (orphenadrine hydrochloride), the accompanying antiparkinsonian drug, to control the extrapyramidal symptoms. Moreover, in an attempt to be sympathetic, Dr B said that he did believe in Linda's story. In response, Linda said: 'Then, if you believe in my story, you, being my psychiatrist, must come to the police station, say that I am not mad and get them to restrain Roger!'. When Dr B said that he could not meet her request, Linda felt let down and decided not to have anything more to do with psychiatrists. However, she accepted regular visits by Mrs Ambar Vitae, our community psychiatric nurse, whom she trusted.

Gradually, Linda began to show signs of depression and became suicidal. At that point, Ambar suggested that perhaps I would be able to engage Linda in some form of working alliance. Linda agreed to attend our out-patient department once more and to meet with me.

When I interviewed this patient, my main concern was how to enlist her co-operation. Obviously, neither telling her that she was deluded nor validating her delusion was going to be effective. At that point I remembered that Moreno had devised psychodramatic techniques aimed at working with psychotic patients without initially challenging or colluding with their delusions. I thought that psychodrama, by creating an 'as if' space in between the psychotic world of the patient and external reality, could provide the indispensable link between one and the other.

Thus when the patient asked me: 'Do you agree with Dr X or with Dr B?', I replied: 'Probably with neither of them. I want to know more about the situation. In order to obtain more information, I would like to use a form of theatre. You, me and some other members of staff will become actors and actresses, and then illustrate your story as if it were a play. Do you want to help me?'. Linda accepted my suggestion. So I formed a psychodrama group with one patient (Linda) and five staff members, Wanda Irwin being one of them.

The day Linda arrived to have her first psychodrama session, she was almost as bad as she was when I first met her: very anxious and panicky. Once the session was underway, as we expected, Linda wanted to talk about Roger and his plot. I asked her how it all started. She said, 'One day, in Roger's shop...'. She explained that one day she went to Roger's shop to buy fruit and vegetables. On that occasion, Roger invited Linda to meet for a drink and Linda refused. Since then, Roger, out of hurt, had organized a plot to disturb her.

I then invited Linda to re-create the scene in Roger's shop. She chose a male nurse to act as Roger. She instructed this man to show sexual interest towards her. At some point, I suggested reversing the roles, so that Linda could become Roger, and Roger, Linda. Then, to our great surprise, Linda's anxious state completely faded away. She became sensuous, alive, seductive, almost joyful.

Then, I said: 'This time you go back to play your own role, you are Linda again, but now you decide to accept Roger's advances'.

Linda responded: 'I can't, I am married!'.

I then said: 'Look, Linda, in psychodrama everything is possible, women can become men and men women, young people can become old and old people can become young, dead people can be resurrected and people who are not yet born can be brought to life. This is only theatre! So, let us pretend that you are not married, that you like Roger and that you decide to start a relationship with him'.

Linda accepted my suggestion. In this new scene, she spontaneously behaved in an engaged, sensuous and relaxed manner. She seemed to enjoy the temporary freedom to show a part of herself. This reaction gave me a possible clue: her delusional state had at least two defensive components: projection and reactive formation. The next step would be the exploration of the underlying anxieties. However, I ended the session and invited Linda to come back two days later.

From then on we had three sessions a week for ten weeks. Through psychodrama, we engaged Linda in analytic work. Ten weeks after we started these sessions we felt confident enough to include Linda in a weekly out-patient analytic group. Treatment continued for five years in this group. Occasional marital sessions were also held.

Linda was one of seven children born on a farm. Her mother was often depressed and oscillated between being indifferent towards her children and being punitive, often to the extent of physically abusing them. Linda was the oldest sister and often had to look after her younger siblings. She had no opportunity to play. She felt deprived and resentful. However, looking after her younger siblings ensured her mother's approval.

Linda had to repress any rebellious ideas that she might have had.

Her father was neglectful. He began to abuse Linda sexually when she was 10 and continued to do so until she was 15. Linda felt that the only way she could attract her father's love and attention was through incestuous sex. This she could not discuss with anyone.

Linda did not have peer friendships and never felt she could emotionally rely on anyone. In construing an interpretation of life experiences, she could not rely on others for shared reflective thinking. She perceived herself to be fundamentally bad, someone who did bad things or deserved bad things to happen to her. These feelings, which she could not explain logically, only diminished when she felt persecuted by Roger. So Roger's 'badness' was a projection of her own badness.

At the same time, Linda – because of her past experiences with her father – made an unconscious link between seeking a caring response and seeking sex. Her erotic fantasies compensated for her sense of emotional deprivation but had to be opposed because of their incestuous quality.

At 19, Linda came to live in London and met her husband, the only man she had ever had a relationship with. Her husband was jealous, stern, rigid and lacking in erotic aliveness, empathy and playfulness, but did give her a sense of superficial security because he was always there.

Linda was the only psychotic patient in the slow-open analytic group in which she stayed for five years. The other group members did not treat her as essentially different from themselves and made a good effort to help her explore and reflect upon her attachment history. Linda did make good use of the group. When she decided to leave, her delusions were encapsulated and no longer affected her emotional states. She was calmer and more reflective.

SHEELA, THE UGLIEST WOMAN IN THE WORLD

Sheela was a 20-year-old, articulate, red-haired, tall, slim and pretty English woman who was a student nurse in a well-known London hospital. While undergoing her nursing training, she gradually developed the conviction that she was the ugliest woman in the world.

Sheela began to attract the attention of some of her colleagues and tutors at the hospital where she was training. One of her tutors suggested a psychiatric consultation and Sheela was consequently seen by one of my colleagues, who – being aware of my area of interest – referred her to me.

At the time, in the early 1980s, part of my duties involved working in a psychotherapy in-patient unit for young people. I admitted Sheela to this unit, and for a period of 18 months we held three-times-a-week individual sessions. In addition, she attended community meetings twice weekly as well as art-therapy sessions. Subsequently, for another year, Sheela had once-a-week individual therapy with me as an out-patient.

When I discussed this patient with John Bowlby, he said:

'Look Mario, I don't know very much about psychosis. I guess there may be genetic, neurochemical and early developmental components. However, I would advise you to help this patient to explore her attachment history and elicit her episodic memories. You may find that, by doing so, her symptoms may look after themselves'.

Following Bowlby's advice, I focused on the patient's episodic memories. Sheela was an only child. Her mother died when she was six. The information given to her about the death of her mother was tardy, misleading and scant. Her father was a lonely policeman. He never remarried, had a risky job, was always tense and behaved violently at home. He used to lose his temper easily, particularly if Sheela did not clean the house, cook and keep everything in strict order.

Violence and role reversal dominated the father–daughter relationship. Sheela was intimidated and had 'the ugliest feelings in the world' against her father, but she could not express them.

When Sheela remembered in detail some scenes from her childhood she burst into tears and her sense of fear, humiliation and oppression came alive again. She was able to describe in great detail scenes such as this: 'I was alone, after school, and accidentally spilt milk on the table. I must have forgotten to clean it. My father came back from work, saw the milk on the table, his face went red. He started screaming and threw the bottle over my head. The bottle hit the wall and broke into pieces. I felt terrified. Still it was me who had to say sorry'.

By the end of her therapy, Sheela's idea that she was physically ugly had not completely gone, but there was a waxing and waning of her preoccupation about her belief. She was relaxed and friendly with me, and yet she often challenged me with a very nice sense of humour.

EILEEN, THE CHRONICALLY DEPRESSED WOMAN WHO HAD A SECRET

Eileen was a foreign working-class woman, aged 59. She had never had a child and was married to a cold and unsupportive man towards whom she felt very ambivalent. She was referred to me by another psychiatrist, who sought my clinical opinion. Eileen had suffered from recurrent depression over a period of many years. For two years prior to her consultation with me, she had remained in a state of mild to severe depression without psychotic features. She presented subjective feelings of depression, early waking, lack of energy in the morning, loss of appetite and hopelessness. She had an evening job as a school cleaner, which she kept, but otherwise she would spend most of the day watching television or lying in bed. She had no close friends and her relationship with her husband was tense. My colleague had treated her with antidepressants with no good response.

I offered Eileen weekly sessions. One day she said: 'Doctor, I trust you. I am now going to tell you a secret. This is a secret I have kept to myself for 50 years. In the course of the past few days I've been asking myself: should I tell Dr Marrone or should I not tell him? I think it would make a mockery of my therapy if I did not tell you. When I was nine years of age I killed a child'.

Then she told me that, when she was living in her native country, one sunny afternoon, she and a friend (another child) were walking back home from school and started playing on a river bank. Then she accidentally pushed her friend, who fell in the water and drowned. For the next few days the event was widely publicized in the local newspaper and commented on at school. Whenever she saw a police car in the street she felt they were coming to detain her. She never told anyone how she felt. She lived in fear and guilt for many years. At the age of 20 she decided to leave her country and come to London, partly to make sure that she was not arrested. Her guilt followed her like a shadow.

Eileen said that she could never confide in her parents. Her father was distant and a disciplinarian, her mother always critical of her. So early in life she learned not to talk to anyone about her innermost feelings, problems and worries. Since Eileen had never confided in her husband either, this was the first time she had been able to discuss her personal experiences with someone.

Gradually, in the course of her therapy, Eileen began to feel better and her depression subsided. In my view, the key factor in her improvement was the possibility of forming a relationship with me, feeling understood, feeling she could confide. This quality of relating she had never had before.

MARY, THE WOMAN WHO LOST HER HUSBAND

Mary was 72 at the time of her admission into hospital with the diagnosis of 'dissociative fugue'. She was a tall, slim and erect woman with a self-dignified stance. She lived alone. One night, she went out in her pyjamas, leaving the front door open. She walked a long way to a railway station and managed to get a train ticket to Edinburgh. When she was about to board the train, the fact that she was wearing pyjamas was noticed by a policeman, who approached her. As she could not give a rational explanation for her intended trip, she was brought to our casualty department for a psychiatric assessment. I met her for the first time on the ward the following day. She had returned to the pre-fugue state and had no memory of the events leading to her admission.

During the initial interview, Mary told me that she could not understand what had happened. I offered her daily sessions while she was in the acute admissions ward. In the course of these sessions, she told me that she had recently lost her husband. They had been married for 50 years and had no children. They were always together. She defined the marriage as peaceful: they were ideally suited to each other and never had a tense or conflictual moment. They lived entirely for each other and never had friends.

Bowlby (1980) defined this type of marriage as 'Babes in the Wood', following Mattinson and Sinclair (1979). Bowlby said that in these marriages, should disruption occur, due either to desertion or death, the remaining partner is, as we have seen, acutely vulnerable. Colin Murray Parkes (1996) refers to Stengel's (1939, 1943) studies on pathological wandering as an unconscious way of searching for the lost person. Mary's case seemed to fit this description.

Why would a person have such a 'Babes in the Wood' marriage? And why should that person be at risk of a pathological bereavement? In Mary's case, the problem seemed to centre around her inability to face negative feelings. In the context of her account of her early family environment, such inability was probably related to her parents' incapacity to tolerate, contain and process negative feelings, particularly those arising in the family.

Within a few days, I discharged Mary from the in-patient unit and began to see her weekly in my out-patient clinic. There was no recurrence of her former dissociative state. When we had the opportunity to explore her attachment history, initially she was reluctant to co-operate. However, gradually she began to see that in her original family the only way of living was always to be 'OK'. Hence a superficial sense of well-being was created, which was maintained at the cost of denying any conflict or difficulty between persons inside or outside the family.

I offered Mary early psychotherapeutic intervention as an immediate response to her dissociative breakdown. She responded well. I was glad to act in the way I did. Another psychiatrist would have treated her with medication and done no more than that. On the other hand, should she have been referred elsewhere for analytic psychotherapy at that stage, the whole process would have been much too lengthy. However, the main point I wish to make is this: having spent hours in dialogue with Mary, it was her account of her attachment history which gave me the clues I needed to help her.

ANTHONY

Anthony was a short, overweight, unhappy man in his early 40s who had been diagnosed as schizophrenic. He lived in a grotty flat, being unemployed and having little money. Anthony never had a girlfriend and used to say: 'Doctor, I have no future, I'm too damaged!'. I saw Anthony as an out-patient every week for a short session and more often in periods of in-patient treatment. I kept him on antipsychotic depot injections. He also attended a weekly out-patient group for psychotic patients conducted by Wanda Irwin and Tim Root under my supervision. Occasionally, Anthony requested voluntary admission into the in-patient unit, particularly around Christmas and August when Wanda, Tim and I were on holiday.

Work in Wanda's and Tim's group focused on exploring in detail the patients' attachment relationships, past and present. We noticed that since these psychotic patients had joined this out-patient group, the frequency of their re-admissions had lessened considerably.

Anthony spent the earliest years of his life in a dysfunctional family. He felt that his parents never wanted him. At the age of ten he was chucked out of home and was rescued by a prostitute who took him to live in her flat. She gave him free accommodation on the condition that Anthony went to Soho to find clients for her. Anthony never saw his parents again and lived with this woman for many years. He felt confused about this woman's role in his life: sometimes he described her as caring, sometimes as exploitative.

At the age of 19, Anthony began to develop psychotic symptoms. He was admitted into hospital and then discharged into a hostel for young mentally ill people. Eventually, through help from social services, Anthony was housed in a small council flat, where he led his lonely existence for many years.

Anthony's usual mood was dominated by dejection, gloominess, joylessness and hopelessness. His self-concept centred around a deep-seated sense of inadequacy and worthlessness. He had auditory hallucinations, the voices giving him commands that he had to obey. Anthony had the delusion that he could not be in contact with his parents because they were trapped inside his body. On one occasion the voices told him to release his parents from his inside by cutting his abdomen wide open with a kitchen knife, which he did. As a result he was in a surgical ward for a good length of time. Incidents like this re-occurred before he joined the therapy group. Anthony had extensive scars.

Strikingly, Anthony's speech was fairly coherent and he was able to give clear accounts of his experiences. But he could not make good connections between his emotional states, their interpersonal origins and the impulses which emanated from these states. He attended his weekly group therapy sessions and out-patient psychiatric consultations regularly and punctually. For several years we offered this man the only set of genuinely caring relationships he had ever had. We could not undo the damage he had experienced throughout his early development, but we provided an empathic function that regulated his mood and improved his impulse control, judgement and reality-testing. Empathy involved understanding how badly hurt and let down he felt as a child. One day, many years later, Anthony died of a heart attack.

Multiplicity, dissociation and anxious disorganized attachment

As dissociation is a common element in psychiatric disorders, it may be useful to explore briefly this mechanism at this point. As John Southgate says (personal communication), the defence of dissociation has been most graphically described by Ross (1989) as a little girl up on the ceiling watching herself being abused down below... A more technical definition is in the Diagnostic and Statistical Manual of Mental disorders (DSM IV 300.14) is: (a) the presence of two or more distinct identities or personality states (each with its own relatively enduring pattern of perceiving, relating to and thinking about the environment and self); (b) at least two of these identities or personality states recurrently take control of the person's behaviour; (c) inability to recall important information that is too extensive to be explained by ordinary forgetfulness; (d) the disturbance is not due to the direct physiological effects of a substance such as blackouts or chaotic behaviour during alcohol intoxication or a general medical condition (e.g. complex partial seizures).

Towards the latter end of the 19th century through to the 1920s there was considerable interest in dissociation and multiple personality. Freud and Janet's early research was concerned with many aspects of dissociation. From 1920 to around the 1970s this whole field of interest disappeared. A psychoanalyst Connie Wilber started to work with the famous 'Sybil' (Schreiber 1973). A whole group of psychiatrists and psychotherapists started systematic psychotherapy with this client group and this has gathered pace considerably right up to the present time. There is now an International Society for the Study of Dissociation, with a branch in the UK, Holland and elsewhere. Contemporary psychoanalytic account about dissociation can be found in Mollon (1996) and Davis and Frawley (1994).

Over the last decade or so the centre for Attachment-based Psychoanalytic Psychotherapy has developed its own clinical approach to multiplicity originally under the supervision of John Bowlby. They start with a definition of health which they call the 'associating multiple person'. This would be where the person can free-associate and draw upon internally and externally using different parts of the self where appropriate – infant, child, teenager and grown up parts.

The dialectical opposite state they call the 'dissociating multiple person'. Here the person has coped with extreme traumas often throughout childhood by the defence of dissociation, creating multiple selves dissociated from each other, who each hold a small portion of impossible terror. It may be difficult for the person to control which self is 'up front' in consciousness at any particular time. In this context, one of the goals of therapy is to move from being a 'dissociating multiple person' to being an 'associating multiple person'.

The clinical process between therapist and analysand is to communicate with the various selves, and to jointly bring them on to the 'attachment space' created in the partnership. The narrative and stories will be built up over time and the terror and loss dealt with by what Bowlby implied was nature's cure for loss and trauma, i.e. mourning. This is very condensed version of what is an extremely complicated but also rewarding process. This differs from some of the developments started in the USA since the 1980s where the goal is often described as working towards 'integration'.

Conclusions

Our clinical observations, however anecdotal they may seem, suggest that sensitive responsiveness, understanding and continuity of care by key caregivers may in many cases modify the course of a major psychiatric illness in a favourable way. In this context, the use of specific intervention techniques (including various forms of psychotherapy) may prove to be essential. Compared with what is possible in a private psychotherapy practice, the institutional setting has greater resources to help and contain very disturbed patients. Therefore the selection criteria for psychotherapeutic help can be widened.

In this context, case-specific short- and long-term psychotherapeutic interventions seem to be useful. Although various forms of group therapy may be extremely helpful, I am not suggesting that all patients should be placed in groups without discrimination and sense of purpose. Whatever we do with a patient should be based on the specificity of the case. Attachment-based interventions should provide sensitive responsiveness, continuity of care by specific staff members, focus on resolution of trauma and deprivation, and facilitate the development of reflective thinking. Therefore, important issues for future research are highlighted, such as the relationship between psychotic syndromes and mental representations of early attachment.

PART 4

On Bowlby's legacy

CHAPTER 15

On Bowlby's Legacy

Further Explorations

Nicola Diamond[1]

John Bowlby's battle with the psychoanalytic orthodoxy

Despite the importance of Bowlby's theoretical and clinical findings, for decades the psychoanalytic community at large did not acknowledge his work. As Arieta Slade (1998) points out, it was rare 'to find Bowlby's name or attachment theory mentioned in psychiatric and psychoanalytic texts, written between 1955 and the late 1980s'. Bowlby, through this period, was marginalized by most of his colleagues at the British Psycho-Analytical Society.

Bowlby challenged fundamental tenets of psychoanalytic orthodoxy and did this with directness and clarity. However, in the polarization of the conflict, there have been misunderstandings, such as in relation to Bowlby's rejection of the Kleinian concept of phantasy. This has led some to believe that Bowlby disregarded any role for phantasy in its entirety.

Bowlby was up against the closed nature of the psychoanalytic circles of his time, and he offered a radically different theoretical and clinical orientation, which really went against and questioned prevailing assumptions. Bowlby disagreed with many well-established concepts and language deployed in psychoanalysis. He had a tendency not to linger too long in a language he did not

1   The author of this chapter acknowledges the help provided by Mario Marrone and Malcolm Pines in preparing the manuscript, and is also grateful to Hans Cohn, whose article 'John Bowlby's Concern with the Actual' (1998) provided a useful reference.

fully accept and tended to introduce new premises and vocabulary. He did not have a compromising style; he was an outspoken thinker and writer.

This can be seen in Bowlby's outright rejection of key psychoanalytic presuppositions. As part of his polemic stance, he affirmed attachment as a primary motivational force and relegated sexuality into the background. He rarely interpreted clinical material in oedipal terms. By arguing that attachment is the primary motivator and is independent of feeding and sexuality, Bowlby challenged Freud and Klein on fundamental grounds.

Bowlby rejected the outmoded biology of Freud's day. He particularly found the dynamic and economic points of view untenable. He noted the inadequacy of the notion of instinct gratification as a motivational force for human behaviour because it is based on an energetic discharge model derived from what Bowlby viewed as an out-of-date nineteenth century physics. Bowlby went on to suggest an innovative and necessary shift, that is, to modern developments in biology, evolutionary theory, ethology, cybernetics and information systems, to support his arguments. He concluded that there is a biological disposition in humans to become attached to specific figures, of infant to caretaker, and that the interaction which ensues moderates and modulates the infant's biological, emotional and behavioural responses.

However, perhaps above all, it was Bowlby's criticism of Freud's 1897 about turn – the rejection of seduction theory and the centrality placed on phantasy – that separated him from the psychoanalytic establishment.

As Bowlby stated:

> Ever since Freud made his famous, and in my view disastrous volte-face in 1897, when he decided that the childhood seductions he had believed to be aetiologically important were nothing more than the products of his patients' imaginations, it has been extremely unfashionable to attribute psychopathology to real life experiences. (1986, p.78)

Bowlby's phrase 'extremely unfashionable' is an understatement. This turning point in Freud's thought was seized upon by the emergent psychoanalytic orthodoxy and flourished. It has even been signposted as the key moment of the birth of psychoanalysis proper, the fundamental tenet of what psychoanalysis is about: the study and exploration of phantasy life and 'psychic reality'. In Britain, the exploration of phantasy life is often equated with the study of the internal workings of the mind.

Freud said:

> When I had pulled myself together, I was able to draw the right conclusions from my discovery: namely, that the neurotic symptoms were not related to actual events but to wishful fantasies, and that as far as the neurosis was concerned psychical reality was of more importance than material reality. (1925, p.34)

Here, psychic reality takes precedence over external reality. Bowlby thought that this emphasis is both theoretically incorrect and clinically unproductive. He said: 'the concentration of analytic circles on fantasy and the reluctance to examine the impact of real life events has much to answer for' (1986, p.78). Bowlby disregarded the sacred cow: the primacy of phantasy over and above reality. This has led to some accusing Bowlby of being pre-psychoanalytic in his views, that he was returning to the Freud of the seduction theory.

For Bowlby, however, it was a matter of interaction between the individual and the environment, and – more than that – as a psychiatrist engaged in work with families and children, he observed the impact that the parents' emotional problems had on their children: disturbances in the parents' functioning (and hence in the forming of attachment relationships) will lead to the child's emotional distress and eventual psychopathology. Bowlby placed stress on the effect of real relationships on the child and he rejected the notion that psychopathology emerges from intrapsychic reality.

What perhaps needs to be taken account of is the fact that in the nineteenth century there was a mushrooming of various fields of the human sciences, such as sociology and psychology. The different disciplines fought to be considered distinct fields in their own right, to build an identity that would distinguish one body of knowledge from another. This led to polarization of the fields. Social science claimed social facts as utterly distinct from the study of the individual, the latter being the domain of psychology. Psychoanalysis, in contrast to psychology, has had its unique object of knowledge: the nature of psychic reality. The rigidity of these fields of knowledge had a lot to do with the struggle to preserve a sense of identity.

Some points of contention: a critical exploration

Although Bowlby was right to examine Freud's early discharge model critically, a model which has also been questioned by other quarters of psychoanalysis, it is also the case that Bowlby's reading of Freud was based on the Anglo-American understanding of Freud, this being very much influenced by James Strachey's translation of Freud's work. As Mario Marrone (this volume, Chapter 2) has pointed out, there has been much debate over the translation of the German words *instinkt* and *triebe* ('instinct' and 'drive'). However, this has been made more confusing by James Strachey's slip of the pen, dropping 'drive' and substituting 'instinct' throughout Freud's writings. In the Anglo-American context, this gives a much more biological reductionistic flavour to Freud's writings.

Freud rarely referred to *instinkt* when he described human behaviour. When he used *triebe* he alluded to a pressure that is somewhat indeterminate as regards behaviour and 'object'. The term can be related to the way Freud described the 'instinct' (English translation) as 'lying on the frontier between the mental and the physical' (Freud 1905, p.168), and the way he linked the drive to representation, whereby the human infant represents an object symbolically in its absence.

The drive is oriented to the experience of loss when the breast (and caretaker in the context of the overall relationship) goes absent and the infant develops the capacity to represent the 'object' *in absentia*. Here, the drive is linked to a longing for the 'object' lost (absent 'other'). Reference to the discharge model alone does not capture the inseparable link between the somatic pressure and representation.

French understanding of Freud has a greater appreciation of the sense of drive as not reducible to instinct. The French have, of course, developed their own readings, of great interest but outside the scope of this inquiry.

Another bone of contention with Bowlby's thinking is the very secondary status he gave to sexuality because of his primary emphasis on attachment. Although serving a purpose – to make clear that attachment is a primary motivational system in its own right – Bowlby's position had an unintended consequence: a far too clean division between attachment and sexuality. Although Bowlby recognized the importance of further exploring sexuality, he also realized that he did not have time to examine all aspects of human behaviour that he felt had significance. However, to date, the relationship between sexuality and attachment has not been sufficiently marked on the map.

Bowlby's force of argument for the autonomy of the attachment system has to be seen in the context of the times. Nowadays we do not have to be caught in a 'chicken before the egg' type of argument. Attachment and sexuality are not discrete phenomena in human development. What can be said is that sexuality emerges in the developing infant in the context of the attachment tie. Attachment and sexuality become fundamentally interrelated and overlie each other. This is particularly so considering the fact that actual development is not temporally linear or singular in content, but temporally complex and multifaceted.

Enough has been said to raise sexuality as an issue in the context of attachment theory. I shall return later to elaborate further on this theme, in an attempt to rectify Mario Marrone's omission of this vital topic.

On phantasy

As I have already mentioned, another concern brought up is Bowlby's rejection of the concept of phantasy, which has led some to believe that, since Bowlby disregarded such a fundamental tenet in such an off-hand way, he must have understood very little about what psychoanalysis is all about.

However, what Bowlby rejected is the Kleinian concept of phantasy, and any idea that phantasy is auto-generated from within the individual *ex nilo*. For Klein, phantasy emerged from inherent tendencies. This, for Bowlby, was simply implausible.

Although Bowlby, in public meetings (for instance in his visits to the Institute of Group Analysis), vigorously denounced the place given to phantasy, in supervision he was more moderate (Marrone, personal communication). While rejecting the Kleinian view of phantasy, he would think of phantasy as a way of trying to make sense out of experience. He would also refer to phantasy as a form of secondary elaboration of psychic material, which was used as a way of defending oneself against a damaged sense of self-esteem. Here, we would think more of day-dream and wish-fulfilment types of phantasy.

Of course, Bowlby was not alone in criticizing the Kleinian position for what was seen as its neglect of interpersonal factors. During the 'controversial discussions' (1941–1945; see Chapter 1, this volume) and later in other fora, various psychoanalysts highlighted the importance of interpersonal factors. For instance, in the course of the Freud–Klein controversies, the debate between Susan Isaacs and analysts such as Edward Glover, Sylvia Payne and S.H. Foulkes, was in part about the role of experience in the formation of phantasy perceptions.

Following Susan Isaacs' ideas, phantasy was often conceived of as a pre-verbal expression of body sensations, these becoming the mental representation of instinctual urges. Here, body sensations arise from internal experiences; there is no clear reference to the way these sensory states are experienced in relation to the environment. Edward Glover hotly contended these presuppositions, arguing that phantasy needs to be viewed as a response to frustration, induced as a reaction to real experiences. For Glover, 'experience is before phantasy'. Furthermore, 'to regard phantasy as primary neglected the basic significance of reality factors that were involved in laying down memory traces of sensory experiences' (in Hayman 1994, p.351).

In Glover's view, sensory experience did not arise directly from an internally generated source, but was always mediated by a real experience, which was to do with contact with the real world (i.e. a real feed), which in turn gave rise to a memory trace. It was this memory trace, linked to past experience, that made up the raw material on which phantasy was built.

The 'real feed' to which Glover referred, from the point of view of contemporary developments, cannot be seen as an unmediated experience, because the experience is mediated – and more than that, construed – through the overall quality of relationship and its representational construction.

In the course of a symposium on 'Envy and Jealousy', held at the British Psycho-Analytical Society in 1969, Winnicott and others (unpublished documents) criticized Melanie Klein in what they saw as her determination to make a complete statement of the individual's development without reference to the environment. Winnicott predicted that the problem that Klein's followers were going to have would be that they would not only have to proceed on the basis of her valuable contributions but also on the basis of her denial of something that is nevertheless a fact: the actual influence of the quality of environmental provision.

So far, I have been spelling the word 'phantasy' with a 'ph' rather than an 'f'. The use of the word 'phantasy' (Isaacs 1943) implies that it is the primary content of unconscious mental processes. The term, as it was used by Bowlby, should be spelt with an 'f'.

In fact, from a perspective influenced by Bowlby, it could be argued that, to begin with, what matters a great deal are the parents' fantasies of the child, which are derivatives of their own working models. These pre-conceived ideas (which are not in contact with the child's responses and experiences), that parents bring from their past, directly affect the child's growing self-perceptions.

Fantasy is not opposed to external reality because external reality is not a concrete and unmediated reality, but is construed as a meaning-laden interpersonal field, where language, culture and the interpersonal creation of significance play important roles. Preceding working models and particular ways of elaborating meaning also need to be mentioned. Fantasy emerges in the context of a relationship; it can be seen as part of a transmitted communication. There are intergenerational fantasies which can be pre-verbal – even unsymbolized – and difficult to articulate, which can be powerful and affect the interpersonal exchange.

It is not true to say that Klein disregarded external reality, because in a number of her writings she made sensitive comments about the quality of care and other environmental factors that a child receives and the impact that this may have on the child. For example, Klein said:

> Unpleasant experiences and the lack of enjoyable ones, in the young child, especially lack of happy and close contact with loved people, increase ambivalence, diminish trust and hope and confirm anxieties about inner annihilation and external persecution; moreover, they slow down and perhaps permanently check the beneficial processes through which in the long run inner security is achieved. (1988, p.347)

Here, in this example, she seems to be saying that anxiety and ambivalence can be enhanced, rather than created, by negative interpersonal experiences. Implicitly, she is also suggesting that when this happens resolution is harder to achieve. This is a comment that Bowlby could have partially agreed with. Where he would have differed is in the emphasis given to internal factors in the first place. Evidently, Bowlby would have placed greater stress on the interpersonal situations which created the child's disturbance. He would also have wanted to identify in detail the specific form of interpersonal and family dysfunction.

It is of course true that – within the Kleinian tradition – Bion's work (1959b, 1962b, 1967) has developed an analysis of the relation between the caretaker and the infant and the power of the other in containing and processing the child's emotions. Yet Bowlby put greater emphasis on interactional processes throughout the life cycle. The type of psychoanalysis that Bowlby was questioning (which places emphasis on internal factors over and above interpersonal ones) still has an influence among some psychoanalysts and therapists of different schools.

An independent analyst said in a clinical seminar that she was leading: 'We cannot know if the patient's account of her relationship with her parents is right. We only have her word on it!'. Following this statement, the analyst launched into a series of presuppositions about the patient's destructive intentions. However, the analyst did not convey these presuppositions as such, but made her point as if it were an unquestionable fact. Here she implied that what was valid was not the patient's account but her own wild hunches. This is perhaps a crude example, but it is from life and illustrates what can go wrong.

Some thoughts on exploring the past

Mario Marrone refers to Bowlby's emphasis on the value of exploring the patient's past (see, for instance, Chapter 12). This issue inevitably touches upon complex aspects of psychoanalytic thinking, from Freud onwards. One model in Freud's writings refers to the exploration of the past in terms of 'digging up', using the metaphor of the archaeologist retrieving buried material (Freud 1937b).

Freud, at different points in his life, changed the emphasis on the importance and value of exploring the past. In this later paper (1937b), he returned to some views which have a resemblance to what Bowlby said, because they are based on recollection.

In this paper, Freud also said that both analyst and analysand 'have an undisputed right to reconstruct by means of supplementing and combining the surviving remains' (1937b, p.259). Freud here allowed for a more creative process. The analyst and analysand work together to build a narrative and reflect upon it. We could say that there is a retroactive reconstruction and that the work of 'deferred action' is in operation here – *'nachtraglichkeit'*. This is a term that Freud used to describe a temporality: time is in movement (whereby the recollection of the past takes place as an on-going process, so that the possibility of revision is always there). In other words, the concept of deferred action can be understood as the process of active recollection, which allows for the material to be re-worked. This is a move away from a linear determinism of the past on to the present. What we call 'deferred action' is a process of recall which is not in itself a psychotherapeutic technique but can be used sensitively as part of the analytic dialogue.

However, more than this, what I am suggesting is an understanding of the experience of time: time experienced not as clock time, or as a series of fixed points (representing moments of time) on a line, but rather a temporal process, of time in passing, where the past is not fixed as such but is in movement, re-formed in an on-going organization of experience from the present, which refers to a sense of possibility in the future. Such insights on the question of time and temporality were brought to the fore by developments in phenomenological philosophy that help to make sense of deferred action.

If childhood events dominate the patient's experience, then they do so in the context of what sense the person has made of them, and this involves the narrative that has so far been woven and is still being weaved. However, the capacity to create meaning out of one's experience relates to the kind of understanding received from others, a crucial and central point that cannot be overstressed from an attachment perspective. It is important to note here that Peter Fonagy and colleagues (in their seminal contribution to the topic) put a great deal of emphasis on narrative, the organization of experience and the capacity of reflection which this reveals (see Chapter 6 of this book).

It is of relevance here to mention another and more specific meaning given to 'deferred action': the re-emergence of the trauma later on in life. Laplanche and Pontalis (1983, pp.112–13), in their dictionary, argue that often a trauma cannot be assimilated and comprehended at the time. In their view, it is only at a later date, through complex developmental processes (including sexual-biological maturation and the reshaping of past impressions) that a fresh response to the event emerges and the unassimilated traumatic response is made evident.

A homosexually abused boy I treated (see Diamond 1992a), at the age of 12 had no recollection of the sexual abuse, which occurred when he was 8. It was only one day – when he was 13 – while watching a programme on AIDS (now being a sexually awakened adolescent), that the traumatic response came to life. A series of somatic symptoms then emerged and the boy was eventually admitted to a psychiatric hospital (see discussion of somatic symptoms, Diamond 1992a).

Bowlby's writings did not reflect on the enormous complexity of the problem of recollection and construction in analysis. However, Bowlby was reacting against the denial of lived historical experience in the context of relationships.

As Mario Marrone describes in this book (Chapter 12), such a stance led to an extreme instance, whereby an analyst responded to a patient (who recalled past scenes of his life in a session) by saying: 'I don't know, I wasn't there. I only know what is going on between you and me now!'. In contrast, Bowlby said, 'the stance I advocate is one of "you know, you tell me"' (1988b, p.151).

Attachment theory: a different philosophy

It may sound strange to bring up the subject of philosophy as a theme to be taken up in its own right. Bowlby would more comfortably refer to the biological and behavioural sciences in describing his particular developments and innovations. Yet he was also re-thinking basic assumptions as to the nature and workings of human beings. In doing this, he was making implicit philosophical claims. He radically moved away from the psychoanalytic paradigm he was questioning and began with very different founding principles. Bowlby summarized his views in an elegant passage which recapitulates what we have so far discussed, but which provides the opportunity to take some of the points further:

> When I qualified in psychoanalysis in 1937, members of the British Society were preoccupied in exploring the fantasy world of adults and children, and it was regarded as almost outside the proper interest of an analyst to give systematic attention to a person's real experiences. That was the time when Freud's about turn of 1897 regarding the aetiology of hysteria had led to the view that anyone who places emphasis on what a child's real experiences may be, and perhaps still are being, was regarded as pitifully naive. Almost by definition it was assumed that anyone interested in the external world could not be interested in the internal world, indeed was almost certainly running away from it. To me as a biologist this contrast of internal with external, of organism with environment, never appealed. Furthermore as a psychiatrist engaged in work with children and families... I was daily confronted with the impact on children of the emotional problems from which their parents suffered. (1988b, p.142)

Bowlby broke away from a one-person psychology, which takes the individual as the primary unit of analysis. In so doing, he dispensed of the Cartesian model. Descartes made a split between the individual and the world. This split included a division between the mind and the body. Descartes viewed the individual as an isolate, relating to itself and not to others. The idea of 'intrapsychic reality', distinct from the social world, is implicitly based on Descartes' assumptions, as is the view that the thinking person is separate from the material body.

In the Cartesian frame of reference, these divisions are irreducible. Rather than highlighting certain areas for the purpose of studying them (the mind, the world, the body), these areas are sharply divided. This division is so sharp that it prohibits any connection between different areas. Descartes made an *a priori* distinction, prior to experience and existence.

Indirectly, the Cartesian division has subtly infiltrated modern Western thought, including psychoanalysis. A psychoanalytic perspective which assumes a substantial division between inner and outer, and the idea that experience can be auto-generated, uphold a Cartesian division (Diamond 1996).

Bowlby started off from a different position. For Bowlby the object of study that makes up psychoanalysis is the link itself, the relational tie between persons. There is no split, what is absolutely primary is interpersonal reality.

This means that any reference to 'inner' and 'outer' world is always placed within this relational context. Inner experience is not viewed as a private world which exists in itself, it is fundamentally connected with interpersonal communication. Here, there is a philosophical shift, for inner experience or – for that matter – fantasy, do not precede the experience of being-in-the-world with others, but fully emerge in this context.

Although Bowlby never used the term 'intersubjectivity', he implied its sense. The conception and understanding of intersubjectivity derives from phenomenological philosophy. However, the term 'intersubjectivity' has also been used by developmental psychologists and psychoanalysts (particularly by American psychoanalysts). Nevertheless, the philosophical breadth of the notion has been sometimes misunderstood and misused.

In philosophical terms, intersubjectivity is a basic condition of existence. It is not a quality that can be achieved like a developmental acquisition. It is not a state of relating or a disposition to relate. It is not a psychotherapeutic approach or technique open to choice. It is an inherent state of being-in-the-world.

Intersubjectivity depicts the interactive space itself, as a co-habited space and the foundational opening of human beings to one another. Without a notion of intersubjectivity, psychoanalysis is in difficulty, for it is impossible to envisage how feelings belonging to one individual pass into another. If an individual is conceived of as a discrete entity, inhabiting its own private world, it is certainly difficult to conceive of how a world of others can get into an enclosed individual.

Psychoanalysis has tried to bridge the gap between persons, between inner and outer world, by formulating concepts such as internalization, projection and projective identification. However, without a fundamental link, we have to play at jumping over what is in fact – from an ontological point of view – an irreconcilable gulf (Diamond 1996).

In philosophical terms, this problem rests on the notion of space seen from a geometric Euclidian perspective. In this formulation each individual is assumed to exist as a physical point in space, with a measurable distance existing between one individual and another. The inner space of each individual is likewise situated in this physical geography of space. The 'inner content' of each individual is conceived to be like water inside a glass, which can only be relocated in another glass through some passage procedure. However, we do not exist in relation to each other as mere physical bodies positioned according to distance arrangements (Heidegger 1962, p.79–80). We dwell together. From an intersubjective perspective we exist in a shared space of affective intercourse: there is a fundamental overlapping between one and another.

It needs to be said, as Thomas Ogden (1982, 1994) points out, that – in fact – the process of projection cannot be accounted for without consideration of the fundamental nature of the interpersonal relationship. For what is required for projection is an intersubjective communication of a type whereby feeling states of one person are received (and can be processed) by another.

Certainly, clinical terms such as 'projection' and 'projective identification', deserve recognition for what they are trying to describe. Yet my concern here is with the formulations underlying such concepts: there has to be a basis in intersubjective being.

I suggest that philosophical work had to be done, in order to move away from Descartes' split between the thinking subject and the rest of the world (which made 'thinking' into an introspective, internal, mental affair, separate from our being and doing in the world: a proposition which still haunts important aspects of psychoanalytic theory).

Husserl, the originator of phenomenology (influenced by his teacher Bretano, who introduced the concept of intentionality), argued that thinking is always thinking of something. It is directed to something outside itself (Cohn 1997, pp.10–11). It was Heidegger (1962) who related this orientation towards something, to being in relation to others and the world.

The French phenomenologist Merleau-Ponty, in his paper 'The Child's Relations to Others' (1964), questioned the idea of a psyche that is only accessible to the individual. The subject is not in itself, in some autogenic interiority, but outside – located in a world with others. Merleau-Ponty showed how the infant is primordially open towards others, inhabiting a shared space with fellow humans, expressed directly as an inter-corporeality. It is interesting to note that philosophers such as Merleau-Ponty made it possible to establish links between philosophy and developmental psychology.

Merleau-Ponty and research in early infant development

Merleau-Ponty described how the infant primarily lives in the gestures and meaning of others. He noted that the infant's body is pre-reflectively paired with others. There is direct imitation of facial and bodily gestures. As Nick Crossley (1996) points out, this notion is backed up by recent research into infants' imitation (see, for instance, Meltzoff and Moore 1977, 1983, 1991). Infants are able to imitate adult gestures and are motivated to do so. As early as 42 minutes of age they are able to copy sticking out the tongue.

Crossley (1996, p.51) says:

> It effectively shows that the infant's (lived) body is pre-reflectively paired and thus intersubjectively bonded with that of its other. It sticks out its tongue, in reply to the same action by the other, before it has even realized that it has a tongue, thereby demonstrating a lived sense of corporeal equivalences (your tongue/my tongue) at the very earliest stages of development.

It is in the gestures of others where the infant comes to view its own gesticulations. Donald Winnicott (1971) also considered the way the infant is imaged in the mother's smile. Similarly, Peter Hobson (1993) makes the following comment: 'Merleau-Ponty (1964)… proceeds to stress the simple fact that I live in the facial expression of the other as I see him living in mine' (p.232).

Recent developmental research confirms the notion of the inter-corporeal exchange between infant and caretaker. The infant has a potential for an active role in the interaction. There are many researchers who have contributed to understanding this interaction – Barry Brazelton, Bertrand Cramer, Lynn Murray and Daniel Stern to name some of the most famous – however, it is most pertinent to mention Colwyn Trevarthen's work here. As both a biologist and developmental psychologist, he was the first to import the term 'intersubjectivity' into developmental psychology from phenomenology.

Trevarthen (1979) describes what he calls 'primary intersubjectivity' and the early proto-conversation, which is precisely made up through the interplay of corporeal equivalences between caretaker and infant, based on facial and bodily mimicry, that builds from an intent to communicate into a meaningful exchange. The infant and adult imitate each other's gestures. The adult picks up on the infant's gestures and sounds and perhaps slightly exaggerates them in the return response. The infant mimics the movement and/or sound and adds to it. Through this exchange an understanding and definite communication develops. This interaction cannot be reduced to either participant.

Trevarthen and Hubley (1978) go on to describe 'secondary intersubjectivity', which develops at around six months to a year. This is when the infant can relate to both a person and an object simultaneously, in a way that involves shared references to meaning. Following on from this, games and nursery rhymes become possible. The infant can show greater initiative, and joking (implying an understanding of shared references) or being cheeky come to the fore. He can begin to show an awareness of himself being an actor or taking his mirror image as a playful partner (Reddy et al. 1997). Towards the end of the year, the infant shows increased sensitivity to others, to their emotions and intentions.

Trevarthen stresses that the intersubjective pre-verbal exchange underlies all subsequent communication. He also emphasizes that the human infant is motivated by a need for companionship with other human beings. Before nine months the infant will strike up an interaction with any familiar adult. The singling out of a specific attachment relationship needs to be viewed as only part of the wider motivational focus, the infant's fundamental striving to seek out companionship (Reddy et al. 1997, pp.247–74).

Intersubjectivity in the context of infant development implies specific types of interaction. As a result, intersubjectivity takes on a particular meaning and moves away from the general philosophical description (describing the foundations and fact of our interrelationship with one anther as basic to human existence). In developmental psychology, intersubjectivity has often come to refer to a quality of relating, where sharing, mutuality and attunement are experienced between infant and caretaker (see Stern 1985, pp.128–33). (Trevarthen implies a greater capacity for mutual understanding in secondary intersubjectivity.) However, there has also been an examination of the difficulties that arise in intersubjective relating. When these occur, the experience of shared understanding can be replaced by forms of misattunement.

From an attachment perspective, when there is an emotional impairment in the caretaker's capacity to be sensitively responsive, then the intersubjective conversation will also be disturbed. The still-face procedure, where the mother (or father) holds a blank expression for a short period in the midst of an otherwise normal interaction, will result in the baby's eventual withdrawal. This happens in infants as young as two and three months old (Murray and Trevarthen 1985; Tronick *et al.* 1978). Daniel Stern aptly calls early intersubjective disturbances, 'missteps in the dance' (Stern 1977, p.71). An intrusive caretaker who cannot perceive the infant's cue to reduce stimulation, or in the opposite case under-stimulation, can lead to the infant cutting of human interaction. Lynne Murray and colleagues (Murray 1992; Murray *et al.* 1996) found that postnatal depression was correlated with greater infant insecurity and poorer cognitive performance. Such deterioration in infants' mental functioning has been more generally related to the caretaker's lack of psychological availability and cognitive deficits in the quality of intersubjectivity exchange. There are many forms of attachment disturbance and intersubjective styles of misattunement; what cuts across them all is the difficulty the caretaker has in being sensitive to the infant's feeling states.

Intersubjectivity is the context in which individual development takes place. This means that any reference to 'inner' experience always has a relation to the person's interaction with others.

Organism and environment

Trevarthen and Aitken (1994) document biological findings that the human infant is predisposed to relating to others, to intentionally seeking out contact and communication. The brain already has the neuro-physiological capacities that enable the infant to interact productively with others and their feeling states. Meltzoff and Moore (1977, 1991) provide evidence to show that intercorporeality is innate.

In other words, the human infant is inherently oriented towards sociality and is equipped with physiological resources for that purpose. These findings recast the nature/nurture division, because the human infant is biologically predisposed to sociality.

Bowlby (1986) had been aware, 'that there is potential in the healthy neonate to enter into an elemental form of social interaction' (p.7). For him, the organism always interacts with the environment. In this context, the debate on the 'innate and acquired' dichotomy is entirely false (cf. Bowlby 1969). A biological trait, albeit morphological, physical or behavioural, is a result of interaction with the environment. Some traits become more stable, often due to evolutionary outcome; others are more unstable, malleable and modifiable in the context of cultural influences.

Following the Robertsons' studies of the 1960s (see Chapter 4, this volume), it was noted that prolonged separation increased the child's proneness to infection: the child's immunity to disease was reduced, leading to growth failure, and propensity to ill-health and premature death (see Taylor 1987). Similarly, contemporary attachment research has observed that there is a significant correlation between physiological responses and frequent separations and unstable care of the infant (see, for instance, de Zulueta 1993). As Mario Marrone indicates (see Chapter 4, this volume), there is evidence that biological regulatory functions are reliant on attachment relationships. This is crucial in infancy but important throughout the entire life cycle.

Bowlby was advanced in suggesting that psychoanalysis could benefit from modern biological findings. However, it does need to be pointed out that, within psychoanalysis itself, Freud made reference to the physiological immaturity of the newborn's basic bodily functions, which in turn required a nursing dependency lasting longer than in other mammals. This means that the infant, in attempting to satisfy any biological need, is dependent on a response from a caretaker, who provides what Freud (1895, p.315) calls, 'a secondary function of the highest importance, that of communication'.

Laplanche stresses the way in which the biological processes essential for life (digestion, excretion, homeostasis, and so on) are premature and incomplete in the infant. (Lacan (1966) refers to a 'vital insufficiency'; cf. Evans 1997, pp.85–6.) Laplanche then notes how these functions have to pass, 'from the beginning through intersubjectivity, ie. by way of another human' (1985, p.60); see also Diamond (1992b, pp.22–5). Thus in this context, the environmental provision plays a crucial and deeply influential role.

Mind, body and environment are all intricately connected. In contemporary biological understanding, the traditional splits between mind and body are no longer viable. Paul Martin (1997) explores how thoughts and emotional states can have profound effects on bodily processes, including susceptibility to disease. He examines how the brain and immune system operate in the context of the social environment. Robert Damasio and Gerald Edelmen, both eminent neurobiologists, offer convincing arguments as to the dependency of the mind on the whole body and not the brain alone (Damasio 1994; Edelman 1992).

'Mind', of course, signifies different notions, depending on context. In psychoanalysis, 'mind' relates to a capacity to think, involving an ability to symbolize experience, to put emotions and cognitions into reflective thought. I have been questioning a mind considered in isolation in any sense (even if we work with an interpersonal conception of mind). For that reason Mario Marrone and I think that the use of the word 'mentalization' to refer to reflective processes may need more discussion.

In psychoanalysis, often language can become associated with verbal mental acquisitions alone. What I want to remind us of is the rich nature of language. The 'proto-conversation' that Trevarthen (1979) refers to, is a form of language. Meaning is also created in the non-verbal exchange. In the interaction between caretaker and infant, communication takes place through gestures, movements and sounds well before the baby can articulate words. The non-verbal cannot simply be subsumed to verbal language. Thinking and action develop together.

Attachment and sexuality

From an attachment perspective, sexuality cannot be seen to derive from impulses in a singular body. Attachment locates sexuality in a relationship where the quality of affectionate tie is in play. Attachment moves sexuality away, once and for all, from a one-person psychology.

When there are extreme deprivations of an attachment tie then there will be severe impoverishment in the capacity to engage sexually. We move now to looking at early attachment research. The follow-up study of the Harlow experiment observed that monkeys who had not experienced a living mother could not perform sexually as adolescents or as adults.

The males were completely unable to perform intercourse, even when provided with opportunities to learn from observation. A female monkey would collapse hopelessly on the floor, allowing an able male monkey to penetrate her, but without any active response from her. It was also the case that these female monkeys were unable to mother, rejecting and physically abusing their infants (Harlow and Zimmerman 1959; McKinney 1975; Scharff 1982).

If inferences are to be made from monkey behaviour to that of human behaviour, then the suggestion is that our capacity to make love is related to the emotional and physical bond that was experienced in early infancy. However later relationships can influence the effect of early experiences for better or worse.

A human's capacity to link sexuality to a relationship is bound up with the quality of the attachment experience. The quality of attachment relations have a profound effect on the direction sexuality will take. The nature of the attachment tie(s) affects whether sexuality is organized around 'part-objects' or is connected to an appreciation and concern for the other.

The development of sexuality will be affected by the actual interaction which shapes the affectionate tie or, in other cases (as in sexual abuse), transgresses it altogether. In the latter case, the language of passion is confounded with the language of affection, to borrow from Ferenczi. In this case, a friendly touch is equated with sexual intrusion.

In more subtle situations, under- or over-stimulation can take place. Under-stimulation, which is associated with neglect, involves privation of sensory contact and communication. On the other hand, in over-stimulation (where, for instance, a tickling game can become a definite eroticization), the child is brought to a state of extreme excitement. There is a relationship between the quality of early attachments and the development of bodily experience, including sexuality. This area deserves further discussion and exploration. To develop a relationship between some useful Freudian thinking and attachment understanding, would seem a fruitful field for further thought.

Disturbances in early attachment relationships may correlate with difficulties in forming a relationship with a sexual partner in adulthood. For instance, studies carried out by Hazan and Shaver (1987) indicate that the working models of childhood are likely to influence deeply the type of attachment relationship established with an adult sexual partner. In their findings, secure individuals reported warmer childhood relations with both parents; they were more comfortable with intimacy and more able to trust and depend on other people. In contrast, avoidant individuals experienced greater discomfort with intimacy and closeness and also showed resistance to accepting the partner and depending on him/her.

On the other hand, the anxious-ambivalently attached person expressed feelings of closeness, combined with fears of being abandoned and of not being loved sufficiently. However, Hazan and Shaver also found that if an insecure individual becomes involved with a securely attached partner, then the prospects for the insecure partner are more hopeful.

Sexuality can be used in adult relationships in different ways. Erotization can be an expression of underlying anxious clinging or a substitute for a more substantial sense of intimacy. In other words, erotization can be defensive, a means of trying to deal with emotional disturbances originating in early failures and difficulties in the attachment relationship. This can result in a desperate search for emotional love and a need to be looked after by the other, which underlies the need to be sexually desired, and indeed can take precedence over a sexual means of relating.

Freud's term, 'anaclitic object-choice', refers to the selection of a sexual partner on the basis of the early relation to parental figures as providers of care and protection. These caretaker qualities are what are sought after in the partner. An anaclitic object-choice can be seen to relate to the kind of attachment dilemma referred to above (Freud 1901–1905, p.222; 1914–1916, p.87).[2]

The person may feel that there is no real connection and closeness with the other. He/she may use sex, excitement and seduction to try and make up for a lack of stability and substance in the relationship. Sexual activity can also be associated with avoidance of intimacy, as in the case of a split being made between sex and an emotional relationship: the person can indulge in sex frequently without further involvement. Alternatively, sexual, emotional relationships can be avoided altogether.

Disturbances in attachment ties can be felt not only in the overall mode of relating, but also in sexual affect. This may be apparent, for example, in being unable to orgasm in the sexual act, in withholding (for fear of letting oneself go) or in preferring masturbation (because it is felt to be safer and there is no fear of losing control to the other).

If the parent failed to treat the child as a separate subject with feelings and thoughts, then the growing individual will have serious problems in how he treats himself and others. As shown in previous chapters, attachment research notes that the child recognizes its own feelings through the caregiver's understanding.

Peter Fonagy and colleagues state that the child has the opportunity 'to find himself in the other' (Fonagy *et al.* 1995, p.257). What this means is that, as the parent endeavours to understand and contain the child, through this process the child builds a picture of itself. This occurs when the child and the parent have direct access to each other's subjective states (based in intersubjectivity).

If the parent lacks the capacity to understand that the child has feeling states of his own, then problems arise. As a result, for instance, the child may be unable to perceive subjective emotional states in himself or in others. As an adult, this person is likely to have an impaired capacity to treat himself and others with sensitivity and understanding, as people with independent feeling states. Of course, this impairment is going to show in the sexual relationship.

This situation could be worse. If a child was consistently abused or treated with extreme insensitivity, as an adult this person is likely to treat his sexual partner in the way he was treated. As a result, the sexual partner will not be imbued with subjective feelings, and may even be treated as an object – as in the case of some perversions. Although the trajectory leading to perversion is highly complex, the association between disturbance of early attachment and sexual behaviour is an important area that requires further examination.

---

2   Anaclisis is a specific term which Freud uses. Laplanche (1985) makes it clear that the concept refers to the way sexuality emerges out of the self-preservative functions essential for life, by initially leaning on the biological functions (cf. Diamond 1992b, pp.22–5). Laplanche categorically states that 'anaclisis' is not to be confused with meaning a, 'leaning on the mother…even if such a leaning is observable elsewhere' (Laplanche 1985, p.16). I am not challenging Laplanche's terminological reading of Freud but instead emphasizing that 'such a leaning' is indeed observable elsewhere. For all the self-preservative functions are 'met' in the (intersubjective) situation of an interaction between infant and caretaker. This is the wider context, where the attachment relationship between parent and baby takes place. So even though anaclisis does not refer to attachment in the Bowlby sense, the attachment relationship nevertheless structures the meeting of the infant's biological 'needs' and sexuality develops in this interactive context.

Sexual excitement can also be a way of re-enacting childhood trauma. As Robert Stoller (1986) argues, in certain circumstances hostility acts as a trigger for sexual excitement. Here, hostility in eroticism (the need to induce harm in another person), is understood as a way of trying to deal with childhood traumas. The traumatized person disowns his feelings of being utterly helpless and vulnerable by making the other feel these emotions. The eroticized pleasure is associated with the achievement of 'total' control, of being in the position of master of what is happening.

The choice of sexual partner is another area where repetition of disturbed patterns of attachment are relived. For example, this may be the case with the person who had a cruel father (or mother) and always chooses a cruel partner, repeating the same pattern. Another case would be the individual who had a controlling mother (or father) goes for the controlling lover, re-enacting the experience of infantile helplessness. These observations may seem stereotyped but they are still clinically significant.

In classical psychoanalysis the emphasis was placed on the oedipal relationship and its resolution. Part of this would involve achieving genitality, which was linked to reaching a degree of maturity. From our perspective, 'maturity' in emotional relating and genitality need not go together. Many people have acquired genitality yet they cannot relate with consideration and affection.

Following on from this, a normative assumption has often been made in relation to object choice. Like genitality and its link with maturity, heterosexuality has been associated with a desired and optimal resolution. Yet heterosexuality can involve many types of difficulty in sexual relating. I would argue that what matters most is how each partner treats the other; it is the quality of relating that is important rather than the sex the partner happens to be.

Having said that, I am aware that references to the 'quality of relating' may be interpreted as if I am making moral judgements, as if there were a right way of behaving sexually. What I am stressing here, is that if there is an entire disregard for the feelings and experience of the other in the sexual partnership, then ethical issues arise. Such ethical issues are not to do with moralistic sexual ideas but refer to the sense of responsibility to, and appreciation of, another human being. This specific point does not make reference to, or deny, the fact that sexuality finds very rich and varied forms of human expression.

The role of the mother

Some feminists in the past have been critical of the role given to women as mothers in what is viewed as Bowlby's thought in attachment theory. Bowlby is seen to propagate the idea that women are natural mothers, to encourage women's imprisonment in the home, and thereby to stop women working and achieving greater independence. Also, his views are seen to be part of a movement in psychoanalysis which ends up blaming the mother for all emotional ills.

Bowlby did place an evolutionary link between women and the role of mother in regard to their biological offspring. Moreover, some contemporary attachment theory and research has a tendency to talk too readily about the mother in isolation. Although it is the case that (in the given context of such research work) it is mainly women that mother, this context needs to be treated with critical awareness and the mother should always be situated within her social network.

However, Bowlby's views – taken as a whole – differ from the picture presented by the feminist critique. Moreover, modern attachment research is now taking much more heed of the mother in context and the importance of father and other attachment figures. To sort out this confusion in viewpoints, it is important to offer some brief discussion of the role of mother in Bowlby's thought and in some current developments of feminist understanding.

Bowlby's early paper 'The Nature of the Child's Tie to his Mother' (1958) gave rise to some controversy. In that paper, Bowlby outlined the instinctual responses coming from the child to suck, cling, follow and cry: a repertoire of responses that have an evolutionary basis to ensure the infant's survival. In this paper he implied that the mother is the primary attachment figure. The instinctual behaviour directed to her had the predictable outcome of ensuring the proximity of the mother, resulting in the infant being protected from predators. This behaviour was seen as rooted in an evolutionary heritage from the ancestral days of primitive human beings.

In contrast, Bowlby's later writings showed a change of emphasis. For example, in *A Secure Base* (1988b), although Bowlby still made reference to early mother–infant interaction, he talked much more of both mother and father parenting. Furthermore, he acknowledged that the person who parents can be whoever plays the role of key attachment figure, and he often used the word 'caregiver' rather than 'mother'. He also broadened his position, highlighting the role played by a number of attachment figures and the importance of family processes. He also indicated that parenting does not take place in a vacuum, but is influenced by the social environment. Given the fact that in our society mothers are still likely to be principal caregivers, what matters is the quality of support and sharing of responsibility they receive and are provided with, in forms of child care. This point should not be overlooked.

A note also needs to be made concerning changing ideas in feminism. In the 1970s many feminists tended to reject all biological arguments, as they were associated with justifying the subordination of women on essentialist grounds. That is the argument that women are in nature essentially inferior, and thus there is no possibility of change. Of course, the position which propagates the view of women as naturally inferior to men is still unacceptable to feminists and is implausible in general. However, feminist understanding has become more open to biology, no longer viewing it as a necessary evil.

This shift in view partially relates to changes in the biological sciences, whereby the opposition between nature/nurture is no longer viable, and the interaction of the environment and its effects on biological processes is now recognized. Biology also need not be coupled with reactionary political opinions. In contemporary feminism, the arguments influenced by modern philosophy, which reclaim the importance of the body and its social being, have resulted in a feminism that need no longer deny differences in women's lived bodily experience (cf. Gatens 1983; Young 1990). Such lived differences include pregnancy, giving birth and, for many, taking on the role of mother. This shift in feminist understanding implies that there is space to explore the relation between women's bodily experience and mothering, and that mothering – in this context – is no longer treated as almost a dirty word. However, 'mothering' need not be confined to women, nor should women be confined to such a role (or by it).

Having said this about the feminist argument, I would like to make some critical remarks about Bowlby's evolutionary model. It seems that Bowlby thought that there is compatibility between the biological needs of the child and the mother. However, contemporary evolutionary understanding (see, for instance, Trivers 1974) proposes the existence of genetic conflicts between parent and offspring.

Perhaps Bowlby's evolutionary argument no longer holds. For the environment of primitive man is a far cry from the cultural and ideological modes of organizing the family and justifying the different designations of roles in contemporary society. The imperative of survival to preserve the species is no longer the sole or primary motivating force in our cultural organization of child-rearing.

What is of greater relevance is the interactive model which Bowlby proposed: that although attachment behaviour is in part pre-programmed, it is nevertheless highly influenced by how the child's principal caretakers respond and also who responds to the child's signals. In principle, the father (or any other person for that matter) can be the chief person. Furthermore, as indicated throughout this book, Bowlby always stressed the fact that all years of immaturity (from infancy to adolescence) are most important in the person's developmental history. As the child grows older, the impact of other people in his life will be inevitable. In this social network, cultural factors cannot be underestimated.

Towards a wider perspective

Throughout Bowlby's work, security of attachment is seen to offer the key to well-being and emotional health. Later developments in attachment theory and research have fleshed out the particular features and quality of the early relationship that permits the optimal development of the infant and young child. There is no doubt that this area of work has largely contributed to our understanding of human development and will continue to do so. However, there is the risk – as found with every approach – of closure and reductionism to key axioms if a debate on different perspectives is not kept open.

One such area of different orientation that I wish to mention is the psychoanalytic view that places stress on the fragmentary nature of human experience and fragile sense of personal identity. This is a strand of thinking which exists in various forms throughout psychoanalysis. It is perhaps most evident in French schools of psychoanalytic thought that have a very different understanding of subjectivity from the Anglo-American readings of Freud.

From a more critical perspective it may appear that the notion of attachment security implies a certain ideal of health, where feelings of uncertainty and unsettling states are no longer an issue. However, it needs to be said that even from an attachment viewpoint, parenting is inevitably imperfect and some of the mismatches that take place in interaction are unavoidable.

To repeat the well-known phrase of Winnicott, the most we can expect is that the environmental provision will be 'good enough'. In consequence, there will always be some interplay between stability and instability in subjective states, even in the more secure individual. With greater resources the person is more able to acknowledge less comfortable states and emotionally reflect upon them.

Attachment theory has been consolidated by empirical research, so much so that without research findings the theory would not have the strength it currently has. However, as with any discipline, empirical work has its own limitations. Empirical work without a psychoanalytic understanding may become a system of objective measures devoid of a meaningful context. Bowlby himself never lost sight of the fact that what he was studying also required an interpretive approach. He gave evidence of this approach in his last major work, a book on Darwin (Bowlby 1991).

Bowlby did not fail to recognize the contribution that the humanities and social sciences could make to his paradigm. He was aware of the need for scientific rigour. However, we could call Bowlby a realist rather than a empiricist. A realist believes in scientific method but recognizes that observation involves selection and interpretation as well as theoretical presuppositions. Within this framework, it is held that scientific truths can be discovered and that although facts do not speak for themselves, there are such things. Realists also appreciate the importance of interpreting meaningful behaviour in the study of human interaction. In other words, realism is a more sophisticated scientific approach than pure empiricism.

There is in Bowlby a belief in the scientific method that more accurately conforms to a realist orientation. Yet in his understanding of human experience and relations, he implicitly showed an affiliation with developments in phenomenological thought. This point raises epistemological questions which require further exploration and discussion.

intro

References

Agazarian, Y. and Peters, R. (1981) *The Visible and Invisible Group*. London: Routledge & Kegan Paul.

Ainsworth, M.D.S. (1967) *Infancy in Uganda: Infant Care and the Growth of Love*. Baltimore: The Johns Hopkins University Press.

Ainsworth, M.D.S. (1969) 'Object relations, dependency and attachment: a theoretical review of the infant–mother relationship.' *Child Development 40*, 969–1025.

Ainsworth, M.D.S., Blehar, M.C., Waters, E. and Wall, S. (1978) *Patterns of Attachment: A Psychological Study of the Strange Situation*. Hillsdale, NJ: Erlbaum.

Bakermaus-Kranenburg, M.J. and Van Ijzendoorn, M.H.(1993) 'A psychometric study of the Adult Attachment Interview: reliability and discriminating validity.' *Developmental Psychology 29*, 870–879.

Balint, M. (1952) *Primary Love and Psycho-Analytic Technique*. London: Tavistock.

Bartholomew, K. and Horowitz, L. (1991) 'Attachment styles among young adults: a test of a four-category model.' *Journal of Personality and Social Psychology 61*, 226–244.

Bartrop, K., Luckhurst, E., Lazarus, L., Kiloh, L.G. and Perry, R. (1977) 'Depressed lymphocyte function after bereavement.' *Lancet 1*, 834–836.

Bellak, L., Hurvich, M. and Gediman, H.K. (1973) *Ego Functions in Schizophrenics, Neurotics and Normals*. New York: John Wiley & Sons.

Belsky, J., Woodworth, S. and Crnic, K. (1961) 'Troubled family interaction during toddlerhood.' *Development and Psychopathology 8*, 477–495.

Benedek, T. (1938) 'Adaption to reality in early infancy.' *Psychoanalysis Quarterly 7*, 200–214.

Bifulco, A., Brown, G.W. and Harris, T. (1994) 'Childhood experience of care and abuse (CECA): a Retrospective Interview Measure.' *Child Psychology and Psychiatry, 35*, 1419–1435.

Bifulco, A., Lillie, A. and Brown, G.W. (1994) *Manual of the Attachment Style Interview*.

Bifulco, A.T., Moran, P., Brown, G.W. and Ball, C. (1997) Cognitive coping and onset of depression in vulnerable London women (MS).

Bion, W. (1957) 'Differentiation of the psychotic from the non-psychotic personalities.' *International Journal of Psycho-Analysis 38*, 266–275.

Bion, W. (1959a) *Experiences in Groups*. New York: Basic Books.

Bion, W. (1959b) 'Attacks on linking.' *International Journal of Psycho-Analysis 40*, 308–315.

Bion, W.R. (1962a) *Learning from Experience*. London: Heinemann.

Bion, W.R. (1962b) 'A theory of thinking.' *International Journal of Psycho-Analysis 43*, 306–310.

Bion, W. (1967) *Second Thoughts*. London: Heinemann.

Blatz, W.E. (1966) *Human Security: Some Reflections*. Toronto: University of Toronto Press.

Bowlby, J. (1940) 'The influence of early environment in the development of neurosis and neurotic character.' *International Journal of Psycho-Analysis 1*, 154–178.

Bowlby, J. (1944) 'Forty-four juvenile thieves: their characters and home life.' *International Journal of Psycho-Analysis 25*, 1–57 and 207–228. Reprinted (1946) as monograph. London: Bailiere, Tindall and Cox.

Bowlby, J. (1951) Maternal care and mental health. Geneva: *World Health Organisation Monograph Series* (No. 2).

Bowlby, J. (1958) 'The nature of the child's tie to his mother.' *International Journal of Psycho-Analysis 39*, 350–373.

Bowlby, J. (1960a) 'Separation anxiety.' *International Journal of Psycho-Analysis 41*, 89–113.

Bowlby, J. (1960b) 'Grief and mourning in infancy.' *The Psychoanalytic Study of the Child 15*, 3–39.

Bowlby, J. (1960c) 'Ethology and the development of object relations.' *International Journal of Psycho-Analysis 41* (parts II–III), 313–317.

Bowlby, J. (1965) *Child Care and the Growth of Love*, 2nd edn. London: Penguin Books.

Bowlby, J. (1969) *Attachment and Loss. Vol. I: Attachment*. London: Hogarth Press.

Bowlby, J. (1973) *Attachment and Loss. Vol. 2: Separation*. London: Hogarth Press.

Bowlby, J. (1975) 'Attachment theory, separation anxiety and mourning.' In D.A. Hamburg and K.H. Brodie (eds) *American Handbook of Psychiatry*, 2nd. edn, Vol. IV. New Psychiatric Frontiers.

Bowlby, J. (1977) 'The making and breaking of affectional bonds (I: Aetiology and psychopathology in the light of attachment theory; II: Some principles of psychotherapy).' *British Journal of Psychiatry 130*, 201–210 and 421–431.

Bowlby, J. (1980) *Attachment and Loss. Vol. 3: Loss, Sadness and Depression*. London: The Hogarth Press and New York: Basic Books.

Bowlby, J. (1982) 'Attachment and loss: retrospect and prospect.' *American Journal of Orthopsychiatry 44*, 9–27.

Bowlby, J. (1985a) 'The role of childhood experience in cognitive disturbance.' In M.J. Mahoney and A. Freeman (eds) *Cognition and Psychotherapy*. London and New York: Plenum Publishing Corp.

Bowlby, J. (1988a) 'Developmental psychiatry comes of age.' *American Journal of Psychiatry 145*, 1–10.

Bowlby, J. (1988b) *A Secure Base. Clinical Applications of Attachment Theory*. London: Routledge.

Bowlby, J. (1990) *Charles Darwin: A New Life*. London: Hutchinson.

Bowlby, J. and Durbin, E. (1939) *Personal Aggressiveness and War*. London: Kegan Paul.

Bretherton, I. (1985) 'Attachment theory: retrospect and prospect.' In I. Bretherton and E. Waters (eds) *Growing Points in Attachment Theory and Research. Monograph of the Society for Research in Child Development 50*, (Serial No. 209).

Bretherton, I. (1991) 'The roots and growing points of attachment theory.' In C.M. Parkes, J. Stevenson-Hinde and P. Marris (eds) –Attachment Across the Life-Cycle. London: Routledge.

Brown, G.W. and Harris, T.O. (1993) 'Aetiology of anxiety and depressive disorders in an inner-city population. 1. Early adversity.' *Psychological Medicine 23*, 143–154.

Brown, G.W. and Moran, P. (1994) 'Clinical and psychological origins of chronic depressive episodes (I: A community survey).' *British Journal of Psychiatry 165*, 447–456.

Brown, G.W., Harris, T.O., Hepworth, C. and Robinson, R. (1994b) 'Clinical and psychosocial origins of chronic depressive episodes (II: A patient enquiry).' *British Journal of Psychiatry 165*, 457–465.

Byng-Hall, J. (1985) 'The family script: a useful bridge between theory and practice.' *Journal of Family Therapy 7*, 301–305.

Byng-Hall, J. (1986) 'Family scripts. A concept which can bridge child psychotherapy and family therapy thinking.' *Journal of Child Psychotherapy 12*, 2, 3–13.

Byng-Hall, J. (1988) 'Scripts and legends in families and family therapy.' *Family Process 27*, 167–179.

Byng-Hall, J. (1991) 'The application of attachment theory to understanding and treatment in family therapy.' In C.M. Parkes, J. Stevenson-Hinde and P. Marris (eds) *Attachment Across the Life Cycle*. London: Routledge.

Byng-Hall, J. (1995) *Rewriting Family Scripts*. New York: The Guilford Press.

Carlson, V., Cicchetti, D., Barnett, D. and Braunwold, K. (1989) 'Disorganised/disoriented attachment relationships in maltreated infants.' *Developmental Psychology 25*, 525–531.

Cicchetti, D. (1994) 'Advances and challenges in the study of the sequelae of child maltreatment.' *Development and Psychopathology 6*, 1–3.

Cicchetti, D. and Bukowski, W.M. (1995) 'Developmental processes in peer relationships and psychopathology.' *Development and Psychopathology 7*, 587–589.

Cichetti, D., Cummings, M., Greenberg, M. and Marvin, R. (1990) 'An organizational perspective on attachment theory beyond infancy: implications for theory, measurement and research.' In M. Greenberg, D. Cicchetti and M. Cummings (eds) *Attachment in the Preschool Years*. Chicago: University of Chicago Press.

Cohn, H. (1997) *Existential Thought and Therapeutic Practice*. London: Sage.

Cohn, H. (1998) 'John Bowlby's concern with the actual.' *Journal of the Society for Existential Analysis (published by the Society of Existential Analysis).* In press.

Coie, J., Terry, R., Lennox, K., Lochman, J. and Hyman, C. (1995) 'Childhood peer rejection and aggression as predictors of stable patterns of adolescent disorder.' *Development and Psychopathology 7,* 697–713.

Colin, V.L. (1996) *Human Attachment.* Philadelphia: Temple University Press.

Couch, A. (1995) 'Anna Freud's adult psychoanalytic technique: a defence of classical analysis.' *International Journal of Psycho-Analysis 76,* 153–171.

Craik, K. (1943) *The Nature of Explanation.* Cambridge: Cambridge University Press.

Crittenden, P. (1992) 'Treatment of anxious attachment in infancy and early childhood.' *Development and Psychopathology 4,* 575–602.

Crossley, N. (1996) *Intersubjectivity.* London: Sage Publications.

Damasio, A.R. (1994) *Descartes' Error.* New York: Crosset Putnam.

Davies, J.M. and Frawley, M.G. (1994) *Diagnostic and Statistical Manual of Mental Disorders* (DSM IV 300.14).

de Clerambault, C.G. (1942) *Les Psychoses Passionelles. Oeuvre Psychiatrique.* Paris: Presses Universitaires.

de Maré, P., Piper, R. and Thompson, S. (1991) *Koinonia: From Hate through Dialogue, to Culture in the Large Group.* London: Karnac.

de Zulueta, F. (1993) *From Pain to Violence.* London: Whurr Publishers.

Diamond, N. (1992a) 'Sexual abuse: the bodily aftermath.' *Free Association 25,* 71–83.

Diamond, N. (1992b) 'Biology.' In E. Wright (ed) *Feminism and Psychoanalysis: A Critical Dictionary.* Oxford: Blackwell.

Diamond, N. (1996) 'Can we speak of internal and external reality?' *Group Analysis, 29,* 303–316.

Dozier, M. and Kobak, R.R. (1992) 'Psychophysiology in attachment interviews: converging evidence for deactivating strategies.' *Child Development 63,* 1473–1480.

Durkin, H.E. (1964) *The Group in Depth.* New York: International Universities Press.

Edelman, G.M. (1992) *Bright Air, Brilliant Fire.* New York: Basic Books.

Eagle, M. (1984) *Recent Developments in Psychoanalysis.* Cambridge, MA: Harvard University Press.

Eagle, M. (1995) 'The developmental perspectives of attachment and psychoanalytic theory.' In S. Goldberg, R. Muir and J. Kerr (eds) *Attachment Theory: Social, Developmental and Clinical Perspectives.* New York: Analytic Press.

Enoch, M.D. and Trethovan, W.H. (1979) *Uncommon Psychiatric Syndromes.* Bristol: John Wright & Sons Ltd.

Evans, D. (1997) *An Introductory Dictionary of Lacanian Psychoanalysis.* London and New York: Routledge.

Ezriel, H. (1963) 'Experimentation within the psycho-analytic session.' In L. Paul (ed) *Psychoanalytic Interpretation.* New York: The Free Press of Glencoe (The Macmillan Co.).

Fairbairn, W.R.D. (1952) *Psychoanalytic Studies of the Personality.* London: Routledge & Kegan Paul.

Fonagy, P. (1996) 'Discussion of Peter H. Wolff's paper "Irrelevance of infant observation for psychoanalysis".' *Journal of the American Psychoanalytic Association 44,* 2, 404–422.

Fonagy, P., Steele, M., Steele, H., Moran, G. and Higgitt, A. (1991) 'The capacity for understanding mental states: the reflective self in parent and child and its significance for security of attachment.' *Infant Mental Health Journal 13,* 201–218.

Fonagy, P., Steele, H. and Steele, M. (1991) 'Maternal representation of attachment during pregnancy predicts infant–mother attachment at one year.' *Child Development 62,* 891–905.

Fonagy, P., Higgitt, A., Moran G., Steele, H. and Steele, M. (1991) 'Measuring the ghosts in the nursery: a summary of main findings of the Anna Freud Centre–University College London Parent–Child Study.' *Bulletin of the Anna Freud Centre 14,* 115–131.

Fonagy, P., Steele, M., Steele, H., Leigh, T., Kennedy, R., Mattoon, G. and Target, M. (1995). 'Attachment, the Reflective Self and Borderline States: the predictive specificity of the Adult Attachment Interview and pathological emotional development.' In S. Goldberg, R. Muir and J. Kerr (eds) *Attachment Theory: Social, Developmental and Clinical Perspectives.* Hillsdale, NJ: The Analytic Press.

Fonagy, P., Steele, M., Kennedy, R., Mattoon, G., Leigh, T., Steele, H., Target, M. and Gerber, A. (1996) 'The relation of attachment states, psychiatric classification and response to psychotherapy.' *Journal of Consulting and Clinical Psychology 64*, 22–31.

Fonagy, P., Steele, M., Steele, H. and Target, M. (1997) *Reflective-Functioning Manual (version 4.1) for Application to Adult Attachment Interviews.* Unpublished manual. Sub-Department of Clinical Health Psychology, University College London.

Foulkes, E. (ed) (1990) *S.H. Foulkes, Selected Papers: Psychoanalysis and Group Analysis.* London: Karnac.

Foulkes, S.H. (1964) *Therapeutic Group Analysis.* London: George Allen & Unwin Ltd.

Foulkes, S.H. (1974) 'My philosophy in psychotherapy.' *Journal of Contemporary Psychotherapy 6*, 109–114. In S.H. Foulkes (1990) *Selected Papers.* London: Karnac Books.

Foulkes, S.H. (1975) *Group Analytic Psychotherapy.* London: Interface (Gordon and Breach Science Publishing Ltd).

Foulkes, S.H. (1977) 'Notes on the concept of resonance'. In L.R. Wolberg and M.L. Aronson (eds) *Group Therapy 1977: An Overview.* New York: Stratton.

Fraiberg, S., Adelson, E. and Shapiro, V. (1975) 'Ghosts in the nursery: a psychoanalytic approach to the problems of impaired mother–infant relationships.' *Journal of the American Academy of Child Psychiatry 14*, 387–421. Reprinted in S. Fraiberg (ed) (1980) *Clinical Studies in Infant Mental Health: The First Year of Life.* London: Tavistock Publications.

Franz, C.E., McClelland, D.C. Weinberg, J. and Peterson, P. (1994) 'Parenting antecededents of adult adjustment: a longitudinal study.' In C. Perris, W.A. Arrindell and M. Eisemann (eds) *Parenting and Psychopathology.* Chichester: Wiley.

Freud, A. (1972) *Problems of Psycho-Analytic Technique and Therapy.* London: The Hogarth Press.

Freud, S. (1893–1895) *Studies on Hysteria.* SE 2. London: The Hogarth Press.

Freud, S. (1895) *Project for a Scientific Psychology.* In J. Strachey (ed) *The Standard Edition of the Complete Psychological Works of Sigmund Freud.* SE 1. London: The Hogarth Press.

Freud, S. (1901–1905) *Three Essays on Sexuality.* SE 11. London: The Hogarth Press.

Freud, S. (1905 [1901]) *Fragment of an Analysis of a Case of Hysteria.* SE 7. London: The Hogarth Press.

Freud, S. (1911) *Formulations on the Two Principles of Mental Functioning.* SE 12. London: The Hogarth Press.

Freud, S. (1914–1916) *On Narcissism: An Introduction.* SE 14. London: The Hogarth Press.

Freud, S. (1916–1917) 'Some thoughts on development and regression.' In *Introductory Lectures on Psycho-Analysis.* Part III. SE 16. London: The Hogarth Press.

Freud, S. (1920) *Beyond the Pleasure Principle.* SE 23. London: The Hogarth Press.

Freud, S. (1925) *An Autobiographical Study.* SE 20. London: The Hogarth Press.

Freud, S. (1926) *Inhibitions, Symptoms, and Anxiety.* SE 20. London: The Hogarth Press.

Freud, S. (1937a) *Analysis Terminable and Interminable.* SE 23. London: The Hogarth Press.

Freud, S. (1937b) *Constructions in Analysis.* SE 23. London: The Hogarth Press.

Gatens, M. (1983) 'A critique of the sex/gender distinction.' *Intervention* (Beyond Marxism?) *17*.

George, C., Kaplan, N. and Main, M. (1985) *Adult Attachment Interview* Unpublished manual. Department of Psychology, University of California, Berkeley.

Goldstein, W.N. (1991) 'Clarification of Projective Identification.' *American Journal of Psychiatry 148*, 2, 153–161.

Greenson, R.R. (1994) *The Technique and Practice of Psychoanalysis.* London: The Hogarth Press.

Gribbin, J. (1985) *In Search of Schrodinger's Cat.* London: Corgi Books.

Grinberg, L. (1956) 'Sobre algunos problemas de tecnica psicoanalitica determinados por la identificacion y contraidentificacion proyectiva.' *Revista de psicoanalisis 13*, 507–511.

Grinberg, L. (1979) 'Projective counteridentification and countertransference.' In L. Epstein and A. Feiner (eds) *Countertransference.* New York: Jason Aronson.

Grosskurth, P. (1987) *Melanie Klein: Her World and Her Work.* Cambridge, MA: Harvard University Press.

Hamilton, V. (1985) 'John Bowlby: an ethological basis for psychoanalysis.' In J. Reppen (ed) *Beyond Freud: A Study of Modern Psychoanalytic Theorists.* New York: Analytic Press.

Harlow, H. (1958) 'The nature of love.' *The American Psychologist 3,* 673–685.

Harlow, H.F., and Harlow, M.K. (1966) 'Learning to love.' *American Scientist 54,* 244–272.

Harlow, H.F. and Zimmerman, R.R. (1959) 'Affectional responses in infant monkeys.' *Science 130,* 421–432.

Harris, T., Brown, G.W. and Bifulco, A. (1990) 'Loss of parent in childhood and adult psychiatric disorder: a tentative overall model.' *Development and Psychopathology 2,* 311–328.

Harris, T. (1992) 'Some reflections on the process of social support and the nature of unsupportive behaviour.' In H.O.F. Veiel and V. Bauman (eds) *The Meaning and Measurement of Social Support.* Washington: Hemisphere Publishing Corporation.

Harris, T., Brown, G.W. and Robinson, R. (1997) Befriending as an intervention for chronic depression among women in an inner city (MS).

Harwood, I.N.H. and Pines, M. (1998) *Self Experiences in Group.* London: Jessica Kingsley Publishers.

Haymann, A. (1994) 'Some remarks about the "Controversial Discussions".' *International Journal of Psycho-Analysis 75* (2), 343–358.

Hazan, C. and Shaver, P. (1987) 'Romantic love conceptualised as an attachment process.' *Journal of Personality and Social Psychology 52,* 511–524.

Heidegger, M. (1962) *Being and Time.* Oxford: Blackwell.

Hobson, P. (1993) *Autism and the Development of Mind.* Hove (East Sussex): Lawrence Erlbaum Associates Ltd.

Hoffer, M.A. (1984) 'Relationships as regulators: a psychobiologic perspective on bereavement.' *Psychosomatic Medicine 46,* 3, 183–197.

Hoffman, M. (1994a) 'Le role de l'initiative dans le developpment emotionel precoce.' *Psychiatrie de L'enfant 37,* 1, 179–213.

Hoffman, M. (1994b) 'De la iniciativa a la experiencia.' *Clinica Psicologica 3,* 249–261.

Hoffman, M. (1995) 'Espejamiento.' *Revista de la Asociacion Argentina de Psicoligia y Psicoterapia de Grupo 18,* 1, 81–115.

Hopper, E. (1981) *Social Mobility: A Study of Social Control and Insatiability.* Oxford: Blackwell.

Isaacs, S. (1948) 'The nature and function of phantasy.' *International Journal of Psycho-Analysis 29,* 73–97.

Karen, R. (1990) 'Becoming attached.' *The Atlantic,* February, 35–70.

Karen, R. (1994) *Becoming Attached.* New York: Warner Books.

Khan, J. and Wright, S. (1980) *Human Growth and the Development of Personality* (3rd. ed.). London: Pergamon Press.

Khan, M. (1963) 'The concept of cumulative trauma.' *Psychoanalytic Study of the Child 18,* 283–306.

King, P. and Steiner, R. (1991) *The Freud–Klein Controversies 1941–45.* London & New York: Tavistock/Routledge.

Klein, M. (1952) 'The origins of transference.' *International Journal of Psycho-Analysis, 33,* 433–438.

Klein, M. (1975) 'Notes on some schizoid mechanisms.' In M. Klein, *Envy and Gratitude and Other Works: 1946–1963.* New York: Basic Books.

Kohut, H. (1971) *The Analysis of the Self.* New York: International Universities Press.

Kohut, H. (1977) *The Restoration of the Self.* New York: International Universities Press.

Kohut, H. (1979) 'The two analyses of Mr. Z.' *International Journal of Psycho-Analysis 60,* 3–27.

Kohut, H. (1980) 'Summarizing reflections.' In A. Goldberg (ed) *Advances in Self Psychology.* New York: International Universities Press.

Kohut, H. (1984) *How Does Analysis Work?* Chicago: The University of Chicago Press.

Kraemer, G.W. (1985) 'Effects of differences in early social experience on primate neurobiological-behavioural development.' In M. Reite and T. Field (eds) *The Psychobiology of Attachment and Separation.* London: Academic Press.

Kuhn, T.S. (1962) *The Structure of Scientific Revolutions.* Chicago: University of Chicago Press.

Lacan, J. (1953–1954) *Le Seminaire. Livre 1. Les ecrits techniques de Freud, 1953–1954.* J.-A. Miller. Paris: Seuil, 1975. *The Seminar. Book I. Freud's Papers on Technique, 1953–1954.* (translation and notes by John Forrester). Cambridge: Cambridge University Press, 1987.

Lacan, J. (1954–1955; published 1988) *The Seminar. Book II. The Ego in Freud's Theory: 1954–1955.* Translation by Sylvana Tomasell, notes by John Forrester. New York: Norton.

Lacan, J. (1966) *Ecrits.* Paris: Sevil.

Lacan, J. (1981) *The Four Fundamental Concepts of Psycho-Analysis.* New York: W.W. Norton and Co.

Laing, R.D. (1960) *The Divided Self.* London: Tavistock.

Laing, R.D. (1961) *The Self and Others.* London: Tavistock.

Laing, R.D. and Esterson, A. (1964) *Sanity, Madness and the Family.* London: The Hogarth Press.

Laplanche, J. (1985)*Life and Death in Psychoanalysis* (translated and introduced by J. Mehlman). Baltimore and London: Johns Hopkins University Press.

Laplanche J. and Pontalis, J.B. (1983) *The Language of Psycho-Analysis.* London: The Hogarth Press.

Lichtenberg, J. and Wolf, E.S. (1997) On self-psychology. Unpublished paper presented at the meeting of British independent psychoanalysts and American self-psychologists, London, July 1997.

Lieberman, A. (1992a) 'Attachment theory and infant–parent psychotherapy: some conceptual, clinical and research considerations.' In D. Cicchetti and S. Toth (eds) *Models and Integrations: Rochester Symposium on Developmental Psychopathology.* Rochester: University of Rochester Press.

Lieberman, A.F. (1992b) 'Infant–parent psychotherapy with toddlers.' *Development and Psychopathology* 4, 559–574.

Lindsay, D.S. and Read, J.D. (1994) 'Psychotherapy and memories of childhood sexual abuse: a cognitive perspective.' *Applied Cognitive Psychology 8,* 281–338.

Locke, J. [1693] (1964) 'Some thoughts concerning education.' In P. Gay (ed) *John Locke on Education.* New York: Bureau of Publications, Teacher's College, Columbia University.

Lorenz, K. (1952) *King Solomon's Ring.* London: Methuen.

Lyons, R.K., Connell, D., Zoll, D. and Stahl, J. (1987) 'Infants at social risk: relationship among infant maltreatment, maternal behaviour and infant attachment behaviour.' *Development and Psychopathology 23,* 223–232.

Mahler, M.S., Pine, F. and Bergman, A. (1975) *The Psychological Birth of the Human Infant.* New York: Basic Books.

Main, M. (1991) 'Metacognitive knowledge, metacognitive monitoring, and singular (coherent) vs multiple (incoherent) model of attachment: findings and directions for future research.' In C.M. Parkes, J. Stevenson-Hinde and P. Marris (eds) *Attachment Across the Life Cycle.* London: Routledge.

Main, M. (1995) 'Recent studies in attachment: overview, with selected implications for clinical work.' In S. Goldberg, R. Muir and J. Kerr (eds) *Attachment Theory: Social, Developmental and Clinical Perspectives.* Hillsdale, NJ: The Analytic Press.

Main, M. and Goldwyn, R. (1985) *Adult Attachment Scoring and Classification System.* Unpublished scoring manual. Department of Psychology, University of California, Berkeley.

Main, M. and Hesse, E. (1990) 'Parents' unresolved traumatic experiences are related to infant disorganised attachment status: is frightened and/or frightening parental behaviour the linking mechanism?' In M. Greenberg, D. Cicchetti and E.M. Cummings (eds) *Attachment in the Preschool Years.* Chicago: University of Chicago Press.

Main, M. and Solomon, J. (1986) 'Discovery of a new, insecure–disorganized–disoriented attachment pattern.' In T.B. Brazelton and M. Yogman (eds) *Affective Development in Infancy.* Norwood: Ablex.

Main, M. and Solomon, J. (1990) 'Procedures for identifying infants as disorganized/ disoriented during the Ainsworth Strange Situation.' In M. Greenberg, D. Cicchetti and E.M. Cummings (eds) *Attachment in the Preschool Years: Theory, Research and Intervention.* Chicago: University of Chicago Press.

Main, M. and Stadtman, J. (1981) 'Infant response to rejection of physical contact with the mother: aggression, avoidance and conflict.' *Journal of the American Academy of Child Psychiatry 20,* 2992–3007.

Main, M. and Weston, D. (1981) 'The quality of the toddler's relationship to mother and father: related to conflict behaviour and the readiness to establish new relationships.' *Child Development 52*, 932–940.

Marineau, R.F. (1989) *Jacob Levy Moreno 1989–1974*. London and New York: Tavistock/Routledge.

Marris, P. (1991) 'The social construction of uncertainty.' In C. Murray Parkes, J. Stevenson-Hinde and P. Marris (eds) *Attachment Across the Life Cycle*. London: Routledge.

Marris, P. (1996) *The Politics of Uncertainty: Attachment in Private and Public Life*. London and New York: Routledge.

Marrone, M. (1982) 'Notas acerca del nivel proyectivo en analisis de grupos.' *Acta Psiquiatrica y Psicologica de America Latina 28*, 319–327.

Marrone, M. (1984) 'Aspects of transference in group analysis.' *Group Analysis 17*, 3, 179–194.

Marrone, M. (1994) 'Attachment theory and group analysis.' In D. Brown and L. Zinkin (eds) *The Psyche and the Social World*. London and New York: Routledge.

Marrone, M. and Pines, M. (1990) 'Group analysis.' In I.L. Kutash and A. Wolf (eds) *Group Psychotherapist's Handbook*. New York: Columbia University Press.

Martin, P. (1997) *The Sickening Mind*. London: Harper Collins.

Martinez Bouquet, C., Moccio, F. and Pavlovsky, E. (1970) *Psicodrama Psicoanalitico en Grupos*. Buenos Aires: Kargieman.

Marvin, R.S. (1977) 'An ethological-cognitive model for the attention of mother–child attachment behaviour.' In T. Alloway, P. Pliner and L. Krames (eds) *Attachment Behaviour*. New York: Plenum.

Mattinson, J. and Sinclair, I.A.C. (1979) *Mate and Stalemate: Working with Marital Problems in a Social Services Department*. Oxford: Blackwell.

McKinney, W.T. (1975) 'Psychoanalysis revisited in terms of experimental primatology.' In E.T. Adelson (ed) *Sexuality and Psychoanalysis*. New York: Brunel Mazel.

Meares, R.A. and Hobson, R.F. (1977) 'The persecutory therapist.' *British Journal of Medical Psychology 50*, 349–359.

Meltzoff, A. and Moore, M. (1977) 'Imitation of facial and manual gestures by human neonates.' *Science 198*, 75–78.

Meltzoff, A. and Moore, M. (1983) 'Newborn infants imitate adult facial gestures.' *Child Development 54*, 702–709.

Meltzoff, A. and Moore, M. (1991) 'Cognitive foundations and social functions of imitation and intermodal representation in infancy.' In M. Woodhead, R. Carr and P. Light (eds) *Becoming a Person*. London: Routledge.

Merleau-Ponty, M. (1964) *Phenomenology of Perception*. London: Routledge and Kegan Paul.

Mollon, P. (1996) *Multiple Selves, Multiple Voices*

Moreno, J.L. (1972) 'Psychodrama.' In H.I. Kaplan and B.J. Sadock (eds) *Sensitivity through Encounter and Marathon*. New York: E.P. Dutton and company

Murray, L. (1992) 'The impact of postnatal depression on infant development.' *Journal of Child Psychology and Psychiatry 33*, 543–561.

Murray, L., Fiori-Cowley, A., Hopper, R. and Cooper, P. (1996) 'The impact of post-natal depression and associated adversity on early mother–infant interactions and later outcome.' *Child Development 67*, 2512–2526.

Murray, L. and Trevarthen, C. (1985) 'Emotional regulation of interactions between 2 month olds and their mothers.' In T.M. Field and N.A. Fox (eds) *Social Perception in Infants*. Norwood, NJ: Ablex.

Ogden, T.H. (1982) *Projective Identification and Psychotherapeutic Technique*. New York: Jason Aronson.

Ogden, T.H. (1994) *Subjects of Analysis*. London: Karnac.

O'Connor, M.J., Sigman, M. and Brill, N. (1987) 'Disorganization of attachment in relation to maternal alcohol consumption.' *Journal of Consulting and Clinical Psychology 55*, 831–836.

Parkes, C.M. (1991) 'Attachment, bonding and psychiatric problems after bereavement in adult life.' In C.M. Parkes, J. Stevenson-Hinde and P. Marris (eds) *Attachment Across the Life Cycle*. London: Routledge.

Parkes, C.M. (1995) 'Edward John Mostyn Bowlby 1907–1990.' *Proceedings of the British Academy 87*, 247–261.

Parkes, C.M. (1996) *Bereavement: Studies of Grief in Adult Life., Third Edition.* London: Routledge.

Parr, M. (1997) Description of a study evaluating a new approach to preparation for parenting for women and men in the transition to parenthood (unpublished).

Patrick, M., Hobson, P., Castle, D. Howard, R. and Maugham, B. (1994) 'Personality disorder and the mental representation of early social experience.' *Development and Psychopathology 6*, 375–388.

Paulley, J.W. (1982) Pathological mourning: a key factor in psychopathogenesis of auto-immune disorders. Paper presented at the 14th European Congress on Psychosomatic Research, 1982.

Pavlovsky, E. (1988) 'Psicodrama analitico. Su historia. Reflexiones sobre los movimientos frances y argentino.' *Lo Grupal 6*, 11–54.

Pearson, J.L., Cohn, D.A., Cowan, P.A. and Pepe Cowan, C. (1994) Earned and continuous-security in adult attachment: relation to depressive symptomatology and parenting style. *Development and Psychopathology 6*, 359–373.

Perris, C. (1994) 'Linking the experience of dysfunctional parental rearing with manifest psychopathology: a theoretical framework.' In C. Perris, W.A. Arunell and M. Eisemann (eds) *Parenting and Psychopathology.* Chichester: John Wiley & Sons.

Peterfreund, E. (1978) 'Some critical comments on psychoanalytic conceptualizations of infancy.' *International Journal of Psycho-Analysis 59*, 427–441.

Peterfreund, E. (1983) *the Process of Psychoanalytic Therapy.* Hillsdale, NJ: The Analytic Press (Lawrence Erlbaum Associates).

Pettingale, K.W., Hussein, M. and Tee, D.E.H. (1994) 'Charges in immune status following bereavement.' *Stress Medicine 10*, 3, 145–150.

Phares, V. and Compas, B.E. (1992) 'The role of fathers in child and adolescent psychopathology: make room for daddy.' *Psychological Bulletin 3*, 3, 387–412.

Piaget, J. (1952) *The Origins of Intelligence.* New York: International Universities Press.

Piaget, J. (1954) *The Construction of Reality in the Child.* New York: Basic Books.

Quinton, D. and Rutter, M. (1976) 'Early hospital admission and later disturbances of behaviour: an attempted replication of Douglas' findings.' *Developmental Medicine and Child Neurology 19*, 447–459.

Rapaport, D. (1960) 'The structure of psychoanalytic theory.' *Psychological Issues.* Monograph 6. New York: International University Press.Rayner, E. (1990) *the Independent Mind in British Psychoanalysis.* London: Free Association Books.

Rayner, E. (1990) *The Independent Mind in British Psychoanalysis.* London: Free Association Books.

Reddy, V., Hay, D. Murray, L. Trevarthen, C. (1997) 'Communication in infancy: mutual regulation of affect and attention.' In G. Bremmer, A. Slader and G. Butterworth (eds) *Infant Development: Recent Advances.* Hove: Psychology Press.

Roberts, J. and Kraemer, S. (1996) 'Introduction: holding the thread.' In S. Kraemer and J. Roberts (eds) *The Politics of Attachment.* London: Free Association Books.

Robertson, J. (1953) *A Two-Year-Old Goes to Hospital.* Film. University Park, PA: Penn State Audio Visual Services. UK, Ipswich: Concord.

Robertson, J. and Robertson, J. (1967) 'Kate, aged two years five months, in foster care for twenty-seven days.' Film. Young Children in Brief Separation Film Series. University Park, PA: Penn State Audio Visual Services. UK, Ipswich: Concord.

Robertson, J. and Robertson, J. (1968) 'Jane, aged seventeen months in foster care for ten days.' Film. *Young Children in Brief Separation Film Series.* University Park, PA: Penn State Audio Visual Services. UK, Ipswich: Concord.

Robertson, J. and Robertson, J. (1969) 'John, aged 17 months, for nine days in a residential nursery.' Film. *Young Children in Brief Separation Film Series.* University Park, PA: Penn State Audio Visual Services. UK, Ipswich: Concord.

Robertson, J. and Robertson J. (1971) 'Thomas, aged two years four months, in foster care for ten days.' Film. *Young Children in Brief Separation Film Series.* University Park, PA: Penn State Audio Visual Services. UK, Ipswich: Concord.

Roberston, J. and Robertson, J. (1973) 'Lucy, aged twenty-one months in foster care for nineteen days.' Film. *Young Children in Brief Separation Film Series.* University Park, PA: Penn State Audio Visual Services. UK, Ipswich: Concord.

Robertson, J. and Robertson, J. (1989) *Separation and the Very Young.* London: Free Association Books.

Ross, O.A. (1989) *Multiple Personality Disorder.* New York: John Wiley and Sons

Rousseau, J.J. (1762) *Emile, or Education.* (B. Foxley trans.) London (1948): J.M. Dent and Sons.

Rutter, M. (1981) *Maternal Deprivation Reassessed.* 2nd Edition. London: Penguin.

Rutter, M. (1995) 'Clinical implications of attachment concepts: retrospect and prospect.' *Journal of Child Psychology and Psychiatry 36,* 4, 549–571.

Sandler, J. with Anna Freud (1985) *The Analysis of Defense: The Ego and the Mechanisms of Defense Revisited.* New York: International Universities Press.

Scharff, D.E. (1982) *The Sexual Relationship.* London: Routledge.

Schleifer, S.J., Keller, S.E., Meyerson, A.T., Raskin, M.D., Davis, K.L. and Stein, M. (1983) 'Lymphocyte function in major depressive disorder.' *General Psychiatry 42,* 129–133.

Schreiber, F.R. (1973) *Sybil.* London: Penguin

Slade, A. (1997) 'The implications of attachment theory and research for the theory and practice of adult psychotherapy.' In J. Cassidy and P.R. Shaver (eds) *Handbook of Attachment Theory and Research.* New York: Guilford.

Slade, A. (1998) 'Representaion, symbolization and affect regulation in a concomitant treatment of a mother and child: Attachment theory and child psychotherapy.' *Psychoanalytic Inquiry.* In press.

Smith, P.B. and Pederson, D.R. (1988) 'Maternal sensitivity and patterns of infant–mother attachment.' *Child Development 59,* 1097–1101.

Spitz, R.D. (1950) 'Anxiety in infancy: A study of its manifestations in the first year of life.' International Journal of Psycho-Analysis, 31, 138–143.

Spratt, M.L. and Denney, D.R. (1991) 'Immune variables, depression and plasma cortisol over time in suddenly bereaved patients.' *Journal of Neuropsychiatry and Clinical Neuroscience 3,* 299–306.

Spreker, S.J. and Booth, C.L. (1988) 'Maternal antecedents of attachment quality.' In J. Belsky and T. Nezworski (eds) *Clinical Implications of Attachment.* Hillsdale, NJ: Lawrence Erlbaum Associates.

Sroufe, L.A. and Waters, E. (1977a) 'Attachment as an organizational construct.' *Child Development 48,* 1184–1189.

Sroufe, L.A. (1988) 'A developmental perspective on day care.' *Early Childhood Research Quarterly 3,* 283–291.

Sroufe, L.A. (1997) Lecture at St George's Hospital, London.

Stengel, E. (1939) 'Studies on the psychopathology of compulsive wandering.' *British Journal of Medical Psychology 18,* 150.

Stengel, E. (1943) 'Further studies on pathological wandering.' *Journal of Mental Sciences 89,* 224.

Stephen, K. (1941) 'Aggression in early childhood.' *British Journal of Medical Psychology 18,* 178–190.

Stern, D.N. (1977) *The First Relationship.* Cambridge, MA: Harvard University Press.

Stern, D.N. (1985) *The Interpersonal World of the Infant.* New York: Basic Books.

Stern, D.N. (1995) *The Motherhood Constellation.* New York: Basic Books.

Stoller, R.J. (1986) *Perversion: The Erotic Form of Hatred.* London: Karnac Books. (First printed: Maresfield Library, London).

Sutherland, J.D. (1980) 'The British object relations theorists: Balint, Winnicott, Fairbain, Guntrip.' *Journal of the American Psychoanalytic Association 28,* 4, 829–860.

Szasz, T.S. (1963) 'The concept of transference.' *International Journal of Psycho-Analysis 44,* 432–443.

Taylor, G.J. (1987) *Psychosomatic Medicine and Contemporary Psychoanalysis.* Madison: International University Press.

Thomas, P., Romme, M. and Hamellijnck (1996) 'Psychiatry and the politics of the underclass.' *British Journal of Psychiatry 169,* 401–404.

Trevarthen, C. (1979) 'Communication and co-operation in early infancy. A description of primary intersubjectivity.' In M. Bullara (ed) *Before Speech: The Beginning of Human Communication*. London: Cambridge University Press.

Trevarthen, C. and Aitken, K.J. (1994) 'Brain development, infant communication and empathy disorders: intrinsic factors in child mental health.' *Development and Psychopathology 6*, 597–663.

Trevarthen, C. and Hubley, P. (1978) 'Secondary intersubjectivity: confidence, confiding and acts of meaning in the first year.' In A. Lock (ed) *Action, Gesture and Symbol: The Emergence of Language*. London: Academic Press.

Tronick, E., Als, H., Adamson, L., Wise, S. and Brazelton, T.B. (1978) 'The infant's response to intrapment between contradictory messages in face-to-face interaction.' *Journal of Child Psychiatry 17*, 1–13

Troy, M. and Sroufe, L.A. (1987) 'Victimisation among preschoolers: Role of attachment relationship theory.' *Journal of the American Academy of Child and Adolescent Psychiatry 26*, 166–172.

Tulving, E. (1972) 'Episodic and semantic memory.' In E. Tulving and W. Donaldson (eds) *Organization of Memory*. New York: Academic Press.

Tulving, E. (1985) 'How many memory systems are there?' *American Psychologist 40*, 385–398.

Urban, J., Carlson, E., Egeland, B. and Sroufe, L.A. (1991) 'Patterns of individual adaption across childhood.' *Development and Psychopathology 3*, 445–460.

van Ijzendoorn, M.H. (1995) 'Adult attachment representation, parental responsiveness and infant attachment: a meta-analysis of the predictive validity of the Adult Attachment Interview.' *Psychological Bulletin 117*, 3, 387–403.

Waddington, C.H. (1957) *The Strategies of the Genes*. London: Allen and Unwin.

Waelder, P. (1956) 'Introduction to the discussion on problems of transference.' *International Journal of Psycho-Analysis 37*, 366–367.

Watzlawick, P., Helmick B., Jackson, D.D. (1967) *Pragmatics of Human Communication*. New York: W.W. Norton and Co.

Weiner, H. (1984) *Human Relationships in Health, Illness and Disease*. Paper presented at the Fourth Stockholm Conference on 'Person–Environment Interaction', Stockholm, Sweden, 1984.

Weiss, R.S. (1975) *Marital Separation*. New York: Basic Books.

Winefield, H.R., Tiggemann, M. and Winefield, A.H. (1994) 'Parental rearing behaviour, attributional style and mental health.' In C. Perris, W.A. Arrindell and E. Eisenn (eds) *Parenting and Psychopathology*. Chichester: John Wiley & Son.

Winnicott, D.W. (1976) *The Maturational Processes and the Facilitating Environment*. London: The Hogarth Press (first edition 1965).

Winnicott, D.W. (1971) *Playing and Reality*. New York: Basic Books.

Young, I.M. (1990) *Throwing like a Girl and Other Essays in Feminist Philosophy and Social Theory*. Bloomington and Indianapolis: Indiana University Press.

Further Reading

Ainsworth, M.D.S. (1967b) 'The effects of maternal deprivation: a review of findings and controversy in the context of research strategy.' In *Deprivation of Maternal Care: A Reassessment of its Affects.* Public Health Papers No. 4. Geneva: World Health Organization.

Ainsworth, M.D.S. Attachment: retrospect and prospect. In C.M. Parkes and J. Stevenson-Hinde (eds) *The Place of Attachment in Human Behaviour.* London: Tavistock.

Ainsworth, M.D.S. (1984) 'Attachment.' In N.S. Endler and J.McV. Hunt (eds) *Personality and the Behavioral Disorders, Vol.1,* pp.559–602. New York: Wiley.

Ainsworth, M.D.S. (1985) 'Attachments across the life span.' *Bulletin of the New York Academy of Medicine 61,* 792–812.

Ainsworth, M.D.S. (1989) 'Attachments beyond infancy.' *American Psychologist 44,* 709–716.

American Psychiatric Association (1994) *DSM-IV.*

Andrey, R. (1962) 'Paternal and maternal roles in delinquency.' In *Deprivation of Maternal Care: A Reassessment of its Effects.* Geneva: World Health Organization.

Anisfeld, E., Casper, V., Nozyce, M. and Cunningham, N. (1990) 'Does infant carrying promote attachment? An experimental study of the effects of increased physical contact on the development of attachment.' *Child Development 61,* 1617–1627.

Arend, R., Grove, F. and Sroufe, L.A. (1979) 'Continuity of individual adaption from infancy to kindergarten: a predictive study of ego-resiliency and curiosity in preschoolers.' *Child Development 50,* 950–959.

Arsenian, J.M. (1943) 'Young children in an insecure situation.' *Journal of Abnormal and Social Psychology 38,* 225–229.

Auerbach, J.S. and Blatt, S.J. (1996) 'Self-representation in severe psychopathology: the role of reflexive self-awareness.' *Psychoanalytic Psychology 13,* 297–341.

Bacal, H.A. and Newman, K.M. (1990) *Theories of Object Relations: Bridges to Self Psychology.* New York: Columbia University Press.

Bakwin, H. (1942) 'Loneliness in infants.' *American Journal of Diseases of Children 63,* 30–40.

Balint, M. (1964) *Primary Love and Psychoanalytic Technique.* London: Tavistock.

Balint, M. (1968) *The Basic Fault.* London: Tavistock.

Balint, M. (1986) 'The unobtrusive analyst.' In G. Kohon (ed) *The British School of Psychoanalysis.* London: Free Association.

Bartholomew, K. (1990) 'Avoidance of intimacy: the attachment perspective.' *Journal of Social and Personal Relationships 17,* 147–178.

Bates, J., Maslinh, C. and Frankel, K. (1985) 'Attachment security, mother–child interaction, and temperament as predictors of behaviour problem ratings at age three years.' In I. Bretherton and E. Waters (eds) *Growing Points in Attachment Theory and Research. Monographs of the Society for Research in Child Development. 50 (Serial No. 209).*

Bell, R. (1968) 'A reinterpretation of the direction of effects in studies of socialization.' *Psychological Review 75,* 81–95.

Bell, R. and Ainsworth, M.D.S. (1972) 'Infant crying and maternal responsiveness.' *Child Development 43,* 1171–1190.

Belsky, J. (1984) 'The determinants of parenting: a process model.' *Child Development 55,* 83–96.

Belsky, J. and Isabella, R.A. (1988) 'Maternal, infant and social-contextual determinants of attachment security.' In J. Belsky and T. Nezworski (eds) *Clinical Implications of Attachment.* Hillsdale, NJ: Erlbaum.

Belsky, J. and Nezworski, T. (1988) *Clinical Implications of Attachment.* Hillsdale, NJ: Erlbaum.

Belsky, J., Youngblade, L. and Pensky, E. (1990) 'Childrearing history, marital quality, and maternal affect: intergenerational transmission in a low-risk sample.' *Development and Psychopathology 1,* 291–304.

Birtchnell, J. (1984) 'Dependence and its relation to depression.' *British Journal of Medical Psychology 57,* 215–225.

Blum, H.P. (1996) 'Seduction trauma: representation, deferred action, and pathogenic development.' *Journal of the American Psychoanalytical Association 44,* 4, 1147–1164.

Bornstein, M. and Lamb, M. (1992) *Development in Infancy: An Introduction,* 3rd edn. New York: McGraw-Hill, Inc.

Bouchard, T.J. and McGue, M. (1990) 'Genetic and rearing environmental influences on adult personality; an analysis of adopted twins reared apart.' *Journal of Personality 58,* 1, 263–292.

Bowlby, J. (1949) 'The study and reduction of group tension in the family.' *Human Relations 2,* 2, 123–128.

Bowlby, J. (1956) 'Psychoanalytic instinct theory.' In J.M. Tanner and B. Inhelder (eds) *Discussions in Child Development.* London: Tavistock Publications.

Bowlby, J. (1961) 'Processes of mourning.' *International Journal of Psychoanalysis 42,* 4–5, 317–340.

Bowlby, J. (1967) 'Foreword.' In M.D.S. Ainsworth (ed) *Infancy in Uganda: Infant Care and the Growth of Love.* Baltimore: Johns Hopkins.

Bowlby, J. (1978) 'Attachment theory and its therapeutic implications.' In S.C. Feinstein and P.L. Giovacchini (eds) *Developmental and Clinical Studies.* New York: Jason Aronson.

Bowlby, J. (1979) *The Making and Breaking of Affectional Bonds.* London and New York: Routledge.

Bowlby, J. (1981a) 'Contribution to symposium "E. Peterfreund on information and systems theory".' *The Psychoanalytic Review 68,* 187–190.

Bowlby, J. (1981b) 'Psychoanalysis as a natural science.' *International Review of Psychoanalysis 8,* 3, 243–256.

Bowlby, J. (1984a) 'Discussion of paper "Aspects of transference in group analysis" by Mario Marrone.' *Group Analysis 17,* 191–194.

Bowlby, J. (1984b) 'Violence in the family as a disorder of the attachment and caregiving systems.' *American Journal of Psychoanalysis 44,* 9–27.

Bowlby, J. (1985b) The role of the psychotherapist's personal resources in the treatment situation. Unpublished manuscript.

Bowlby, J. (1987) Early days at the London child guidance clinic and training centre. Unpublished manuscript.

Bowlby, J. (1989a) 'The role of attachment in personality development and psychopathology.' In S. Greenspan and G. Pollock (eds) *The Course of Life.* Madison: International University Press.

Bowlby, J. (1989b) Foreword to Emmy Gut's book. *Productive and Unproductive Depression.* London: Tavistock/Routledge.

Bowlby, J., Figlio, K. and Young, R. (1990) 'An interview with John Bowlby on the origins and reception of his work.' *Free Associations 21,* 36–64.

Brazelton, T.B. (1983) *Infants and Mothers: Differences in Development.* New York: Delta (rev. edn.).

Brazelton, T.B. and Cramer, B. (1991) *The Earliest Relationship.* London: Karnak.

Brazelton, T.B., Koslowski, B. and Main, M. (1974) 'The origins of reprocity: The early mother–input interaction.' In M. Lewis and L. Rosenblums (eds) *The Effect of the Infant on its Caregiver.* New York: Wiley.

Bretherton, I. (1987) 'New perspectives on attachment relations: security, communication, and internal working models.' In J. Osofsky (ed) *Handbook of Infant Development, 2nd edn. New York: Wiley.*

Bretherton, I. (1992) 'The origins of attachment theory: John Bowlby and Mary Ainsworth.' *Developmental Psychology 28,* 759–775.

Brooks Brenneis, C. (1996) 'Memory systems and the psychoanalytic retrieval of memories of trauma.' *Journal of the American psychoanalytical Association 44,* 4, 1165–1187.

Brown, G. and Harris, T. (1978) *The Social Origins of Depression.* London: Tavistock.

Brown, G.W., Harris, T.O. and Eales, M.J. (1993) 'Aetiology of anxiety and depressive disorders in an inner-city population. 2. Comorbidity and adversity.' *Psychological Medicine 23*, 155–165.

Bryer, J., Nelson, B., Miller, J. and Krol, P. (1987) 'Childhood sexual and physical abuse as factors in adult psychiatric illness.' *American Journal of Psychiatry 144*, 1426–1430.

Burlingham, D. and Freud, A. (1942) *Young Children in Wartime London.* London: Allen & Unwin.

Burlingham, D. and Freud, A. (1944) *Infants without Families.* London: Allen & Unwin.

Burnham, D.L. (1965) 'Separation anxiety.' *Archives of General Psychiatry 13*, 346–358.

Byng-Hall, J. (1980) 'Symptom bearer as marital distance regulator.' *Family Process 19*, 335–365.

Byng-Hall, J. (1991) 'An appreciation of John Bowlby: his significance for family therapy.' *Journal of Family Therapy 13*, 5–16.

Byng-Hall, J. and Stevenson-Hinde, J. (1991) 'Attachment relationships within a family system.' *Infant Mental Health Journal 12*, 187–200.

Calverley, R.H., Fisher, K.W. and Ayoub, C. (1994) 'Complex splitting of self-representations in sexually abused adolescent girls.' *Development and Psychopathology 6*, 195–213.

Campbell, S., Pearce, E., Mardi, E., Ewing, L. and Szumowski, E. (1994) 'Hard to manage preschool boys: symptomatic behaviour contexts and time.' *Child Development 65*, 836–851.

Casler, L. (1961) 'Maternal deprivation: a critical review of the literature.' *Monographs of the Society for Research in Child Development 26* (Serial No. 80).

Cassidy, J. (1988) 'The self as related to child–mother attachment at six.' *Child Development 59*, 121–134.

Cassidy, J. (1990) 'Theoretical and methodological considerations in the study of attachment and the self in young children.' In M. Greenberg, D. Cicchetti and E.M. Cummings (eds) *Attachment in the Preschool Years: Theory, Research and Intervention.* Chicago: University of Chicago Press.

Cassidy, J. and Kobak, R.R. (1988) 'Avoidance and its relation to other defensive processes.' In J. Belsky and T. Nezworski (eds) *Clinical Implications of Attachment.* Hillsdale, NJ: Erlbaum.

Crittenden, P. (1988a) 'Relationships at risk.' In J. Belsky and T. Nezworski (eds) *Clinical Implications of Attachment.* Hillsdale, NJ: Erlbaum.

Crittenden, P. (1988b) 'Maternal antecedents of attachment quality.' In J. Belsky and T. Nezworski (eds) *Clinical Implications of Attachment. Hillsdale, NJ: Erlsbaum.*

Crockenberg, S. (1981) 'Infant irritability, mother responsiveness, and social support influences on the security of infant mother attachment.' *Child Development 7*, 169–176.

Dawson, G., Hessl, D. and Frey, K. (1994) 'Social influences on early developing sociological and behavioural systems related to risk for affective disorder.' *Development and Psychopathology 6*, 759–779.

Denham, S.A., McKinlay, M., Couchoud, E.A. and Holt, R. (1990) 'Emotional and behavioural predictors of preschool peer ratings.' *Child Development 61*, 1145–1152.

Dozier, M. and Lee, S.W. (1995) 'Discrepancies between self- and other-report of psychiatric symptomatology: effects of dismissing attachment strategies.' *Development and Psychopathology 7*, 217–226.

Durbin, E. and Bowlby, J. (1938) *Personal Aggressiveness and War.* London: Kegan Paul.

Easterbrooks, M.A. and Goldberg, W.A. (1990) 'Security of toddler–parent attachment: relation to children's sociopersonality functioning during kindergarten.' In M. Greenberg, D. Cicchetti, and E.M. Cummings (eds) *Attachment in the Preschool Years: Theory, Research and Intervention.* Chicago: University of Chicago Press.

Egeland, B. and Faber, E. (1984) 'Infant–mother attachment: factors related to its development and changes over time.' *Child Development 55*, 753–771.

Egeland, B., Jacobvitz, D. and Sroufe, L.A. (1988) 'Breaking the cycle of abuse: relationship predictions.' *Child Development 59*, 1080–1088.

Elicker, J., Englund, M. and Sroufe, L.A. (1992) 'Predicting peer competence and peer relationships in childhood from early parent–child relationships.' In R. Parke and G. Ladd (eds) *Family–Peer Relationships: Modes of Linkage Hillsdale, NJ:* Erlbaum.

Erickson, M.F., Sroufe, L.A. and Egeland, B. (1985) 'The relationship between quality of attachment and behaviour problems in preschool in a high risk sample.' In I. Bretherton and E. Waters (eds) *Growing Points in Attachment Theory and Research. Monograph of the Society of Research in Child Development. 50.* (Serial No. 209, Nos. 1–2), 147–186.

Fairbairn, W.R.D. (1956) 'Considerations arising out of the Schreber case.' *British Journal of Medical Psychology 29*, 2, 113–127.

Feeney, J. and Noller, P. (1986) *Adult Attachment.* London: Sage.

Field, T. (1992) Infants of depressed mothers. *Development and Psychopathology.* 4, 49-66.

Fisher, K.E. And Ayoub, C. (1993) Affective splitting and dissociation in normal and maltreated children: Developmental pathways for self in relationships. In D. Cichetti and S.L. Toth (eds) *Rochester Symposium on Development and Psychopathy. Vol.5: Disorders and Dysfunctions of the Self.* New York: University of Rochester Press.

Freud, A. (1960) Discussion of John Bowlby's paper. *The Psychoanalytic Study of the Child 15*, 53-62.

Freud, A. (1978) A study guide to Freud's writings. In *Psychoanalytic Psychology of Normal Development: Writings of Anna Freud.* London: The Hogarth Press.

Freud, S. (1929) *Civilisation and its Discontents.* London: The Hogarth Press.

Gewirtz, J.L. (1961) A learning analysis of the effects of normal stimulation, privation and deprivation on the acquisition of social motivation and attachment. In B.M. Foss *Determinants of Infant Behaviour.* London: Methuen and New York: Wiley.

Glenn, L. (1987) Attachment Theory and group analysis: the group matrix as a secure base. *Group Analysis 20.* 109–117.

Goldberg, S. (1991) Recent developments in attachment theory. *Canadian Journal of Psychiatry 36*, 393–400.

Good, M.I. (1996) Suggestion and veridicality in the reconstruction of sexual trauma, or can a bait of suggestion catch a carp of falsehood? *Journal of the American Psychoanalytical Association 4*, 44, 1189–1224.

Greenberg, J.R. and Mitchell, S.A. (1983) *Object Relations in Psychoanalytic Theory.* Cambridge, MA: Harvard University Press.

Greenberg, M. Cummings, M. and Cicchetti, B. (1988) *Attachment in the Preschool: Research and Intervention.* Hillsdale, NJ: Erlbaum.

Greenson, R. (1967) *The Technique and Practice of Psychoanalysis.* New York: International Universities Press.

Grossman, K., Grossman K.E., Spangler, G., Suess, G. and Unzer, J. (1985) Maternal sensitivity and newborns' orientation responses as related to quality of attachment in Northern Germany. In I. Bretherton and E. Waters (eds) *Growing Points in Attachment Theory and Research. Monographs for Society for Research in Child Development, 50* (Serial no. 209), 233–256.

Grotjahn, M. (1977) *The Art and Technique of Analytic Group Therapy.* New York: Jason Aronson.

Guntrip, H. (1961) *Personality Structure and Human Interaction.* New York: International Universities Press.

Guntrip, H. (1974) *Schizoid Phenomena, Object Relations and the Self.* London: Hogarth Press.

Gutt, E. (1985) *Productive and Unproductive Depression .* London: Tavistock.

Haft, W. and Slade, A. (1989) Affect attunement and maternal attachment: a pilot study. Infant Mental Health Journal 10, 157–172.

Hamilton, V. (1982) *Narcissus and Oedipus.* London: Routledge and Kegan Paul

Hamilton, V. (1996) *The Analyst's Preconscious.* Hillsdale, NJ: The Analytic Press.

Harris, T., Brown, G. and Bifulco, A. (1987) 'Loss of parent in childhood and adult psychiatric disorder: the role of social class position and premarital pregnancy.' *Psychological Medicine 17*, 163–183.

Harris, T. and Bifulco, A. (1991) 'Loss of parent in childhood, attachment style and deprivation in adulthood.' In C.M. Parkes, J. Stevenson-Hinde and P. Marris (eds) *Attachment Across the Life Cycle.* London: Routledge.

Hart, J., Gunnar, M. and Cicchetti, D. (1996) 'Altered neuroendocrine activity in maltreated children related to symptoms of depression.' *Development and Psychopathology 8*, 201–214.

Harwood, I.N.H. and Pines, M. (1998) *Self Experiences in Group*. London: Jessica Kingsley Publishers.

Heard, D. (1978) 'From object relations to attachment theory: a basis for family therapy.' *British Journal of Medical Psychology 51*, 67–76.

Heard, D. (1982) 'Family systems and the attachment dynamic.' *Journal of Family Therapy 4*, 99–116.

Heard, D. and Lake, B. (1986) 'The attachment dynamic in adult life.' *British Journal of Psychiatry 149*, 430–438.

Herman, J., Perry, C. and Kolk, B. (1989) 'Childhood trauma in borderline personality disorder.' *American Journal of Psychiatry 146*, 490–495.

Herman, J. (1992) *Trauma and Recovery*. New York: Basic Books.

Hinde, R. (1982) *Ethology*. Glasgow: Fontana Paperbacks.

Hinshelwood, R.D. (1991) *A Dictionary of Kleinian Thought*. London: Free Associations Books.

Hoffman, M. (1993) 'Algunos comentarios sobre la vida y la obra de Heinz Kohut.' *Revista Argentina de Clincia Psicologica 2*, 1, 80–90.

Holmes, J. (1993) *John Bowlby and Attachment Theory*. London & New York: Routledge.

Hopkins, J. (1990) 'The observed infant of attachment theory.' *British Journal of Psychotherapy 6*, 460–470.

Horowitz, M.J. (1972a) 'Image formation: clinical observations and a cognitive model.' In D.N. Sheehan (ed) *The Function and Nature of Imagenery*. New York: Academic Press.

Horowitz, M.J. (1972b) 'Modes of representation and thought.' *Journal of the American Psychoanalytical Association 20*, 793–819.

Isabella, R.A. and Belsky, J. (1991) 'Interactional synchrony and the origins of infant–mother attachment: a replication study.' *Child Development 62*, 373–384.

Isabella, R.A., Belsky, J. and von Eye, A. (1989) 'Origins of mother–infant attachment: an examination of interactional synchrony during the infant's first year.' *Developmental Psychology 25*, 12–21.

Jacobson, S.W. and Frue, K.F. (1991) 'Effect of maternal social support on attachment: experimental evidence.' *Child Development 62*, 572–582.

Kagan, J. (1979) 'Overview: perspectives on human infancy.' In J. Osofsky (ed) *Handbook of Infant Development*. New York: Wiley.

Kagan, J. (1982) *Psychological Research on the Human Infant: An Evaluation Summary*. New York: W.T. Grant.

Kagan, J., Kearsley, R.B. and Zelazo, P. (1980) *Infancy: Its Place in Human Development*. Cambridge, MA: Harvard University Press.

Kagan, J. and Klein, R. (1973) 'Cross-cultural perspectives on early development.' *American Psychologist 28*, 947–961.

King, P. (1978) 'Affective response of the analyst to the patient's communications.' *International Journal of Psycho-Analysis 59*, 2–3, 329–334.

Kiser, L., Bates, J., Maslin, C. and Bayles, K. (1986) 'Mother–infant play at six months as a predictor of attachment security at thirteen months.' *Journal of the American Academy of Child Psychiatry 25*, 168–175.

Klein, M. (1975) *The Psychoanalysis of Children*. New York: Free Press.

Klein, M. (1988) *Love, Guilt and Reparation*. London: Virago Press.

Lamb, M.E., Thompson, R.A., Gardner, W.P., Charnov, E.L. and Estes, D. (1984) 'Security of infantile attachment as assessed in the "Strange Situation".' *Behavioural and Brain Sciences 7*, 127–171.

Laplanche, J. (1989) *New Foundation for Psychoanalysis*. Oxford: Blackwell.

Lewis, M., Feiring, C., McGuffog, C. and Jaskir, J. (1984) 'Predicting psychopathology in six-year-olds from early social relations.' *Child Development 55*, 123–136.

Lieberman, A.F. and Pawl, J.H. (1990) 'Disorders of attachment and secure base behaviour in the second year of life: conceptual issues and clinical intervention.' In M. Greenberg, D. Cicchetti, and E.M.

Cummings (eds) *Attachment in the Preschool Years: Theory, Research and Intervention*. Chicago: University of Chicago Press.

Levenson, R.W. (1992) 'Autonomic nervous system differences among emotions.' *Psychological Science 3*, 23–27.

Lieberman, A.F., Weston, D. and Paul, J.H. (1991) 'Preventive intervention and outcome with anxiously attached dyads.' *Child Development 62*, 199–209.

Limentani, A. (1977) 'Affects and the psychoanalytic situation.' *International Journal of Psycho-Analysis 58*, 171–182.

Mackie, A.J. (1981) 'Attachment theory: its relevance to the therapeutic alliance.' *British Journal of Medical Psychology 54*, 203–212.

Main, M. and Cassidy, J. (1988) 'Categories of response with the parent at age six: predicted from infant attachment classifications and stable over a one month period.' *Developmental Psychology 24*, 415–426.

Main, M., Kaplan, N. and Cassidy, J. (1985) 'Security in infancy, childhood and adulthood: a move to the level of representation.' In I. Bretherton and E. Waters (eds) *Growing Points in Attachment Theory and Research. Monographs of the Society for Research in Child Development, 50*. (Serial No. 209), 66–104.

Main, M. and Weston, D. (1982) 'Avoidance of the attachment figure in infancy: descriptions and interpretations.' In C.M. Parkes and J. Stevenson-Hinde (eds) *The Place of Attachment in Human Behaviour*. New York: Basic Books.

Malan, D.H. (1979) *Individual Psychotherapy and the Science of Psychodynamics*. London: Butterworths.

Malin, A. and Grostein, J. (1966) 'Projective identification in the therapeutic process.' *International Journal of Psycho-Analysis 17*, 26–31.

Marrone, M. (1987) 'La teoria del "attachment" en el contexto del pensamiento psicoanalitico.' In J.A. Ozamiz (ed) *Psicosociologia de la Salud Mental*. San Sebastian: Ttartalo Ediciones.

Marrone, M. (1992) 'La teoria del apego en el contexto del pensamiento psicoanalitico contemporaneo.' *Vertex (Revista Argentina de Psiquiatria) 3*, 7, 66–70.

Marrone, M. (1992) 'Los modelos representacionales.' *Vertex (Revista Argentina de Psiquiatria) 3*, 8, 145–148.

Marrone, M. (1992) 'La teoria del apego y sus aplicaciones a la psicoterapia.' *Vertex (Revista Argentina de psiquiatria) 3*, 9, 229–230.

Marrone, M. (1993) 'Los modelos representationales. La teoria del apego en el contexto del pensamiento analitico contemporaneo.' In M.J. Ortiz Baron and S. Yarnoz Yaben (eds) *Teoria del Apego y Relaciones Afectivas*. Bilbao: Servicio Editorial de la Universidad del Pais Vasco.

Marrone, M. (1994) 'Biografia: John Bowlby.' *Revista Argentina de Clinica Psicologica 3*, 197–208.

Martinez Bouquet, C. (1977) *Fundamentos para una Teoria del Psicodraman*. Buenos Aires and Mexico: Siglo Veintiuno Editores.

Matas, L., Arend, R.A. and Sroufe, L.A. (1978) 'Continuity and adaption in the second year: the relationship between quality of attachment and later competence.' *Child Development 49*, 547–556.

Mineka, S. and Sutton, S.K. (1992) 'Cognitive biases and emotional disorders.' *Psychological Sciences 3*, 65–69.

Moreno, J.L. (1954) 'Transference, countertransference and tele.' In *Psychodrama*. New York: Beacon House.

Morris, D. (1983) 'Attachment and intimacy.' In G. Stricker and M. Fisher (eds) *Intimacy*. New York: Plenum.

Moss, E., Parent, S., Gosselin, C., Rousseau, D. and St. Laurent, D. (1996) 'Attachment and teacher reported behaviour problems during the pre-school and early school-age period.' *Development and Psychopathology 8*, 511–525.

Murray, L. (1991) 'Intersubjectivity, object relations theory and empirical evidence from mother–infant interactions.' *Infant Mental Health Journal 12*, 3, 219–232.

Norman, D.A. (1976) *Memory and Attention: Introduction to Human Information Processing*. New York: Wiley.

Ornstein, A. (1974) 'The dread to repeat and the new beginning.' *The Annual of Psychoanalysis 2*, 231–248. New York: International Universities Press.

Osofsky, J. (1988) 'Attachment theory and research in psychoanalytic process.' *Psychoanalytic Psychology 5*, 159–177.

Parkes, C.M. (1972) *Bereavement.* London: Tavistock (Third edition published by Routledge in 1996).

Peterfreund, E. (1971) 'Information, system and psychoanalysis.' *Psychological Issues.* Vol. III. Monogr. 25/26. New York: International Universities Press.

Peterfreund, E. (1980) 'On information and systems models for psychoanalysis.' *International Review of Psycho-Analysis 7*, 327–345.

Pines, M. (1993) 'The world according to Kohut.' *Journal of the British Association of Psychotherapists 25*, 47–63.

Ricks, M. (1985) 'The social transmission of parental behaviour: attachment across generations.' In I. Bretherton and E. Waters (eds) *Growing Points in Attachment Theory and Research. Monographs of the Society for Research in Child Development.* 50 (Serial No. 209), 211–227.

Rioch, J. (1988) 'The transference phenomenon in psychoanalytic therapy.' In B. Wolstein (ed) *Essential Papers on Countertransference.* New York: New York University Press. (Reprinted from *Psychiatry*, 1943, *6*, 147–156).

Riviere, J. (1927) 'Contribution to symposium on child analysis.' *International Journal of Psychoanalysis 8*, 373–377.

Robertson, J. (1962) *Hospitals and Children: A Parents'-Eye View.* New York: Gollancz.

Rubinstein, B.B. (1965) 'Psychoanalytic theory and the mind–body problem.' In W.S. Greenfield and W.C. Lewis (eds) *Psychoanalysis and Current Biological Thought.* Madison: University of Wisconsin Press.

Rubinstein, B.B. (1967) 'Explanation and mere description: a metascientific examination of certain aspects of the psychoanalytic theory of motivation.' In R.R. Holt (ed) 'Motives and Thought.' *Psychological Issues.* (Monograph 18/19). New York: International University Press.

Rycroft, C. (1985) *Psychoanalysis and Beyond.* London: Hogarth Press.

Sander, L. (1964) 'Adaptive relationships in early mother–child interactions.' *Journal of the American Academy of Child Psychiatry 1*, 141–166.

Schaffer, H.R. and Emerson, P.E. (1964) 'The development of social attachments in infancy.' *Monographs of the Society for Research in Child Development 29*, (3, Serial No. 94).

Slade, A. (1997) 'Representation, symbolization and affect regulation in the concomitant treatment of a mother and child.' *Psychoanalytic Inquiry* in press.

Solomon, I. (1992) *The Encyclopedia of Evolving Techniques in Dynamic Psychotherapy.* New Jersey and London: Jason Aronson.

Southgate, J. (1996) *An Attachment Perspective on Dissociation and Multiplicity.* (Paper presented at the Third Annual John Bowlby Memorial Lecture). London: Centre for Attachment-based Psychoanalytic Psychotherapy.

Spitz, R.A. (1945) 'Hospitalism. An enquiry into the genesis of psychiatric conditions in early childhood.' *The Psychoanalytic Study of the Child 1*, 53–74.

Sroufe, L.A. (1979) 'Socioemotional development.' In J. Osofsky (ed) *Handbook of Infant Development.* New York: Wiley.

Sroufe, L.A. (1983) 'Infant–caregiver attachment and patterns of adaption in preschool: the roots of maladaption and competence.' In M. Perlmutter (ed) *Minnesota Symposium in Child Psychology* (Vol. 16, pp.41–81). Hillsdale, NJ: Erlbaum.

Sroufe, L.A., Cooper, R.G. and DeHart, G.B. (1992) *Child Development: Its Nature and Course.* 2nd edn. New York: McGraw-Hill.

Sroufe, L.A., Egeland, B. and Kreutzer, T. (1990) 'The fate of early experience following developmental change: longitudinal approaches to individual adaption in childhood.' *Child Development 61*, 1363–1373.

Sroufe, L.A. and Waters, E. (1977b) 'Heart rate as a convergent measure in clinical and developmental research.' *Merrill-Palmer Quarterly 23*, 3–27.

Stern, D.N. (1977) *The First Relationship.* Cambridge, MA: Havard University Press.

Suess, G.J., Grossman, K.E. and Sroufe, L.A. (1992) 'Effects of infant attachment on mother and father quality of adaption in preschool: from dyadic to individual organisation of self.' *International Journal of Behavioural Development 15*, 1, 42–65.

Suomi, S.J. and Harlow, H.F. (1972) 'Social rehabilitation of isolate-reared monkeys.' *Developmental Psychology 6*, 487–496.

Suomi, S.J. and Harlow, H.F. (1978) 'Early experience and social development in rhesus monkeys.' In M. Lamb (ed) *Social and Personality Development.* New York: Holt, Reinehart & Winston.

Toth, S.L., Manly, J.T. and Cicchetti, D. (1992) 'Child maltreatment and vulnerability to depression.' *Development and Psychopathology 4*, 97–112.

Trivers, R.L. (1974) 'Parent–offspring conflict.' *American Zoologist 14*, 249–264.

Tronick, E., Als, H., Adamson, L., Wise, S. and Brazelton, T.B. (1978) 'The infant's response to entrapment between contradictory messages in face-to-face interactions.' *Journal of Child Psychiatry 17*, 1–13.

Turner, P.J. (1991) 'Relationship between attachment, gender, and behavior with peers in preschool.' *Child Development 2*, 1475–1488.

Usandivaras, R.J. (1993) *De Lider a Chaman.* Buenos Aires: Editorial Docencia.

Vaughn, B., Lefever, G. Seifer, R. and Barglow, P. (1989) 'Attachment behaviour, attachment security, and temperament during infancy.' *Child Development 60*, 728–737.

Waters, E. (1978) 'The stability of individual differences in infant–mother attachment.' *Child Development 49*, 483–494.

Weiss, R.S. (1982) 'Attachment in adult life.' In C.M. Parkes and J. Stevenson-Hinde (eds) *The Place of Attachment in Human Behaviour.* New York: Basic Books.

Winnicott, D.W. (1958) *Through Paediatrics to Psycho-Analysis.* New York: Basic Books.

Wolf, E.S. (1988) *Treating the Self.* New York and London: The Guildford Press.

Wolff, C.T., Friedman, S.B., Hofer, M.A. and Mason, J.W. (1964) 'Relationship between psychological defences and mean urinary 17-hydroxycorticosteroid excretion rates: a predictive study of parents with fatally ill children.' *Psychosomatic Medicine 26*, 576–591.

Zeanah, C.H. and Zeanah, P.D. (1989) 'Intergenerational transmission of maltreatment: insights from attachment theory and research.' *Psychiatry 52*, 177–196.

Subject Index

Author Index